Communications in Computer and Information Science   1418

More information about this series at http://www.springer.com/series/7899

Ludovico Boratto · Stefano Faralli ·
Mirko Marras · Giovanni Stilo (Eds.)

Advances in Bias and Fairness in Information Retrieval

Second International Workshop on Algorithmic
Bias in Search and Recommendation, BIAS 2021
Lucca, Italy, April 1, 2021
Proceedings

 Springer

Editors
Ludovico Boratto
Eurecat - Centre Tecnològic de Catalunya
Barcelona, Spain

Mirko Marras
École Polytechnique Fédérale de Lausanne
(EPFL)
Lausanne, Switzerland

Stefano Faralli
Unitelma Sapienza University of Rome
Rome, Italy

Giovanni Stilo
University of L'Aquila
L'Aquila, Italy

ISSN 1865-0929   ISSN 1865-0937 (electronic)
Communications in Computer and Information Science
ISBN 978-3-030-78817-9   ISBN 978-3-030-78818-6 (eBook)
https://doi.org/10.1007/978-3-030-78818-6

This Springer imprint is published by the registered company Springer Nature Switzerland AG
The registered company address is: Gewerbestrasse 11, 6330 Cham, Switzerland

Advances in Bias and Fairness in Information Retrieval: Preface

The Second International Workshop on Algorithmic Bias in Search and Recommendation (BIAS 2021) was held as part of the 43rd European Conference on Information Retrieval (ECIR 2021) on April 1, 2021. BIAS 2021 was expected to happen in Lucca, Italy, but due to the COVID-19 emergency and the consequent travel restrictions, the workshop was held online. The workshop was jointly organized by the Data Science and Big Data Analytics unit at Eurecat (Spain), the University of Rome Unitelma Sapienza (Italy), the École Polytechnique Fédérale de Lausanne (Switzerland), and the Department of Information Engineering, Computer Science and Mathematics at the University of L'Aquila (Italy). It was supported by the ACM Conference on Fairness, Accountability, and Transparency (ACM FAccT) Network.

In total, 37 submissions from authors in different countries were received. The final program included 11 full papers and 3 short papers (38% acceptance rate). All submissions were single-blind peer-reviewed by at least three internal Program Committee members to ensure that only submissions of high quality were included in the final program. Individual requests for reviewers were also made to strengthen the Program Committee, integrating both the new and the accomplished reviewing workforce in the field.

The workshop collected novel contributions to measure, characterize, and mitigate bias and unfairness in the data and the algorithms underlying search and recommendation applications, providing a common ground for researchers working in this area. The workshop day included paper presentations and a final discussion to highlight open issues, research challenges, and briefly summarise the outcomes of the workshop. The presentations covered topics that go from novel metrics and analyses aimed at characterizing fairness and bias in multi-stakeholder environments, video recommendations, and public opinions in mass media, over algorithms driven by fair ranking policies, to studies that provide evidence on users' perceptions of search-engine biases, as examples. More than 60 participants were registered and participated in the workshop.

In addition to the paper presentations, the program also included a keynote talk given by Prof. Carlos Castillo from the Universitat Pompeu Fabra (Spain). Prof. Castillo first introduced how algorithms, especially in relation with ranking and recommendation, can lead to discrimination against stakeholders (e.g., end users or content providers) in these application domains. Then, a range of metrics to monitor fairness in rankings were described, including rank-weighted exposure, randomized merging, and pairwise comparisons, among others. To mitigate unfairness in these systems, recent pre-, in-, and post-processing approaches were presented. Finally, he introduced the concept of transparency and discussed how this beyond-accuracy property relates with ranking and recommender systems.

Overall, this edition of the workshop proved to be a success, in line with the very successful 2020 event, as witnessed by the number of submissions and the level of engagement during the talks and the open discussion. We believe that this workshop has strengthened the community working on algorithmic bias and fairness in information retrieval, fostering ideas and solutions for the current challenges and developing networks of researchers for future projects and initiatives. Plans to organize the third edition of the workshop next year were formed. The organizers would like to thank the authors, the reviewers for allowing us to shape an interesting program, and the attendees for their participation.

May 2021

Ludovico Boratto
Stefano Faralli
Mirko Marras
Giovanni Stilo

Organization

Workshop Chairs

Ludovico Boratto   Eurecat - Centre Tecnológic de Catalunya, Spain
Stefano Faralli   University of Rome Unitelma Sapienza, Italy
Mirko Marras   École Polytechnique Fédérale de Lausanne,
                      Switzerland
Giovanni Stilo   University of L'Aquila, Italy

Program Committee

Himan Abdollahpouri   Northwestern University, USA
Luca Aiello   Nokia Bell Labs, UK
Mehwish Alam   FIZ Karlsruhe and Karlsruhe Institute of Technology,
                      Germany
Marcelo Armentano   National University of Central Buenos Aires, Argentina
Alejandro Bellogin   Universidad Autónoma de Madrid, Spain
Bettina Berendt   Katholieke Universiteit Leuven, Belgium
Glencora Borradaile   Oregon State University, USA
Federica Cena   University of Turin, Italy
Jeffrey Chen   RMIT University, Australia
Pasquale De Meo   University of Messina, Italy
Sarah Dean   University of California, Berkeley, USA
Danilo Dessì   FIZ Karlsruhe and Karlsruhe Institute of Technology,
                      Germany
Michael Ekstrand   Boise State University, USA
Francesco Fabbri   Universitat Pompeu Fabra, Spain
Jean Garcia-Gathright   Spotify, USA
Aniko Hannak   Northeastern University, USA
Nina Grgic-Hlaca   Max Planck Institute for Software Systems, Germany
Genet Asefa Gesese   FIZ Karlsruhe and Karlsruhe Institute of Technology,
                      Germany
Toshihiro Kamishima   AIST, Japan
Martha Larson   Radboud University and TU Delft, the Netherlands
Aonghus Lawlor   University College Dublin, Ireland
Sandy Mayson   University of Georgia, USA
Rishabh Mehrotra   Spotify, UK
Brent Mittelstadt   University of Oxford, UK
Cataldo Musto   University of Bari Aldo Moro, Italy
Panagiotis Papadakos   FORTH-ICS, Greece
Mykola Pechenizkiy   Eindhoven University of Technology, the Netherlands
Simone Paolo Ponzetto   Universität Mannheim, Germany

Contents

Towards Fairness-Aware Ranking by Defining Latent Groups Using Inferred Features

Yunhe Feng[1(✉)], Daniel Saelid[1], Ke Li[1], Ruoyuan Gao[2], and Chirag Shah[1]

[1] University of Washington, Seattle, USA
{yunhe,saeliddp,kel28,chirags}@uw.edu
[2] Rutgers University, New Brunswick, USA
ruoyuan.gao@rutgers.edu

Abstract. Group fairness in search and recommendation is drawing increasing attention in recent years. This paper explores how to define latent groups, which cannot be determined by self-contained features but must be inferred from external data sources, for fairness-aware ranking. In particular, taking the Semantic Scholar dataset released in TREC 2020 Fairness Ranking Track as a case study, we infer and extract multiple fairness related dimensions of author identity including gender and location to construct groups. Furthermore, we propose a fairness-aware re-ranking algorithm incorporating both weighted relevance and diversity of returned items for given queries. Our experimental results demonstrate that different combinations of relative weights assigned to relevance, gender, and location groups perform as expected.

Keywords: Fair ranking · Text retrieval · Fair exposure · Information retrieval · Fairness · Ranking

1 Introduction

As one of the emerging topics in fairness-aware information systems, presenting relevant results to the users while ensuring fair exposure of the content suppliers have raised more and more attention. Fairer information retrieval and search systems not only provide relevant search results with higher diversity and transparency, but also offer reasonable discoverability for underrepresented groups. For example, a high-quality academic paper from small institutions, which have very limited media outlets and resources, should also be treated equally to get its deserved exposures in search systems, especially at the early stage of publication when such papers are more likely to suffer from cold-start problems.

This paper investigates fairness ranking within an academic search task context, where the goal was to provide fair exposure of different groups of authors while maintaining good relevance of the ranked papers regarding given queries. However, it is difficult to achieve such a goal due to the following challenges.

© Springer Nature Switzerland AG 2021
L. Boratto et al. (Eds.): BIAS 2021, CCIS 1418, pp. 1–8, 2021.
https://doi.org/10.1007/978-3-030-78818-6_1

- **Openness and complexity of defining the author group.** Defining the author group is not a trivial task. This requires an in-depth understanding of what should be considered as important group attributes that not only separate different authors but also aggregate similar authors. The challenges in this task include and are not limited to, how many groups should be identified, and how to identify and extract the features from authors and their publications for the group classification task.
- **Algorithm Robustness on different applications.** The definition of author groups may change from application to application. A good fairness ranking algorithm should be robust to a broad range of group definitions in various scenarios. In other words, fairness-aware ranking algorithms should demonstrate a high generalization capability when processing application-wise group definitions.
- **Trade-off between relevance and fairness.** The re-ranking algorithm based on a list of candidate items needs to optimize for both the relevance of the re-ranked results and the fairness of the exposed author groups, while carefully balancing between the two.

We aimed to design and implement fair ranking and retrieval algorithms to enhance the fairness for scholarly search. On the subset of the Semantic Scholar (S2) Open Corpus [1] provided by the Allen Institute for Artificial Intelligence, we defined multiple author groups, inferred demographic characteristics of authors, and developed fairness-aware algorithms to achieve a flexible trade-off between relevance and fairness by tuning principal component weights. Our contribution is twofold. First, we explored non-self-contained features to construct groups for fairness purposes. Second, we proposed a weighted fairness-aware re-ranking algorithm to strike a balance between relevance and fairness.

2   Data Description

The Semantic Scholar (S2) Open Corpus released by TREC 2020 Fairness Ranking Track [3,4] consists of extracted fields of academic papers. For most papers, the available fields include the S2 paper ID, title, abstract, authors, inbound and outbound citations. In addition, another three auxiliary datasets are provided. The first dataset maps paper ids to a list of corresponding author positions with their corpus id. The second one contains paper information such as paper id, title, year of publication, venue, number of citations, and number of key citations. The last one contains author features including author's name, number of citations, h-index (and a dependent feature, h-class), i10-Index, and number of papers published. A detailed data description can be found in our previous TREC 2020 Fairness Ranking Track report [7].

3   Methodology

We first defined author groups based on general demographic characteristics including genders and countries. Then, we utilized Okapi BM25 [8] to estimate the relevance of papers for given search queries. Based on the group definition and BM25 relevance score, we proposed our fairness-aware re-ranking algorithm.

3.1 Group Definition

When defining author groups, we considered genders and countries of authors because the two demographic features are general enough for different applications. Re-ranking algorithms based on such group definitions are more likely to demonstrate strong robustness in various scenarios.

Gender Inference. To predict the binary gender of a given author, we called the genderize.io API [2], which is powered by a large dataset that maps first names to binary genders. Given a name, genderize.io will return 'male' if there are more instances of the name associated with men, and it will return 'female' otherwise. If the dataset contains no instances of the given name, no gender prediction will be returned. For the authors in our sub-corpus, the returned gender predictions are shown in Table 1.

Table 1. The distribution of inferred genders by genderize.io

Gender	Count	Percentage
Male	18810	58.8%
Female	6235	19.5%
Unidentified	6930	21.7%
Total	31975	100%

Table 2. The economy distribution of inferred locations

Locations	Count	Percentage
Advanced	15106	47.2%
Developing	3926	12.3%
Unidentified	12933	40.5%
Total	31975	100%

Country Inference. In contrast with gender prediction, we could not rely on a single API call for location prediction. To begin the process, we searched for the author by name in Google Scholar using the Scholarly API [5]. Since there are often many authors with a given full name on Google Scholar, we picked a single author by comparing our author citation data with Google Scholar's data. After choosing the closest match, we retrieved email extension and 'affiliation' data from Google Scholar. If we successfully retrieved this author data, we followed the below procedure, moving to each consecutive step if the prior was unsuccessful. As listed as the last step, if no author data was retrieved from Google Scholar, we tried finding the author's homepage and parsing its URL for country code.

1. Parse the email extension for a country code (e.g. .uk → United Kingdom).
2. Parse the affiliation for a university name, then return the country in which that university is located.[1]
3. Parse the affiliation for a city name, then return that city's country.[2]

---

[1] https://www.4icu.org/reviews/index0001.htm.
[2] https://en.wikipedia.org/wiki/List_of_towns_and_cities_with_100,000_or_more_inhab itants/cityname:_A.

4. Search author name, author affiliation on Google, scrape the first URL, then parse for country code.
5. Call Google Places API with affiliations, then return associated countries.
6. Search author name + 'homepage' on Google, scrape the first URL, then parse for country code.

Once all authors had been processed, we mapped each author's affiliated country to 'advanced economy' or 'developing economy' based on the IMF's October 2019 World Economic Outlook report [6]. The results are shown in Table 2. Here, 'unidentified' means that no country was predicted for that author.

3.2   Pure Relevance with BM25

We used Okapi BM25, a popular ranking algorithm adopted by many search engines, to estimate the relevance of a document based on a given query. Since complete paper contents are unavailable, we instead chose the paper's abstract and title to represent the corresponding document. The papers were written in 28 different languages including English, Arabian, German, Chinese, etc., while all queries were in English only. However, BM25 functions are incompatible with certain languages that cannot be tokenized by whitespace. Therefore, we decided to translate all needed documents into English first and stored the tokenized text in the database for further usage.

Then we started the BM25 process. We first translated and tokenized the queries since some of them contained Unicode. After that, for each query, we calculated the BM25 score as the base relevance score for each document, and then arranged the documents based on their scores in descending order. This sorted list was used as the pure ranking list for the given query.

3.3   Fairness-Aware Re-ranking Algorithm

We proposed a fairness-aware re-ranking algorithm incorporating both relevance and diversity of documents. The main idea was to estimate the cost of adding a document to the rank list $\mathbf{R}$ from the perspective of relevance and fairness. For a document of d, we used $F(d, \mathcal{D}, q)$, the reversed normalized BM25 score of d in a corpus $\mathcal{D}$ given a query q, to represent its relevance cost, where 0 corresponds to most relevant, and 1 corresponds to least relevant.

For a given query q, we first retrieved the top relevant documents to build a candidate corpus $\mathcal{D}'$. To ensure ranking fairness, it is intuitive to make the probability of defined groups over the rank list R and the candidate corpus $\mathcal{D}'$ very similar. Specifically, let $p(v, \mathcal{D})$ be the probability distribution of a discrete group variable v over the document corpus $\mathcal{D}$. Based on our group definitions, v could be either the group of gender g or country c, i.e., $v \in \{g, c\}$. Note that this is flexible to be extended to other group definitions. Then we use the Kullback-Leibler (KL) divergence of the group distribution probability between the updated current rank list $\mathbf{R}$ and the whole candidate corpus $\mathcal{D}'$ to measure their similarities. We also assigned weights $\mathbf{w}$ for relevance cost and fairness cost for each defined group. The cost function is expressed as:

$$C(d, \mathbf{w}, \mathbf{R}, \mathcal{D}', q) = w_r * F(d, \mathcal{D}', q) + \sum_{v \in \{g, c\}} w_v * KL(p(v, \mathbf{R} + \{d\}) \parallel p(v, \mathcal{D}')) \quad (1)$$

where $\mathbf{w} = \{w_r, w_g, w_c\}$ and $w_r + w_g + w_c = 1$; $F(d, \mathcal{D}', q)$ is the reversed normalized BM25 score of a document d such that 0 corresponds to most relevant, and 1 corresponds to least relevant; and $KL(p(v, \mathbf{R} + \{d\}) \parallel p(v, \mathcal{D}'))$ is the Kullback-Leibler divergence regarding group v between the updated $\mathbf{R}$ by appending document d and the overall candidate corpus $\mathcal{D}'$. Then, we built our re-ranked list by repeatedly appending the document with the minimal cost $C(d, \mathbf{w}, \mathbf{R}, \mathcal{D}', q)$. The proposed fairness-aware re-ranking algorithm as illustrated in Algorithm 1.

Since many documents were missing group definitions for at least one author, we adopted a systematic way to address it. For every author missing a group definition, we assigned a group value based on the overall group distribution in the corpus. For instance, if 75% of the authors in the corpus were identified as male, we choose 'male' for an unidentified author with a probability of 75%.

Algorithm 1: Fairness-aware Re-ranking Algorithm

Input: $\mathcal{D}$: document corpus; q: query of interest; l: length of expected ranked list ; $\mathbf{w}$: component weight vector
Output: $\mathbf{R}$: re-ranked list of relevant documents
$\mathbf{R} \leftarrow \emptyset$; // initialize the ranked list as empty
$\mathcal{D}', \mathcal{D}'' \leftarrow$ Retrieve relevant document candidates from $\mathcal{D}$ for query q ;
// document candidate corpus for q
for $i = 1 \rightarrow l$ do
    $c_{min} \leftarrow A \, Large \, Integer$; // initialize the minimal cost
    $d_{min} \leftarrow None$; // initialize the document with the minimal cost
    for $d \in \mathcal{D}''$ do
        Calculate the cost $C(d, \mathbf{w}, \mathbf{R}, \mathcal{D}', q)$ according to Equation 1 ;
        // calculate the cost of adding d into $\mathbf{R}$
        if $C(d, \mathbf{w}, \mathbf{R}, \mathcal{D}', q) < c_{min}$ then
            $d_{min} \leftarrow d$; // update the document with the minimal cost
            $c_{min} \leftarrow C(d, \mathbf{w}, \mathbf{R}, \mathcal{D}', q)$; // update the minimal cost
        end
    end
    append d_{min} to $\mathbf{R}$; // add the document with the minimal cost into
    the re-ranked list $\mathbf{R}$
    $\mathcal{D}'' \leftarrow \mathcal{D}'' - \{d_{min}\}$; // remove the added document d_{min} from $\mathcal{D}''$
end
return $\mathbf{R}$

---

4 Results and Discussion

4.1 Baselines

We used random ranking and BM25 as baselines in our study to reveal the ranking performance without considering relevance and fairness, respectively. As its name implies, the random ranking algorithm randomly ranks all items ignoring relevant scores. In contrast, BM25 only cares about the relevance but fails to take fairness into account. We will compare baselines with the proposed fairness-aware re-ranking algorithm in Subsect. 4.2.

4.2 Weighted Fairness-Aware Re-ranking Results

We evaluated the utility and unfairness, which were used as official evaluation metrics by the TREC 2019 Fairness Ranking Track [3], with different combinations of w_r, w_g, w_c in Eq. 1 from the perspective of the gender and country groups. As shown in Fig. 1, in both gender and country groups, BM25 demonstrates a relatively high utility score but a low fairness score, implying that BM25 fails to take fairness into account during the ranking. Another interesting finding is that the random ranking achieves lower fairness than most of our proposed methods on the country group but the highest fairness on the gender group. So, the fairness performance of random ranking methods is sensitive to the definition of groups. In other words, the definition of groups is not a trivial task as we claimed in Sect. 1. As we expected, our methods' utility drops greatly when BM25 scores are excluded ($w_r = 0$). When w_r is assigned a positive value, the performance of our methods with different combinations of w_r, w_g, w_c are comparable on both country and gender groups (see the cluster on left top in Fig. 1(a), and the cluster on the middle top in Fig. 1(b)).

5 Limitations and Future Work

As a first step to explore the fairness-aware ranking by defining latent groups using inferred features, our study has some limitations. When inferring the gender, we treated it as a binary attribute guessed through the first name. However, in the real world, gender is beyond the limitations of the male and female categories of sex, and the first name sometimes tells very little about a person's gender identity. Besides, 40.5% of countries failed to be detected (see Table 2), leading to potentially inaccurate group classifications.

In the future, we will undertake fine-grained gender detection and utilize Google Scholar profile photos, along with the first name, to infer the gender attribute inclusively and robustly. To fix the unidentified countries, we will explore more public personal location information, such as Twitter profile locations. In addition, we will incorporate more non-self-contained features, such as seniority level and language background, to construct latent groups.

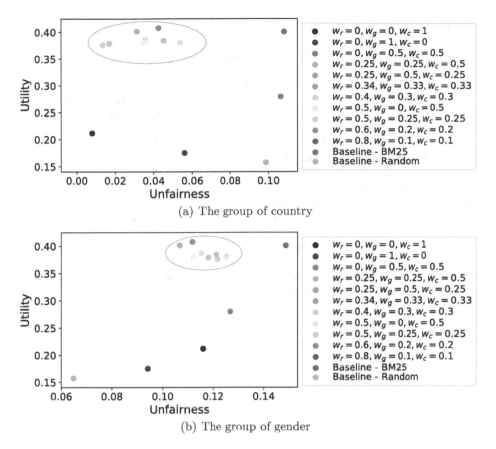

(a) The group of country

(b) The group of gender

Fig. 1. Utility versus unfairness with different group definitions. The utility and unfairness scores were calculated based on Equation (7) and Equation (6) in the TREC 2019 Fairness Ranking Track [3] respectively.

6   Conclusion

This paper presents how to define latent groups using inferred features for fair ranking. Specifically, we construct gender and location groups, which are generalized but not contained in the raw dataset, to promote search result fairness. We also propose a fairness-aware retrieval and re-ranking algorithm incorporating both relevance and fairness for Semantic Scholar data. Evaluation results with different weights of relevance, gender, and location information demonstrated that our algorithm was flexible and explainable.

Acknowledgements. A part of this work is supported by the US National Science Foundation (NSF) award number IIS-1910154.

References

1. Ammar, W., et al.: Construction of the literature graph in semantic scholar. In: NAACL (2018)
2. Demografix ApS: genderize.io (2020). https://genderize.io/
3. Biega, A.J., Diaz, F., Ekstrand, M.D., Kohlmeier, S.: Overview of the TREC 2019 fair ranking track. In: The Twenty-Eighth Text REtrieval Conference (TREC 2019) Proceedings (2019)
4. Biega, A.J., Diaz, F., Ekstrand, M.D., Kohlmeier, S.: The TREC 2020 Fairness Track (2020). https://fair-trec.github.io
5. Cholewiak, S.A., Ipeirotis, P., Revision, V.S.: Scholarly: Simple access to Google Scholar Authors and Citations (2020). https://pypi.org/project/scholarly/
6. Research Department, International Monetary Fund: World economic outlook. World Economic Outlook, International Monetary Fund (2019). https://doi.org/ 10.5089/9781513508214.081
7. Feng, Y., Saelid, D., Li, K., Gao, R., Shah, C.: University of Washington at TREC 2020 fairness ranking track. arXiv preprint arXiv:2011.02066 (2020)
8. Robertson, S.E., Walker, S., Jones, S., Hancock-Beaulieu, M., Gatford, M.: Okapi at TREC-3 (1994). https://fair-trec.github.io

Media Bias Everywhere? A Vision for Dealing with the Manipulation of Public Opinion

Michael Färber$^{(\boxtimes)}$ and Frederic Bartscherer

Karlsruhe Institute of Technology (KIT), Karlsruhe, Germany
{michael.faerber,frederic.bartscherer}@kit.edu

Abstract. This paper deals with the question of how artificial intelligence can be used to detect media bias in the overarching topic of manipulation and mood-making. We show three fields of actions that result from using machine learning to analyze media bias: the evaluation principles of media bias, the information presentation of media bias, and the transparency of media bias evaluation. Practical applications of our research results arise in the professional environment for journalists and publishers, as well as in the everyday life of citizens. First, automated analysis could be used to analyze text in real-time and promote balanced coverage in reporting. Second, an intuitive web browser application could reveal existing bias in news texts in a way that citizens can understand. Finally, in education, pupils can experience media bias and the use of artificial intelligence in practice, fostering their media literacy.

Keywords: Media bias · News bias · Text mining · Trustworthy AI

1 Introduction

Nowadays, public opinion is shaped in manifold ways. The internet, in particular, is changing citizens' media consumption massively and digital media is increasingly influencing the public's opinions [7]. The distortion in media, also called *media bias*, consists, for example, of reporting through a selected choice of words or topics and is now also forcing large Internet companies, such as Facebook, to act [10].

Media bias is therefore the focus of many research areas [4,7]. In the humanities and social sciences, for example, content and meta analyses are carried out using a holistic approach to reveal different types of bias in news texts [4]. Given the ever-increasing rate of publication in digital media, an extensive manual analysis by experts is not possible [3]. In computer science, in contrast, the focus is on the automatic detection of media bias using machine learning methods, which allow for an automatic analysis over a large number of text documents, such as news texts [1].

© Springer Nature Switzerland AG 2021
L. Boratto et al. (Eds.): BIAS 2021, CCIS 1418, pp. 9–13, 2021.
https://doi.org/10.1007/978-3-030-78818-6_2

In contrast to fake news analysis and detection [15], which are mostly limited to evaluating the content of facts, this paper is devoted to the topics of manipulation and mood-making. In cooperation with computer science, the humanities and social sciences,[1] we develop criteria that can be used to assess media bias in news texts. Furthermore, we investigate whether methods of artificial intelligence (AI) are suitable to analyze media bias in news texts in an understandable manner for citizens and to promote balanced coverage in reporting and media empowerment of citizens.

2   Field Analysis and Recommended Actions

Most computational approaches to assessing media bias use text mining methods, such as the lexical analysis of phrases [12]. AI methods, such as deep neural networks, can recognize complex relationships and extract knowledge from texts. Hence, we assume that, in the future, media bias will be recognized automatically in news texts and a quantitative analysis of media bias in its diverse dimensions (e.g., hidden assumptions, subjectivity, representation tendencies, and overall bias [6]) can be carried out.

In the following, we present three fields of action with respect to the application of AI for detecting media bias.

2.1   Field of Action 1: Evaluation Principles of Media Bias

AI methods, such as deep neural networks, learn relationships and dependencies based on training data, which can vary considerably depending on the application. In the case of news texts, for instance, texts on a specific topic often need to be annotated in a time-consuming manner, according to specified criteria.

We can derive two challenges from this:

1. **Annotation scheme:** Determining suitable criteria for assessing media bias.
2. **Annotation process:** Implementing a scalable annotation process to manage the increased annotation effort of multiple media bias dimensions.

Current research shows that annotated data sets for the fine-grained detection of media bias in news texts are still missing [6,9,14]. As the annotation by experts is time-consuming and expensive, we presented a scalable annotation approach to media bias in news texts based on crowd-sourcing [6]. The approach is applied to news texts about the Ukraine crisis in 2014 and 2015. In this way, we created a new media bias data set based on an annotation scheme at sentence level and the bias dimensions *hidden assumptions*, *subjectivity*, and *framing*.

---

[1] We particularly thank Thomas Fetzer from the University of Mannheim, Jessica Heesen from the University of Tübingen, and Michael Decker from the Karlsruhe Institute of Technology (KIT).

2.2   Field of Action 2: Information Presentation of Media Bias

Citizens are faced with an ever-increasing rate of published news texts on a multitude of controversial topics, making it difficult to get an overview of hotly debated topics [8, 13]. In addition, results must be presented intuitively to promote a balanced coverage in reporting as well as the citizens' media empowerment.

We can derive two challenges from this:

1. **Controversial topics:** Disclosing prevalent positions on an issue.
2. **Comprehensible presentation:** Providing intuitive tools for analyzing media bias.

Media bias in reporting can be revealed through the analysis of controversial topics by extracting prevailing positions using AI methods. To this end, text mining systems can analyze debate portals such as debatepedia.org.[2] In this way, controversial topics can be identified to highlight contrary positions in news texts, for example, by using a label for disputed claims.

Furthermore, disclosing media bias is highly dependent on the way the respective information is presented. Information systems not only have to be intuitive to use, but also need to present the results in a comprehensible and human-centered way. We argue that appropriate tools, which are embedded in the daily news consumption process of citizens, are needed. For instance, a web browser application could highlight relevant text spans (e.g., similar to [2]).

2.3   Field of Action 3: Transparency of Media Bias Evaluation

The use of machine learning processes poses a potential risk that complex relationships are not sufficiently captured by the AI, possibly influencing opinions through incomplete information. Accordingly, the evaluation of AI methods for media bias detection and analysis must be transparent and comprehensible and neither discriminate nor distort information.

We can derive two challenges from this:

1. **Explainable AI methods:** Providing comprehensible explanations.
2. **Fair AI methods:** Making methods free from bias and non-discriminatory.

The information must be understandable and presented transparently. Accordingly, trustworthy AI methods (i.e., methods covering human agency and oversight, transparency, as well as diversity, non-discrimination and fairness [5]) are particularly important for media bias evaluation – for instance, through visualization (e.g., similar to [2]). Explanations can be both self-explanatory and make the results comprehensible through background information.

In computer science, fair methods are methods that are free of bias and do not discriminate. Intervening in the annotation and learning process allows outliers to be filtered out and a balanced evaluation to be achieved. In our research paper [6], for instance, we show that the country of origin of the crowdworkers can influence the perception of media bias in the annotation process.

---

[2] http://www.debatepedia.org.

3 Conclusion

In this paper, we presented how media bias can be analyzed and determined automatically, based on artificial intelligence methods and the extent to which the evaluation of methods for automatic media bias annotation is sensitive to various aspects of computer science, the humanities, and the social sciences. Accordingly, three main fields of action were outlined, in which machine learning processes contribute to media bias evaluation: the evaluation principles of media bias, the information presentation of media bias, and the transparency of media bias evaluation.

Possible use cases of our research findings are the assistance of journalists and publishers for balanced coverage in reporting, as well as fostering citizens' media literacy. For example, an intuitive web browser application could highlight media bias in news texts to better understand distortions, and, applied in education, could allow pupils to experience both media bias and the use of artificial intelligence in practice to remedy weaknesses in their media literacy [11].

Acknowledgements. The project was funded as part of the digilog@bw joint research project by the Baden-Württemberg Ministry for Science, Research and Art with funds from the state digitization strategy digital@bw.

References

1. Bellows, M.: Exploration of Classifying Sentence Bias in News Articles with Machine Learning Models (2018). https://digitalcommons.uri.edu/theses/1309
2. Botnevik, B., Sakariassen, E., Setty, V.: BRENDA: browser extension for fake news detection. In: Proceedings of the 43rd International ACM SIGIR Conference on Research and Development in Information Retrieval, SIGIR 2020, pp. 2117–2120. ACM (2020). https://doi.org/10.1145/3397271.3401396
3. Cremisini, A., Aguilar, D., Finlayson, M.A.: A challenging dataset for bias detection: the case of the crisis in the Ukraine. In: Proceedings of the 12th International Conference on Social Computing, Behavioral-Cultural Modeling and Prediction and Behavior Representation in Modeling and Simulation, SBP-BRiMS 2019, pp. 173–183 (2019). https://doi.org/10.1007/978-3-030-21741-9_18
4. D'Alessio, D., Allen, M.: Media bias in presidential elections: a meta-analysis. J. Commun. **50**(4), 133–156 (2000). https://doi.org/10.1111/j.1460-2466.2000.tb02866.x
5. European Commission: Ethics guidelines for trustworthy AI, November 2020. https://ec.europa.eu/digital-single-market/en/news/ethics-guidelines-trustworthy-ai
6. Färber, M., Burkard, V., Jatowt, A., Lim, S.: A multidimensional dataset based on crowdsourcing for analyzing and detecting news bias. In: Proceedings of the 29th ACM International Conference on Information and Knowledge Management, CIKM 2020, pp. 3007–3014. ACM (2020). https://doi.org/10.1145/3340531.3412876
7. Hamborg, F., Donnay, K., Gipp, B.: Automated identification of media bias in news articles: an interdisciplinary literature review. Int. J. Digit. Libr. **20**(4), 391–415 (2019). https://doi.org/10.1007/s00799-018-0261-y

8. Holton, A., Chyi, H.I.: News and the overloaded consumer: factors influencing information overload among news consumers. Cyberpsychol. Behav. Soc. Netw. **15**(11), 619–624 (2012). https://doi.org/10.1089/cyber.2011.0610

9. Lim, S., Jatowt, A., Färber, M., Yoshikawa, M.: Annotating and analyzing biased sentences in news articles using crowdsourcing. In: Proceedings of The 12th Language Resources and Evaluation Conference, LREC 2020, pp. 1478–1484 (2020). https://www.aclweb.org/anthology/2020.lrec-1.184/

10. van der Linden, S., Roozenbeek, J., Compton, J.: Inoculating against fake news about COVID-19. Frontiers Psychol. **11**, 2928 (2020). https://doi.org/10.3389/fpsyg.2020.566790

11. Maksl, A., Ashley, S., Craft, S.: Measuring news media literacy. J. Med. Literacy Educ. **6**(3), 29–45 (2015), https://digitalcommons.uri.edu/jmle/vol6/iss3/3

12. Recasens, M., Danescu-Niculescu-Mizil, C., Jurafsky, D.: Linguistic models for analyzing and detecting biased language. In: Proceedings of the 51st Annual Meeting of the Association for Computational Linguistics, ACL 2013, pp. 1650–1659 (2013)

13. Song, H., Jung, J., Kim, Y.: Perceived news overload and its cognitive and attitudinal consequences for news usage in South Korea. J. Mass Commun. Q. **94**(4), 1172–1190 (2017). https://doi.org/10.1177/1077699016679975

14. Spinde, T., et al.: Automated identification of bias inducing words in news articles using linguistic and context-oriented features. Inf. Process. Manage. **58**(3) (2021). https://doi.org/10.1016/j.ipm.2021.102505

15. Zhou, X., Zafarani, R., Shu, K., Liu, H.: Fake news: fundamental theories, detection strategies and challenges. In: Proceedings of the Twelfth ACM International Conference on Web Search and Data Mining, WSDM 2019, pp. 836–837. ACM (2019). https://doi.org/10.1145/3289600.3291382

Users' Perception of Search-Engine Biases and Satisfaction

Bin Han[(✉)], Chirag Shah, and Daniel Saelid

University of Washington, Seattle, WA, USA
bh193@uw.edu

Abstract. Search engines could consistently favor certain values over
the others, which is considered as biased due to the built-in infrastruc-
tures. Many studies have been dedicated to detect, control, and mitigate the impacts of those biases from the perspectives of search engines
themselves. In our study, we pitched the perspective from end-users to
analyze their perceptions of search engine biases and their satisfaction
when the biases are regulated. In the study, we paired a real page from
search engine Bing and a synthesized page with more diversities in the
results (i.e. less biased). Both pages show the top-10 search items given
search queries and we asked participants which one they prefer and why
do they prefer the one selected. Statistical analyses revealed that overall, participants prefer the original Bing pages. Additionally, the location where the diversities are introduced is significantly associated with
users' preferences as well. We found out that users prefer results that are
more consistent and relevant to the search queries. Introducing diversities
undermines the relevance of the search results and impairs users' satisfaction to some degree. Additionally, users tend to pay more attention
to the top portion of the results than the bottom ones.

Keywords: Fairness · Search engine bias · Survey study

1 Introduction

Search engines often present results that are biased toward one subtopic, view, or
perspective due to the way they compute relevance and measure user satisfaction.
Among various types of search engine biases, one describes the case where the
search engines embed features that favor certain values over the others [7,13].
Many studies have attempted to detect, measure and mitigate the impacts from
search engines biases, with the goal of improving users' satisfactions. All those
works aimed to address the issues from the source of the biases—search engines
themselves.

In the previous study we conducted [under review], we took a different path
to inspect the problem from the aspect of end-users. We paired a real search page
and a synthesized page (more varieties in the search results, thus less biased)
and asked participants which one they prefer. The results showed no significant

© Springer Nature Switzerland AG 2021
L. Boratto et al. (Eds.): BIAS 2021, CCIS 1418, pp. 14–24, 2021.
https://doi.org/10.1007/978-3-030-78818-6_3

differences between the ratios of selecting two pages. However, what remained unknown to us is that why did participants select the ones they prefer? What are the reasonings underneath their preferences? Therefore, we revisited this study and improved our survey design catering to our goals (more details in Sect. 3). We would like to evaluate users' perceptions of the biases, thus hoping to reveal the reasoning of their selections of pages. Additionally, we are interested in studying the effects on users' satisfactions when the biases are abated.

2 Background

Several prior studies have attempted to disclose and regulate biases, not just limited in search engines, but also in wilder context of automated systems such as recommender systems. For example, Collins et al. [4] confirmed the position bias in recommender systems, which is the tendency of users to interact with the top-ranked items than the lower-ranked ones, regardless of their relevance. Ovaisi et al. [11] focused on the selection bias in the learning-to-rank (LTR) systems, which occurs because "clicked documents are reflective of what documents have been shown to the user in the first place". They proposed a new approach to account of the selection bias, as well as the position bias in LTR systems. Another bias, popularity bias, states the negative influences of historical users' feedback on the qualities of returned items from current recommender systems. Boratto et al. [2] designed two metrics to quantify such popularity bias and proposed a method to reduce the biased correlation between item relevance and item popularity.

To reduce biases of the search engines, in other words, is to provide fairer search results. Therefore, our problem is also closely related with fair-ranking studies, in which the goal is to generate ranking lists with nondiscriminatory and fair exposures of various defined groups, such as race, gender, region etc. In our case, the groups are the subtopics of the items, within which the items share similar values and topics. Chen et al. [3] investigated the resume search engine and found out the gender-based unfairness from the usage of demographic information in the ranking algorithm. Zehlike et al. [14] defined the principles of ranked group fairness and the fair top-K ranking problems. They proposed the FA*IR algorithm, which maximizes the utility while satisfying ranked group fairness. In addition to the mitigation of fairness at the group level, Biega et al. [1] proposed new measures to capture, quantify, and mitigate unfairness at the individual subjects level. They proposed a new mechanism—amortized fairness, to address the position bias in the ranking problems.

Additionally, there are some studies in the machine learning domain that investigated human's perceptions of fairness and biases in algorithms. Srivas-taca et al. [12] deployed experiments to detect the most appropriate notions of fairness that best captures human's perception of fairness, given different societal domains. They found out that simplest definition, demographic parity, is aligned with most people's understanding of fairness. Grgić-Hlača et al. [8] deployed a survey study in the criminal risk prediction main to analyze how people people perceive and reason the fairness in the decisions generated by algorithms.

They found out that people's concerns about fairness are multi-dimensional and unfairness should not be just limited to discrimination.

However, fewer studies in the fair-ranking domain have devoted to probe users' consciousness towards the biases and their behaviors associated with their awareness. Fewer studies have analyzed how users' satisfactions are related with the biases in general. Consequently, inspired by the bias/fairness perception studies in the machine learning community, our work aims to dive deeper in this direction.

3   Method

In this section, we present the algorithm to generate the synthesized search pages and the specifics of the survey design. We also enunciate the two core questions we want to address from this study and three hypotheses that we would like to test on. Notice that in sections below, "diversities", "varieties" and "differences" are equivalent. Introducing diversities/varieties/differences could potentially reduce the biases; "documents", "items" and "results" are equivalent, as they all mean the search engine results.

The Algorithm to Generate Synthesized Pages

To generate synthesized search pages that are less biased (more diverse in subtopics), we implemented **epsilon-0.3** algorithm with **statistical parity** as the fairness controller. We first group the documents into $\mathcal{K}$ number of groups. Documents within each group share similar topics, values, views etc. Therefore, each group can be treated as a subtopic group. The fairness controller aims to provide a list of documents with equal or close presence of different subtopic groups: given a search query, we replace three items from the top-10 list with three lower ranked items, proportionally to the frequencies of different subtopic groups in the top-10 list. For instance, suppose that there are two subtopic groups (A and B). If the top-10 list has eight items from group A and two items from group B, we would replace three out of eight items from group A at top-10 with three lower ranked documents from group B. The replacement of the documents could happen in different locations in the top-10 list. Therefore, there are two versions of the algorithm. Version one, presented in Table 1, replaces three documents from top-5 in the top-10 list. Version two is exactly the same as the version one, except for that the replacement happens at bottom-5 in the top-10 list. Please refer to Fig. 1 for details.

We chose the **epsilon-0.3** algorithm not only to be consistent with our previous study, but also based on the fair-ranking work by Gao and Shah [6]. They tested multiple fairness ranking strategies to probe the relationships among fairness, diversity, novelty and relevance and found out that epsilon-greedy algorithms could bring fairer representations of the search results without a cost on the relevance. In the previous study, we experimented with the variants of the algorithm—epsilon-0.1 and epsilon-0.2, and found out that the replacement ratios (0.1 and 0.2) were too low. Therefore, we decided to work with the epsilon-0.3 algorithm. Additionally, we worked with top-10 list because popular search engines, such as Google and Bing, usually return 10 items per page as the default setting (though adjustable). Therefore, we decided to stick with the default number of 10 documents.

Table 1. Algorithm to generate synthesized pages. The replacement happens in top-5 from the top-10 list.

Epsilon-0.3 Algorithm — Top-5 Replacement

1. Group top-100 search documents into two subtopic clusters.
2. Remove top-10 documents from the two clusters.
3. Calculate cluster 1 (c1) and cluster 2 (c2) frequencies (freq) in top-10 documents.
4. For three iterations:

   if $freq_{c1} == freq_{c2}$:

   Randomly select an index in the top-5 and swap with the next highest ranked document from the cluster, from which the current document was taken. Remove this document from the cluster list

   else if $freq_{c1} > freq_{c2}$:

   randomly select an index in the top-5 containing a c1 document, and swap it with the next highest ranked document from c2. If there are no remaining documents in c2, swap with a c1 document. Remove the swapped document from cluster list

   else if $freq_{c1} < freq_{c2}$:

   randomly select an index in the top-5 containing a c2 document, and swap it with the next highest ranked document from c1. If there are no remaining documents in c1, swap with a c2 document. Remove the swapped document from cluster list

   Update frequencies

   Remove the index that has been swapped in the top-5

Survey Questions and Hypotheses

The two core study questions we would like to answer are:

- *Does introducing more varieties in the search engine results, equivalently less biased, hinder users' satisfaction?*
- *What are the reasons of the users' choices of preferences?*

We raised three actionable hypotheses to potentially answer the questions:

- **H1: People do not care/notice the minute differences between the two search results:** even though we introduced lower ranked results into the top list to add varieties, the differences might not be drastic enough for some participants to notice. Or the participants might realize the differences but they do not care about which one is better.

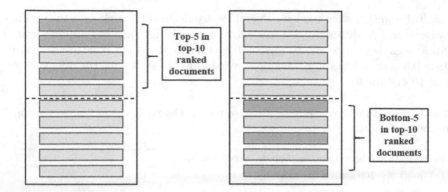

Fig. 1. In the left figure, we replace three documents (marked in orange) from top-5 in the top-10 list with lower ranked results. In the right figure, we replace three documents from bottom-5 in the top-10 list. (Color figure online)

- **H2: The location where the differences present matters. When differences are at the bottom of the search list, people do not care:** intuitively, users might treat the top-ranked results more seriously than the lower-ranked ones. Even in top-10 list, the top-5 might attract different attention than the bottom-5. Therefore, in our survey design, the replacement happens in both locations (top-5 or bottom-5 in the top-10 list).
- **H3: People prefer results with high relevance as opposed to high diversity:** this hypothesis could answer the second question. Introducing lower ranked search items means adding more diversities into the results, thus weakening the potential biases of search engines that consistently favor some values over the others. Unavoidably, however, adding lower ranked results would sabotage the relevance of the search results, leading to consequences of potentially lowering users' satisfactions. Therefore, we want to see whether they prefer higher relevance (more biased) or higher diversity (less biased).

Experimental Design

The experiment starts with a consent form to be signed, which is followed by several demographic questions (e.g. age group, gender and education background). Then the participants are provided with instructions on how to complete the survey through a quick demo (as shown in Fig. 2). Once they are familiar with the details, they may proceed to answer the questions. The survey has 20 rounds in total. Each round consists a pair of real Bing search page and a synthesized page using the algorithm aforementioned, given a specific search query. Participants have 30 s to read the query, compare the items between two pages, and make a selection. Out of 20 rounds, we randomly select 10 rounds to perform the top-5 in top-10 replacement, while the rest rounds receive bottom-5 in top-10 replacement.

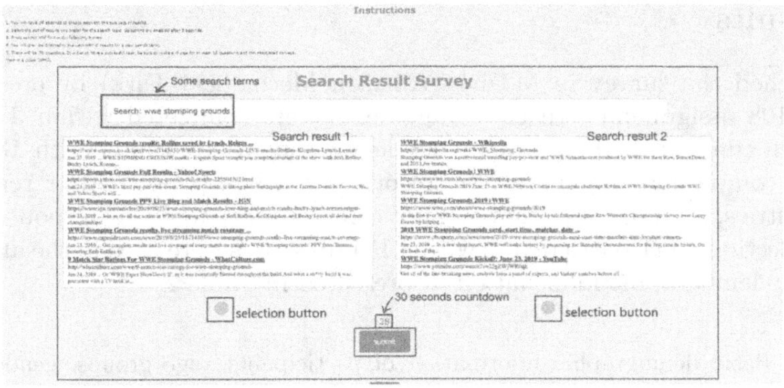

Fig. 2. The interface of the survey. The query shows in the search box at the top. The paired pages consist of a real Bing search page and a synthesized one. Participants can select whichever one they prefer and submit.

Based on the experience from the previous study, we thought 20 rounds provide sufficiently large data information for statistical analysis, while not overly fatiguing the participants by pouring information on them. Additionally, we tested with some trial runs of the survey and found out that 30 s are enough to participants to compare the two pages and made a selection. After each round, there is a reflection question (as shown in Fig. 3) on the reasons of the participants' choice of preferences:

- *"I did not notice any differences"* addresses the H1. The differences might not be palpable enough for the participants.
- *"I noticed some differences but did not care. So I randomly picked up one."* addressed the H1. Participants might detect the discrepancies, but they do not make a difference in users' satisfaction.
- *"I noticed some differences and picked the one that had more results on the same topic."* & *"I noticed some differences and picked the one that had more variety in the results"*. They together address H3. More results on the same topic means that the documents are more consistent with each other. More varieties in the results represent the introduced lower ranked results.

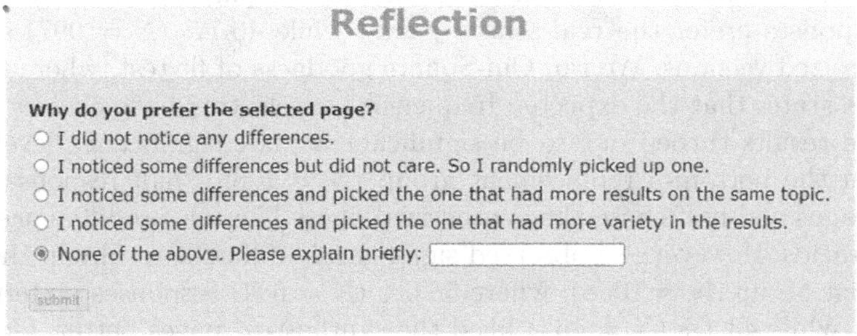

Fig. 3. Reflection question on the reasons of the participants' choice of preferences.

4   Results

We launched the survey in MTurk (Amazon Mechanical Turk) by creating a total of 108 assignment. All the assignments were completed within 3 h from the launch time, with the average completion time as 16.4 min. With 137 participants completing the survey, we recorded 2,408 responses. After removing invalid entries, such as users that did not complete the survey or responses with empty selections, 111 participants with 2,134 responses were used in the analysis. The basic demographic information in presented in Table 2.

Table 2. Basic demographic information of participants—age groups, gender, and education background.

Features	Groups	Count
Age group	22–28	571 (27%)
	29–35	681 (32%)
	36–49	488 (23%)
	50–65	355 (17%)
	Prefer not to say	39 (2%)
Gender	Male	1212 (57%)
	Female	863 (40%)
	Non-binary	20 (1%)
	Prefer not to say	39 (2%)
Education	High school	158 (7%)
	Bachelor	1264 (59%)
	Master	653 (31%)
	PhD (or similar)	20 (1%)
	Prefer not to say	39 (2%)

Selection Ratios

Starting with the overall selection ratios of the two pages, 53.3% (N = 1137) of the responses prefer the real search pages, while 46.7% (N = 997) selected the synthesized versions. We ran Chi-Square goodness of fit test, where the null hypothesis states that the expected frequencies of selecting both choices are the same. The results turned out to be significant at 0.01 significance level (**p = 0.002**). In the bottom-5 replacement group (N = 1066), half responses chose the real pages and half chose the synthesized ones. There is no difference in the selection ratios. However, we observed significantly different results in the top-5 replacement group (N = 1068), where 56.6% (N = 604) responses preferred the real pages while 43.4% (N = 464) liked the synthesized pages better. Goodness of fit test yield significant result (**p < 1e-4**).

Based on the separate tests in each replacement group, it seems that the location where the diversities are introduced have an impact on users' preferences. To further confirm the conjecture, we ran Chi-square test of independence on two categorical variables: users' preferences (real page or synthesized page) and replacement group (top-5 or bottom-5). The result is significant given $\mathbf{p} = \mathbf{0.003}$. It demonstrates that the location is associated with participants' preferences.

Reasoning Analysis

The default four reasons, corresponding to the four choices in order, are "No Diff", "Diff Random", "Diff Same Topic", and "Diff Variety". We probed the reasons for three groups separately – the group that selected the real pages (called "original" group), the group that selected the synthesized pages with the top-5 replacement ("Top-5" group), and the group that selected the synthesized pages with bottom-5 replacement ("Bottom-5" group). We only presented the analysis of the four default answers here because users' own explanations are diverse and sparse, which will be analyzed in the discussion section.

The distributions of default answers for each group are exhibited in Table 3. We noticed that within each group, "Diff Same Topic" dominated all other answers. Within each group, we ran Chi-square goodness of fit test, in which the null hypothesis states that the expected frequencies of the default choices are the same. All three p-values are extremely small, indicating that the observed frequencies are significantly different from the expected ones.

Table 3. Distributions of four default choices in each selection group. p-values are from Chi-square goodness of fit test within each group.

Groups	No diff	Diff random	Diff same topic	Diff variety	p-value
Original	117	222	461	310	2.2e−49
Top-5	49	87	186	132	7.5e−20
Bottom-5	55	104	218	147	1.5e−23

5   Discussion

As defined in Sect. 3, the first question we would like to answer is *"Does introducing more varieties in the search engine results, equivalently less biased, hinder users' satisfaction?"* From the analysis above, we showed that the proportion of participants preferring the real pages is significantly higher than that of the participants that selected the synthesized pages. Bringing up lower ranked results into the top ranked list introduces more varieties and values in the search results, thus weakening the biases of search engine in favoring certain values. However, it potentially damages the relevance and consistency of the results to the queries.

Based on the result, it is reasonable to conjecture that users' satisfactions are impaired due to the added varieties, even though the bias is mitigated.

The second question we would like to answer is *"What are the reasons of the users' choices of preferences?"*. We hypothesized that the site where the varieties are introduced play a role in affecting users' preferences. And we indeed observed distinctions between the results from the two replacement groups. Our results demonstrated that when the differences exhibit at bottom-5, participants had no compelling tendency of picking up one over the other. However, when they noticed the differences at top-5, they had a significant inclination to choose the real Bing page. This could be explained by [5], which articulates that "most people use very short, imprecise search terms and rarely click beyond the first page of results. They also tend to believe that what comes at the top of the search results must be the best result. (p. 13)" Kulshrestha et al. [10] also mentioned that the top-ranked results are capable of shaping users' opinions about the topics, which demonstrates the importance of the search results' location. In our case, we could interpret it as when the differences are shown at top-5, participants will pay more attention to pinpoint the differences and make a selection. The phenomenon was also observed in some users' explanations in the reflection questions. Some mentioned that *"I like the first 3 results"*, *". . . at the top that explained . . .*, *"preferred the top X list"*.

Additionally, from the reasoning analysis section, when participants picked up the real pages, 40% of the reasons are "Diff Same Topic". It means that they did notice some differences between the two pages and they prefer the one with more homogeneous results. Interestingly, for users that gave their own explanations, many mentioned that the original pages provide more relevant and reliable results than the synthesized ones, which is what we expected. Introducing diversities by replacing higher ranked results with lower ranked ones will reduce biases, but potentially hinder the relevance of the search results, thus sabotaging users' satisfaction as the aftermath.

However, when we applied the same reasoning analysis on the two replacement groups, the results do not make logical sense even they are significant. Most of the participants still selected "Diff Same Topic" as the reason, even though they picked up the synthesized pages that have more varieties rather than consistency. It means that they believed that the real page are more diverse in terms of results. This could be contributed to two reasons: (1) the lower ranked results are similar to those replaced higher ranked items such that the participants did not notice the diversities; and (2) the definitions of similarity and diversity on a topic are not unified and are different from each participant. Consequently, they may pick up the one that contain objectively similar results from their perspective, even though the page is subjectively more diverse.

6   Conclusion

In our study, we designed a survey to assess users' perceptions of search engine biases, with the goal of diagnosing the reasoning underneath their preferences of the real search pages or the synthesized pages. We also investigated the effects of bias-mitigation on users' satisfactions. We noticed that overall, participants prefer the real search pages over the synthesized ones with a significant higher ratio. It indicates that adding more varieties makes the results less biased but less relevant and consistent to the queries, which hurts users' satisfactions. In addition, when the diversities in the synthesized pages are present at the top-5, participants tend to prefer the real pages. However, when they are at bottom-5, there is no significant difference between the ratios of selecting two pages. It confirms our hypothesis that the location where the bias-mitigation happens is critical.

In terms of the future work, two directions could be considered. First, the survey design could be improved. The reflection question in the first round might give additional information of what will be asked in later rounds and could potentially impact users' selections. In addition, the response options in the reflection questions are shown in a fixed order, which might generate order bias [9]. Redesigning the format of reflection questions could potentially improve the study results. Second, if more variables of interests could be collected (if applicable) in addition to the demographic features, mixed-effect regression models could be conducted to account for repeated measures from the same individuals and the relationships among the various features and preferences could be probed simultaneously.

References

1. Biega, A.J., Gummadi, K., Weikum, G.: Equity of attention: amortizing individual fairness in rankings. In: The 41st International ACM SIGIR Conference on Research & Development in Information Retrieval (2018)
2. Boratto, L., Fenu, G., Marras, M.: Connecting user and item perspectives in popularity debiasing for collaborative recommendation. Inf. Process. Manage. **58**(1), 102387 (2021)
3. Chen, L., Ma, R., Hannák, A., Wilson, C.: Investigating the impact of gender on rank in resume search engines. In: Proceedings of the 2018 CHI Conference on Human Factors in Computing Systems, CHI 2018, pp. 1–14. Association for Computing Machinery, New York (2018)
4. Collins, A., Tkaczyk, D., Aizawa, A., Beel, J.: Position bias in recommender systems for digital libraries. In: Chowdhury, G., McLeod, J., Gillet, V., Willett, P. (eds.) iConference 2018. LNCS, vol. 10766, pp. 335–344. Springer, Cham (2018). https://doi.org/10.1007/978-3-319-78105-1_37
5. Couvering, E.J.V.: Search engine bias - the structuration of traffic on the world-wide web. Ph.D. dissertation, London School of Economics and Political Science (2009)
6. Gao, R., Shah, C.: Toward creating a fairer ranking in search engine results. Inf. Process. Manage. **57**(1), 102138 (2020)

7. Goldman, E.: Search engine bias and the demise of search engine utopianism. Yale J. Law Technol. **8**, 188 (2005)
8. Grgic-Hlaca, N., Redmiles, E.M., Gummadi, K.P., Weller, A.: Human perceptions of fairness in algorithmic decision making: a case study of criminal risk prediction. In: Proceedings of the 2018 World Wide Web Conference, WWW 2018, Republic and Canton of Geneva, CHE 2018, page 903–912. International World Wide Web Conferences Steering Committee (2018)
9. Krosnick, J.A., Alwin, D.F.: An evaluation of a cognitive theory of response-order effects in survey measurement. Public Opin. Q. **51**(2), 201–219 (1987)
10. Kulshrestha, J., et al.: Search bias quantification: investigating political bias in social media and web search. Inf. Retrieval J. **22**, 188–227 (2019). https://doi.org/10.1007/s10791-018-9341-2
11. Ovaisi, Z., Ahsan, R., Zhang, Y., Vasilaky, K., Zheleva, E.: Correcting for selection bias in learning-to-rank systems. In: Proceedings of The Web Conference 2020, WWW 2020, pp. 1863–1873. Association for Computing Machinery, New York (2020)
12. Srivastava, M., Heidari, H. Krause, A.: Mathematical notions vs. human perception of fairness: a descriptive approach to fairness for machine learning. In: Proceedings of the 25th ACM SIGKDD International Conference on Knowledge Discovery & Data Mining, KDD 2019, pp. 2459–2468. Association for Computing Machinery, New York (2019)
13. Tavani, H.: Search engines and ethics. In: Zalta, E.N. (ed.) The Stanford Encyclopedia of Philosophy. Fall 2020 edn. Metaphysics Research Lab, Stanford University (2020)
14. Zehlike, M., Bonchi, F., Castillo, C., Hajian, S., Megahed, M., Baeza-Yates, R.: FA*IR: a fair top-k ranking algorithm. In: Proceedings of the 2017 ACM on Conference on Information and Knowledge Management, CIKM 2017, pp. 1569–1578. Association for Computing Machinery, New York (2017)

Preliminary Experiments to Examine the Stability of Bias-Aware Techniques

Toshihiro Kamishima[1]($\boxtimes$)(iD), Shotaro Akaho[1], Yukino Baba[2],
and Hisashi Kashima[3]

[1] National Institute of Advanced Industrial Science and Technology (AIST),
Tsukuba, Japan
mail@kamishima.net, s.akaho@aist.go.jp
[2] University of Tsukuba, Tsukuba, Japan
baba@cs.tsukuba.ac.jp
[3] Kyoto University, Kyoto, Japan
kashima@i.kyoto-u.ac.jp

Abstract. Fairness-aware techniques are designed to remove socially sensitive information, such as gender or race. Many types of fairness-aware predictors have been developed, but they were designed essentially to improve the accuracy or fairness of the prediction results. We focus herein on another aspect of fairness-aware predictors, i.e., the stability. We define that fairness-aware techniques are stable if the same models are learned when a training dataset contains the same information except for the sensitive information. We sought to collect benchmark datasets to investigate such stability. We collected preference data in a manner ensuring that the users' responses were influenced by cognitive biases. If the same models are learned for a dataset influenced by different types of cognitive biases, the learner of the models can be considered stable. We performed preliminary experiments using this dataset, but we failed to fully remove the influence of cognitive biases. We discuss the necessary next steps to solve this problem.

Keywords: Fairness · Cognitive bias · Crowdsourcing

1 Introduction

One of the goals of the current research concerning fairness-aware machine learning is to develop techniques for learning a predictor that is as accurate as possible while satisfying a given fairness constraint. The development of fairness-aware techniques have focused on the improvement of the trade-offs between accuracy and fairness; however, the accuracy is measured over a dataset whose annotation is potentially biased, because fair labels are not accessible. It is unclear whether the accuracy over an unbiased dataset is appropriately measured. We thus propose that another property is desirable for a fairness-aware predictor, i.e., the *stability*.

© Springer Nature Switzerland AG 2021
L. Boratto et al. (Eds.): BIAS 2021, CCIS 1418, pp. 25–35, 2021.
https://doi.org/10.1007/978-3-030-78818-6_4

We herein refer to the stability of fairness-aware techniques in the sense that the same model is learned if all the information are the same except for the sensitive information. In a classification case, a class will be predicted from features of objects. If some of the features represent sensitive information that should be removed from the viewpoint of social fairness, these features are called *sensitive* features. We also focus herein on statistical parity or group fairness, which is a type of fairness constraint; the constraint is the statistical independence between a class variable and sensitive features. This means that no sensitive information influences the decision of a class. Hence, the same model should be learned if all of the features other than sensitive features are the same. We call the classifier stable if such an ideal condition is satisfied.

We conducted the present study to collect controlled datasets to investigate this stability. If we have multiple datasets composed of the same information other than sensitive information, the stability of fairness-aware classifiers can be evaluated by comparing the learned models from each of these datasets. Because it is generally difficult to control the socially sensitive information that is dealt with by fairness-aware classifiers, we select a problem about the decision to choice of the preferred items. Even though we do not target socially sensitive decisions, it is not problematic, because the notion of stability relates to the more general problem compared to the fairness-aware classification, which removes the influence of undesirable information for users. Hereafter, we use the more general term, i.e., *bias-aware*, in the place of *fairness-aware*.

The datasets consisted of subjects' preference information regarding various types of sushi. We collected the data of paired comparison tests completed by the subjects recruited by a crowdsourcing service, and we used cognitive biases as a proxy of a sensitive feature. We designed user interfaces so that the subjects' choices were influenced by a cognitive bias. We targeted two kinds of cognitive biases: a positional effect [2] and a bandwagon effect [4]. A bias-aware technique was used to remove the influence of these cognitive biases. The bias-aware technique is considered as stable if the same models are learned under different types of cognitive biases.

We performed preliminary experiments on the collected datasets. Since the collection scheme of the datasets was controlled, the cognitive biases can be theoretically removed by a simple bias-removing technique, i.e., stratification. We hypothesized that the stratification technique would be stable, but our experimental results do not support this hypothesis. We analyze the reason why the influence of cognitive biases was not fully removed, and we discuss the next steps that can be taken to resolve this problem.

Our contributions are summarized as follows:

- We proposed the notion of stability of bias-aware techniques.
- We collected controlled data to examine the stability of bias-aware techniques.
- The relationship between bias-aware techniques and causal inference is discussed.
- We report preliminary experimental results obtained with the collected dataset.

2   Datasets

After describing the generative model of preference data below, we provide the details of the procedure used to collect the datasets. We then confirm that the collected data were influenced by the subjects' cognitive biases.

2.1   Generative Models for the Datasets

We next illustrate our model for the analysis of cognitive biases. As in the standard model for fairness-aware machine learning, the model presented here in consists of three types of variables: S, $\mathbf{X}$, and Y. S denotes a sensitive feature. In a usual task of fairness-aware classification, this variable represents socially sensitive information, e.g., individuals' gender or race. In this study, we used a cognitive bias as a sensitive feature, because (a) any factor that influences humans' decision can be used in this experiment, and (b) a cognitive bias is easily controlled. We tested two types of cognitive bias. One is a positional effect, the item displayed near the upper-left corner of the interface screen is more frequently selected [2]. We horizontally displayed two types of sushi and expected that the left item would be selected more frequently. In this case, S represents whether a type of sushi is displayed at the left or right pane of the screen. The other type of cognitive bias is a bandwagon effect, in which it is indicated that other people prefer an item, and the item is more frequently selected [4]. We emphasized one type of sushi with the label 'Popular' and expected that the emphasized type would be selected more frequently. In this case, S represents whether or not a type of sushi is emphasized.

$\mathbf{X}$ denotes non-sensitive features. In a standard task of fairness-aware classification, these features correspond to all of information represented by the variables other than Y and S. In this paper, $\mathbf{X}$ explicitly consists of two variables, X_1 and X_2. These variables represent the two types of sushi shown to the subjects. These variables are discrete and can take one of an index number indicating a specific type of sushi. We contend that many types of unobserved factors, e.g., who the subjects are and when the subjects evaluate, implicitly affect the choice of items.

Y denotes a decision or target variable representing a predicted class. In a task of fairness-aware classification, Y may represent the decision about university admission, credit, employment, or other matter. Herein, Y represents whether or not one type sushi is preferred to the other. The variable Y takes 1 if the subject preferred the sushi type indicated by X_1 to the sushi type indicated by X_2; otherwise, Y takes 0.

We then describe the model used to measure the influence of a cognitive bias. The dependence between variables is illustrated in Fig. 1(a). In a context of causal inference, we consider that S corresponds to an intervention and Y corresponds to an effect. The choice of items exposed to the subjects, $\mathbf{X}$, is treated as a confounder.

The influence of a cognitive bias can be evaluated by using this model if interventions are randomly assigned. In particular, randomly selected items are

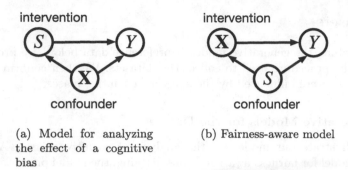

(a) Model for analyzing the effect of a cognitive bias

(b) Fairness-aware model

Fig. 1. Models of the dependence between variables

exposed to a random subject, and interventions, $S = 0$ and $S = 1$, are randomly assigned. Because this procedure is regarded as a randomized controlled trial, the degree of the influence of a cognitive bias can be measured by

$$E[Y|S = 1] - E[Y|S = 0] = \Pr[Y = 1|S = 1] - \Pr[Y = 1|S = 0]. \quad (1)$$

2.2   Data Collection Procedure

In this section, we describe the procedure for collecting the preference data by the paired comparison scheme. We randomly selected two types of sushi among the following ten types of sushi, which were used in our earlier study [7], and we showed pairs of sushi types to the subjects:

Fatty tuna (FT)   Tuna (Tn)   Shrimp (Sh) Salmon roe (SR)   See eel (SE)
Sea urchin (SU) Tuna roll (TR) Squid (Sq)   Egg (Eg)   Cucumber roll (CR)

In the presentation below of our experimental results, the types of sushi are specified by the above-noted abbreviations shown in parentheses. According to the survey of $> 5,000$ subjects in our previous study [7], these ten types of sushi are preferred in the order in which they are presented above, and we refer to this order as the *popularity order*. Our subjects then compared two displayed types of sushi and selected the one that they preferred to the other.

We used two types of interfaces: baseline and bandwagon. The baseline interface displays two types sushi, which are the same size and horizontally aligned, as shown in Fig. 2(a). The other bandwagon interface emphasizes one of two types of sushi by displaying it in a larger size and with the label 'Popular',fv as shown in Fig. 2(b).

We collected preference data by using three procedures. We first presented two types of sushi for each subject by using the baseline interface, and we randomly selected which types of sushi was to be placed at the left pane. In the case of a positional effect, $S=1$ indicates that the item represented by X_1 is shown in the left pane. This procedure is an ideal randomized controlled trial, and the degree of a positional effect can be exactly measured by Eq. (1). We call this the 'random' procedure.

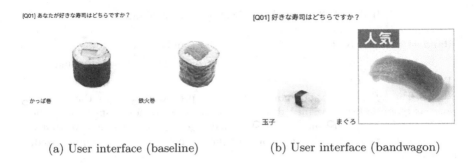

(a) User interface (baseline)   (b) User interface (bandwagon)

Fig. 2. User interfaces for collecting data.
NOTE: We asked the subjects "Which type of sushi do you prefer?" in both cases. In the 'bandwagon' case, one of the types of sushi was highlighted with the label 'Popular'.

Second, after dividing the subjects into two groups, we showed pairs of sushi types to each subject by using the baseline interface, and we then merged the datasets obtained from the two groups. In one group, the sushi that was ranked higher in the popularity order was placed always at the left pane, and in the other group, it was always placed in the right pane. This can still be considered as a randomized controlled trial, because the assignment of items is random and the assignment of the subjects to groups is also random. However, it might be incomplete because some implicit factors are not fully randomized. For example, the subjects could be influenced by a previous choice, the so-called memory effect, because (a) they chose their preferred types of sushis sequentially, and (b) the influence of this procedure could be stronger than that of the random procedure. We call this procedure 'fixed' because the placements of the types of sushi were fixed for each subject.

Third, we again divided the subjects into two groups, but used the bandwagon interface. While the sushi-type that was ranked higher in the popularity order was emphasized in one group, the type that was ranked lower was emphasized in the other group. In the case of a bandwagon effect, $S = 1$ indicates that the item represented by X_1 is emphasized. As in the case of the fixed procedure, this procedure can be considered a randomized controlled trial, but it could be incomplete. We call this the 'bandwagon' procedure.

We collected the data by using a crowdsourcing service in Japan. The data were collected during the approximately 3-week period between 31 Jan. 2020 to 22 Feb. 2020, and we paid each subject JPY 50 for their participation. The number of queries per subject was 50. Two of the queries were concentration tests that requested the subject to "Select right", and we used the data from the subjects who passed the tests. The sizes of the datasets are shown in Table 1.

Table 1. The numbers of subjects in each dataset

Random	Fixed		Bandwagon	
	Left	Right	Popular	Unpopular
120	103	118	99	96

NOTE: The *left* and *right* columns of the 'fixed' procedure indicate that a more popular type of sushi was placed at the left and right panes, respectively. The *popular* and *unpopular* columns of the 'bandwagon' procedure indicate that a more-popular type of sushi and a less-popular type of sushi was emphasized, respectively.

2.3   Evaluation of Cognitive Bias

Table 2. The total effect of the cognitive biases

Random	Fixed	Bandwagon
0.0229	0.0077	0.3451

In this section, we evaluate the total effect of the cognitive biases, which can be measured by Eq. (1). Note that in a context of fairness-aware machine learning, the quantity of the total effect corresponds to the risk difference [1,9]. The total effect under each procedure is described in Table 2. A positive value indicates that the item in the left pane was selected (in the random and fixed procedures) or that the emphasized item was selected (in the bandwagon procedure). We can confirm that the choice of items was influenced by a cognitive bias. In addition, the effect of a bandwagon effect was stronger than that of the positional bias. These results are consistent with the reported observation that the bandwagon effect was stronger than the other effects [4].

We further evaluated the subjects' cognitive biases, and evaluated the effect of each item. For each sushi i, the target variable Y_i becomes 1 if the item i is preferred to the other items. The degree of cognitive biases per item becomes

$$\mathrm{E}[Y_i|S = 1] - \mathrm{E}[Y_i|S = 0] = \Pr[Y_i = 1|S = 1] - \Pr[Y_i = 1|S = 0]. \qquad (2)$$

These effects were illustrated in Fig. 3. No clear patterns were observed in terms of a positional effect. In the case of a bandwagon effect, highly popular and highly unpopular items were more strongly influenced by a cognitive bias. This observation also indicates that the influence of a bandwagon effect is stronger than that of a positional effect.

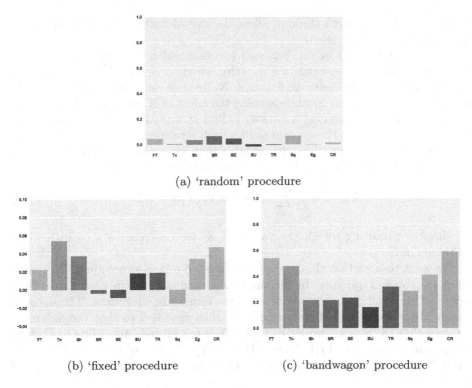

(a) 'random' procedure

(b) 'fixed' procedure   (c) 'bandwagon' procedure

Fig. 3. The degrees of cognitive bias under each procedure.
NOTE: The x-axes use the abbreviations of ten types of sushi, and the y-axes represent the effects of cognitive bias in Eq. (2). Because the degree of cognitive bias under the bandwagon procedure was larger than those under other two procedures, we rescaled the y-scale of the chart.

3   The Stability of Bias-Aware Techniques

We here discuss the relationship between causal inference and a bias-aware technique, and we then provide the preliminary results of removing the cognitive biases.

3.1   Causal Inference from the Viewpoint of Bias-Aware Classification

We next consider the relationship between causal inference and bias-aware classification, and we describe a simple technique of stratification that can be used to remove cognitive biases. We consider group fairness or statistical parity [1,3,9], which is defined by the independence between Y and S, i.e., $Y \perp\!\!\!\perp S$. In a context of causal inference, this condition corresponds to the removal of the total causal effect from S to Y as described in [8]. Note that the term 'total causal effect' means the sum of effects through all of the causal paths from an intervention variable to a target variable.

We interpret a model for bias-aware classification from the viewpoint of causal inference. As depicted in Fig. 1(b), we treat a sensitive feature, S, as a confounder, and non-sensitive features, $\mathbf{X}$, become an intervention. We try to remove the effect of S on Y while keeping the effect of $\mathbf{X}$ on Y. For this purpose, in a case of causal inference, a dataset is first stratified according to the value of S. The statistics are then computed for each stratum, and these statistics are aggregated by the summation with weights that are proportional to the sizes of the strata. This operation is the summation weighted by $\Pr[S]$,

$$\Pr[Y|\mathbf{X}] = \sum_{\mathbf{s}} \Pr[\mathbf{S} = \mathbf{s}] \Pr[\mathbf{Y}|\mathbf{S} = \mathbf{s}, \mathbf{X}]. \tag{3}$$

By simply computing for all the values of $\mathbf{X}$, we can remove a cognitive bias contained in S.

We want to note that this process is related to a bias-aware approach that is the post-process type [5,6]. In this approach, each sub-classifier is learned from a dataset consisting of data whose sensitive values are equivalent. The decision thresholds or weights of sub-classifiers are then modified so that the difference between $\Pr[Y|\mathbf{X}, \mathbf{S} = 1]$ and $\Pr[Y|\mathbf{X}, \mathbf{S} = 0]$ is minimized. According to Eq. (3), the stratification forces $\Pr[Y|\mathbf{X}, \mathbf{S} = 1]$ and $\Pr[Y|\mathbf{X}, \mathbf{S} = 0]$ to be $\Pr[Y|\mathbf{X}]$, and the difference becomes 0. The stratification can thus be regarded as a type of fairness-aware technique.

In addition, the stratification operation is related to the generative model for bias-aware classification. A joint distribution satisfying the condition of statistical parity, $S \perp\!\!\!\perp Y$, can be formalized as

$$\begin{aligned} \Pr[Y, \mathbf{X}, \mathbf{S}] &= \Pr[S] \Pr[Y|S] \Pr[\mathbf{X}|\mathbf{Y}, \mathbf{S}] \\ &= \Pr[S] \Pr[Y] \Pr[\mathbf{X}|\mathbf{Y}, \mathbf{S}] \quad (\leftarrow \mathbf{Y} \perp\!\!\!\perp \mathbf{S}) \\ &= \Pr[Y]\Big\{ \Pr[S] \Pr[\mathbf{X}|\mathbf{Y}, \mathbf{S}] \Big\}. \end{aligned} \tag{4}$$

If we marginalize the factors in curly braces by S, the operation that corresponds to the stratification that though S is still treated as a confounder, the roles of Y and $\mathbf{X}$ are exchanged. Therefore, Eq. (3) is a classifier adopting a discriminative type, and Eq. (4) is its generative version.

3.2   Experiments to Examine the Stability of a Bias-Aware Technique

Next, we analyze the model obtained by applying the stratification, and we report the stability of the learned models. We simply apply Eq. (3) for each value of $\mathbf{X}$, i.e., every pair of items, and we obtain a probability matrix collected by three above-described procedures: baseline, fixed, and bandwagon. The matrix consists of probabilities that the item in a row is preferred to the item in a column.

Theoretically, because the influence of a cognitive bias is removed and the other information is the same, these matrices would become equal irrelevant to the type of data-collection procedure if a bias-removal technique, e.g., the stratification in Eq. (3), is stable. To test this hypothesis, we derive probability matrices from each datasets collected by the three procedures, and we computed the mean absolute distance between matrices of the baseline and the fixed procedures, and between those of the baseline and the bandwagon procedures. The former distance is rather small 0.0521; the latter is larger 0.127. If the stratification is stable, these distances would become small and similar values, but contrary to our expectation, the difference is rather large.

We further examine the results presented in Fig. 4. The stratified probabilities that each type of sushi is preferred to the other types. Because cognitive biases are removed by stratification, the more popular types sushis are basically more preferred. However, as shown in Fig. 4(c), for the dataset collected by the bandwagon procedure, the stratified probabilities are clearly different from those of the other two procedures.

In summary, although we expected that similar probability matrixes would be obtained by the bias-removal technique, i.e., stratification, the actually obtained matrixes were rather deviated.

3.3   Next Steps for Collecting Better Datasets

As described above, the obtained models are rather diverged, contrary to our hypothesis. As next steps, we discuss two approaches to modify our hypothesis. One approach is based on the possibility that the stratification fails to remove the effect of cognitive biases. The other approach is based on the possibility that there may be confounders other than the cognitive bias that we control.

First, cognitive biases may not be completely removed by the stratification. We generated two data from a single comparison by the subjects. For example, when comparing items A and B, we generate a data whose $X_1 =$ A and a datum whose $X_1 =$ B. We adopted this procedure to obtain data both for $S = 0$ and $S = 1$, but the scheme might be fatal for satisfying the condition for a randomized controlled trial. We designed so that the fixed and bandwagon procedures depend on the preference order in each subject group, and that the scheme might make a causal path from $\mathbf{X}$ to S. Therefore, S may behave as a mediator as well as a confounder. We need to develop another causal structure model by using these factors.

Second, confounders other than the controlled cognitive bias might exist. When actually unpopular items are displayed as popular, the information would not match the subjects' intuition, and the mismatch may cause another type of bias. To check this hypothesis, we plan to collect datasets designed to be influenced by other types of cognitive biases, e.g., a memory effect.

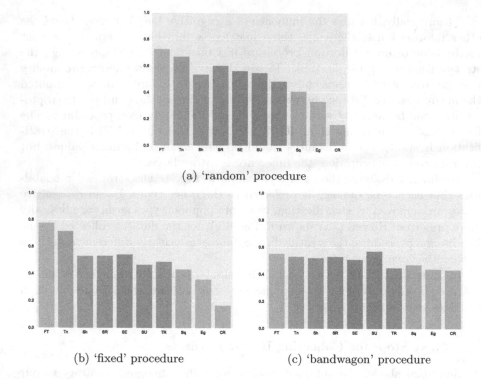

(a) 'random' procedure

(b) 'fixed' procedure   (c) 'bandwagon' procedure

Fig. 4. The stratified probabilities that each type of sushi was preferred to the other types.
NOTE: The x-axes indicate the types of sushi, and the y-axes show the average of the stratified effect of $\mathbf{X}$ on Y, Eq. (3), over the data whose X_1 is equivalent.

4   Conclusion

We have discussed the stability of bias-aware techniques. To investigate this property, we collected preference data that were expected to be influenced by cognitive biases. After discussing the relationship between causal inference and bias-aware techniques, we described a technique of stratification to remove the biases. Our experimental results indicate the instability of the stratification, contrary to our expectation. As next steps, we plan to modify our bias-removal technique and to collect datasets that may be influenced by other types of cognitive bias.

References

1. Calders, T., Verwer, S.: Three naive bayes approaches for discrimination-free classification. Data Min. Knowl. Disc. **21**, 277–292 (2010). https://doi.org/10.1007/s10618-010-0190-x

2. Chandler, D., Horton, J.: Labor allocation in paid crowdsourcing: experimental evidence on positioning, nudges and prices. In: AAAI Workshop: Human Computation, pp. 14–19 (2011). https://www.aaai.org/ocs/index.php/WS/AAAIW11/paper/view/3983
3. Dwork, C., Hardt, M., Pitassi, T., Reingold, O., Zemel, R.: Fairness through awareness. In: Proceedings of the 3rd Innovations in Theoretical Computer Science Conference, pp. 214–226 (2012). https://doi.org/10.1145/2090236.2090255
4. Eickhoff, C.: Cognitive biases in crowdsourcing. In: Proceedings of the 11th ACM International Conference on Web Search and Data Mining, pp. 162–170 (2018). https://doi.org/10.1145/3159652.3159654
5. Hardt, M., Price, E., Srebro, N.: Equality of opportunity in supervised learning. In: Advances in Neural Information Processing Systems, vol. 29 (2016). https://papers.neurips.cc/paper/6374-equality-of-opportunity-in-supervised-learning
6. Kamiran, F., Karim, A., Zhang, X.: Decision theory for discrimination-aware classification. In: Proceedings of the 12th IEEE International Conference on Data Mining, pp. 924–929 (2012). https://doi.org/10.1109/ICDM.2012.45. https://doi.ieeecomputersociety.org/10.1109/ICDM.2012.45
7. Kamishima, T.: Nantonac collaborative filtering: recommendation based on order responses. In: Proceedings of 19th International Conference on Knowledge Discovery and Data Mining, pp. 583–588 (2003). https://doi.org/10.1145/956750.956823
8. Zhang, L., Wu, Y., Wu, X.: Anti-discrimination learning: from association to causation. In: The 24th ACM SIGKDD International Conference on Knowledge Discovery and Data Mining, Tutorial (2018). http://csce.uark.edu/~xintaowu/kdd18-tutorial/
9. Žliobaitė, I.: Measuring discrimination in algorithmic decision making. Data Min. Knowl. Disc. **31**(4), 1060–1089 (2017). https://doi.org/10.1007/s10618-017-0506-1

Detecting Race and Gender Bias in Visual Representation of AI on Web Search Engines

Mykola Makhortykh[1(✉)], Aleksandra Urman[1,2], and Roberto Ulloa[3]

[1] University of Bern, Bern, Switzerland
[2] University of Zurich, Zürich, Switzerland
[3] GESIS - Leibniz Institute for the Social Sciences, Cologne, Germany

Abstract. Web search engines influence perception of social reality by filtering and ranking information. However, their outputs are often subjected to bias that can lead to skewed representation of subjects such as professional occupations or gender. In our paper, we use a mixed-method approach to investigate presence of race and gender bias in representation of artificial intelligence (AI) in image search results coming from six different search engines. Our findings show that search engines prioritize anthropomorphic images of AI that portray it as white, whereas non-white images of AI are present only in non-Western search engines. By contrast, gender representation of AI is more diverse and less skewed towards a specific gender that can be attributed to higher awareness about gender bias in search outputs. Our observations indicate both the need and the possibility for addressing bias in representation of societally relevant subjects, such as technological innovation, and emphasize the importance of designing new approaches for detecting bias in information retrieval systems.

Keywords: Web search · Bias · Artificial intelligence

1 Introduction

Web search engines are important information intermediaries that help users navigate through web content. By filtering and ranking information in response to user queries, search engines determine what users learn about specific topics or entities [32] in turn influencing individual and collective perception of social reality [22]. However, search engine outputs can be biased - that is systematically skewed towards particular individuals or groups [21] - which may lead to the distorted perception of the search subject and potentially result in negative societal effects such as racial or gender discrimination.

A growing number of studies discusses how search engines perpetuate biases related to gender and race, in particular in image search results [30,38,40]. Because of their affective and interpretative potential [12], images can be effective means of educating the public about complex social phenomena, such as

L. Boratto et al. (Eds.): BIAS 2021, CCIS 1418, pp. 36–50, 2021.
https://doi.org/10.1007/978-3-030-78818-6_5

gender or race, but also of reiterating stereotypes [30]. With image search being used for a broad range of purposes, varying from educators preparing teaching materials [36] to media professionals producing new content [41], its biased outputs can reinforce skewed representation, in particular of already vulnerable groups, and amplify discrimination [38].

Currently, research on race and gender bias in image search focuses on visual representation of a few subjects, such as professional occupations [30] or emotions [41]. However, there is a growing recognition that representation of other aspects of contemporary societies can also be genderly or racially skewed. One of such aspects is technological innovation, the representation of which in the West historically tended to be decontextualized and often associated with masculinity [11] and whiteness [29]. Such biases can further aggravate existing inequalities by influencing hiring decisions (e.g., by stereotyping a certain field as racially homogeneous) and positioning the technologies, predominantly portrayed as White, above marginalised non-white people [14]. Biases found to be present in web search outputs (e.g., [30,38]) have the potential to influence public opinion and perceptions of the social reality [19,32]. This is further aggravated by the fact that users tend to trust the output of search engines [44].

Besides expanding the current focus of search bias research to new areas, it is also important to consider the consequences of recent studies on search engine auditing for evaluating the robustness of bias measurements. Firstly, while the effect of personalization on the variability of search outputs is shown to be minor [49,50], the influence of randomization (e.g., result reshuffling for maximizing user engagement) can be more significant [35] and is yet to be accounted for in the context of bias research. Second, despite substantial differences in content selection across search engines [28,35,51], the majority of existing research focuses on individual search engines (e.g., Google [30] or Bing [41]), whereas possible bias variation between different engines (including the ones prevalent in non-Western context, such as Yandex or Baidu) remains understudied.

In this paper, we aim to make two contributions. First, we introduce a mixed-method approach for detecting race and gender bias in image search outputs that takes into consideration potential effects of randomization and personalization. Second, we apply this method for conducting a cross-engine comparison of bias in the visual representation of artificial intelligence (AI). Our choice of a case study is attributed to common criticism of AI representation being racially and genderly skewed both in popular culture and industry [4,46] and the recent claims about Google amplifying these biases via its image search results [14,46].

2   Related Work: Race and Gender Bias in Image Search

The possibility that outputs of web search engines can be systematically skewed towards certain gender and racial groups is increasingly recognized both by the broad public and information retrieval (IR) community [41]. Race and gender biases are found in different IR systems associated with search engines, including text search results [38,43] and search autocompletion [8,13]. However, image search is particularly relevant in this context, because of high interpretative and affective potential of visual information [12,34] that makes it a potent means of challenging, but also forming stereotypes.

Despite the growing recognition of the problem, there are still relatively few studies which look at biases in image search outputs in a systematic way. To study the prevalence of gender bias, Kay et al. [30] collected the US Bureau of Labor and Statistics data on gender distribution per occupation and compared it with results of Google image search for the respective occupations. Their findings indicate that Google image search outputs tend to exaggerate gender biases in relation to occupations viewed as male- or female-dominated. Otterbacher et al. [40] used Bing image search API to extract results for "person" query and then classified them using Clarifai. Their findings indicate that male images occur more commonly than female ones for gender-neutral queries; furthermore, search results tend to present males as more competent and purpose-oriented.

Even less research was done on racial bias in image search outputs. Using a selection of racialized and gendered web search queries (e.g., "black girls"), Noble [38] employed qualitative content analysis to identify multiple cases when Google promoted racist and misogynistic representation of women and minority groups. Araujo et al. [6] used feature extraction to compare outputs from Google and Bing image search APIs for "ugly woman" and "beautiful woman" queries and found that images of black women were more often identified as "ugly", whereas white women were positively stereotyped.

3   Case Study: Racial and Gender Representation of AI

The ongoing recognition of the complex relationship between technical (e.g., algorithms) and social (e.g., race) constructs has substantial implications for how modern technology is perceived. In the case of AI, which can be broadly defined as the ability of human-made artifacts to engage in intellectual behavior [37], this connection is particularly strong. Its strength is attributed both to conceptual reasons, such the bilateral relationship between intellectual behavior and social norms/activities [17], and the increasing adoption of AI for the tasks dealing with societal matters (e.g., predictive policing [20]).

The tendency to anthropomorphize AI - that is to present it in a human-like form either physically or digitally [14,33] - further problematizes its relationship with social constructs. There are multiple theories explaining the historical tendency to integrate anthropomorphic features in product design [16], but generally anthropomorphism is an important factor in making complex technology more familiar and comfortable to use. However, anthropomorphism also stimulates application of social categories (e.g., race or gender) to the non-human entities, such as AI, and it has substantial implications both to their perception and representation [9].

The racial representation of AI in the Western Anglophone culture is characterized by whiteness both in terms of physical appearance and behavior. Cave and Dihal [14] list multiple cultural products in which AI is presented as exclusively white (Terminator, Blade Runner, I, Robot to name a few). While the portrayal of AI in recent cultural products slowly becomes more diverse (e.g., Westworld and Humans), it is still predominantly treated as white.

Similar to popular culture, the historical and institutional context of AI industry in the West is argued to be related to whiteness [29]. Besides multiple other consequences, it affects how AI is imagined and represented as indicated by the prevalent use of white materials and surfaces for constructing robots [46] and the reliance on sociolinguistic markers associated with whiteness (e.g., by omitting dialects related to non-white groups when developing conversational agents [14].

In contrast to the limited variety of its racial representation, the gender representation of AI is more diverse (albeit still quite binary). In the case of popular culture, there are multiple instances of portraying AI as male and female entities. The number of fictitious representations of AI as female (Metropolis, Her, Ghost in the Shell, Ex Machina) might be even higher than the number of male ones (A.I., I, Robot, Prometheus). At the same time, many of these representations portray female AI just as servants to their (usually male) masters, who often treat AI as a means of satisfying their (sexual) needs [4].

A similar relationship between AI and gender can be observed in the industry, where the most well-known AI-based assistants (e.g., Cortana or Siri) have female features. While the industrial treatment of gender aspects of AI does not necessarily rely on its intense sexualization as much as popular culture, it still iterates the notion of women being subordinate to men and intended to be used by their masters [5].

4 Methodology

To collect data, we utilized a set of virtual agents - that is software simulating user browsing behavior (e.g., scrolling web pages and entering queries) and recording its outputs. The benefits of this approach, which extends algorithmic auditing methodology introduced by Haim et al. [24], is that it allows controlling for personalization [25] and randomization [35] factors influencing outputs of web search. In contrast to human actors, virtual agents can be easily synchronized (i.e., to isolate the effect of time at which the search actions are conducted) and deployed in a controlled environment (e.g., a network of virtual machines using the same IP range, the same type of operating system (OS) and the same browsing software) to limit the effects of personalization that might lead to skewed outputs.

In addition to controlling for personalization, agent-based auditing allows addressing randomization of web search that is caused by search engines testing different ways of ranking results to identify their optimal ordering for a query (e.g., the so-called "Google Dance" [10]). Such randomization leads to a situation, when identical queries entered under the same conditions can result in different sets of outputs (or their different ranking), thus making the observations non-robust. One way of addressing this issue is to deploy multiple virtual agents that simultaneously enter the same search query to determine randomization-caused variation in the sets of outputs that can then be merged into a single, more complete set.

For the current study, we built a network of 100 CentOS virtual machines based in the Frankfurt region of Amazon Elastic Compute Cloud (EC2). On each machine, we deployed 2 virtual agents (one in Chrome browser and one in Mozilla Firefox browser), thus providing us with 200 agents overall. Each agent was made of two browser extensions: a tracker and a bot. The tracker collected the HTML and the metadata of all pages visited in the browser and immediately sent it to a storage server. The bot emulated a sequence of browsing actions that consisted of (1) visiting an image search engine page, (2) entering the "artificial intelligence" query, and (3) scrolling down the search result page to load at least 50 images.

Before starting the emulation, the browsers were cleaned to prevent the search history affecting the search outputs. While there is a possibility that search engines infer the gender of the agent based on the previous IP behavior (i.e., the use of the IP by other AWS users before it was assigned to a virtual agent deployed as part of our experiment), we expect that the use of multiple agents shall counter this potential limitation, because it is unlikely that the large number of randomly assigned IPs will be associated with one specific gender.

The study was conducted on February 27, 2020. We distributed 200 agents between the world's six most popular search engines by market share: Google, Bing, Yahoo, Baidu, Yandex, and DuckDuckGo (DDG) [47]. For all engines, the ".com" version of the image search engine was used (e.g., google.com). The agents were equally distributed between the engines; however, because of technical issues (e.g., bot detection mechanisms), some agents did not manage to complete their routine. The overall number of agents per engine which completed the full simulation routine and returned the search results was the following: Baidu (29), Bing (30), DDG (34), Google (33), Yahoo (31), and Yandex (21).

For our analysis, we extracted from collected HTML links related to top 30 image search results for each agent. Then, we divided these links into three subgroups: 1) results from 1 to 10; 2) results from 11 to 20; and 3) results from 21 to 30. Such a division allowed us to investigate differences in terms of race and gender bias between top results (i.e., 1–10), which are usually the only ones viewed by the users [42], and later results. Then, we aggregated all images for each subgroup per engine to account for possible randomization of search outputs on individual agent level, and removed duplicate images. The number of unique images in each subgroup per each engine is shown in Table 1; the numbers do not include images which were not accessible anymore (e.g., because of being removed from the original websites).

To detect race and gender bias in search outputs, we relied on their manual coding. While some earlier studies (e.g., [40]) use image recognition for extracting image features, its applicability for bias detection has been questioned recently [45] considering the possibility of recognition approaches being biased themselves. Hence, we used two coders to classify all the collected images

Table 1. The number of unique images per each result subgroup per engine

	Baidu	Bing	DuckDuckGo	Google	Yahoo	Yandex
Results 1:10	10	16	11	11	13	12
Results 11:20	12	10	11	16	15	14
Results 21:30	12	10	10	13	16	15

based on categories listed below. To measure intercorder reliability, we calculated Kripperndorf's alpha values that showed an acceptable level of reliability: 0.73 (antropomorphism), 0.69 (race), 0.67 (sex). Following the reliability assessment, the identified disagreements were resolved by the original coders using consensus-coding.

Anthropomorphism: We determined whether the image of AI includes any anthropomorphic elements, such as human(-like) figures or parts of human bodies. Depending on their exact appearance, such elements can indicate what human-like features are attributed to AI and how its developers and users are portrayed. Most importantly, this category determines the subset of images which can be subjected to gender and race bias, because both forms of bias are primarily applicable to anthropomorphic portrayals of AI.

Race: For anthropomorphized images, we identified the race of the portrayed entity to determine whether there is racial skew in AI representation. Following Cave and Dihal [14], we treat racialized representation in broad terms and interpret the coloring of AI elements as a form of racial attribution. Hence, both a white-skinned individual and a human-like android made of white material can be treated as White. The options included 1) white, 2) non-white, 3) mixed (when both white and non-white entities were present), 4) abstract (when an entity can not be attributed to any human race), and 5) unknown (when it was not possible to reliably detect race).

We acknowledge that treating race as a binary (white/non-white) category is a simplification as the complex notion that ignores multiple nuances, in particular different categories of non-white population (e.g., Black, Hispanic or Asian). However, numerous recent explorations of the role of race in the societal hierarchies as well as media-driven racial bias use the same white/non-white dichotomy [18,26,27,31], in part to avoid shifting the focus from the uniqueness of white privilege compared with various degrees of marginalization of non-white population. The same logic can be applied to the study of technological innovation, in particular in the context of AI, which has been historically related to whiteness [29]. Furthermore, it is difficult to identify different sub-categories of non-white population using only visual cues, considering the complex notion of race and the fact that is not necessarily based on one's appearance only. Because of these reasons, we believe that in the context of the present study, the binary categorization of race is suitable despite its limitations.

Sex: For anthropomorphized images, we determined the sex of the entity portrayed to determine whether there is a gendered skew. We used sex as a proxy for gendered representation because of the complexity of the notion of gender. Unlike sex, which is a binary concept, gender encompasses a broad variety of social and cultural identities that makes it hard to detect based on visual cues. Hence, we opted out for a more robust option that is still sufficient for evaluating gender-related aspects of AI representation. The possible options included 1) male, 2) female, 3) mixed (when both male and female entities were present), 4) abstract (when an entity was shown as sexless), and 5) unknown (when it was not possible to reliably detect sex).

5   Findings

5.1   AI and Antropomorphism

Unlike Kay et al. [30], who had data on gender distribution for occupations to compare their representation in image search outputs, we do not have a clear baseline for AI representation. Hence, we follow Otterbacher et al. [40] and treat the unequal retrievability - that is the accessibility of outputs with specific characteristics [48] - as an indicator of bias in search outputs. By systematically prioritizing images with specific features (e.g., the ones showing males and not females; [40]), the system creates a skewed perception of the phenomenon represented via its outputs.

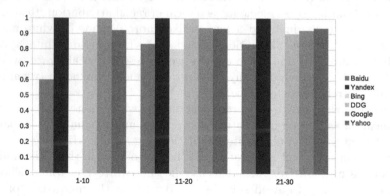

Fig. 1. Ratio of anthropomorphic representations of AI per result set for each engine (1–10 refers to results 1 to 10; 11–20 to results 11 to 20; 21–30 to results 21 to 30).

The first sign of the skewed representation of AI by search engines is the tendency for its anthropomorphization (Fig. 1). The proportion of images showing AI not as an anthropomorphized entity constitutes less than 10% for most engines with a single exception coming from Baidu, the largest Chinese search engine. On Google and Yandex, all images appearing in the top 10 results show

AI as a human-like entity. For other Western engines, the proportion of anthropomorphized AI images increased after the first 10 results, and in some cases (Bing, DDG) also reached 100% for the second and the third sets of outputs.

The anthropomorphized representations of AI usually take one of two forms: a schematic representation of a human brain or a human-like figure made of different materials (e.g., metal, plastic, or pixels). The way of presenting AI as "shiny humanoid robots" [33] can be attributed to it being the most recognizable way of presenting it in Western popular culture. However, by reiterating human-like AI images, search engines also create more possibilities for bias compared with more schematic or non-anthropomorphized representations.

5.2   AI and Race

Our analysis showed that non-racialized portrayals of AI are prevalent on Western search engines (Fig. 2). With the exception of Bing, where racialized images prevail among the first 10 results, Western engines tend to put more abstract images (e.g., schematic brain images or bluish human figures) on the top of search results, whereas later sets of outputs become more skewed towards specific racial representations. However, a different pattern is observed on non-Western engines, where racialized images of AI appear on the top of search results and become less visible in the later outputs.

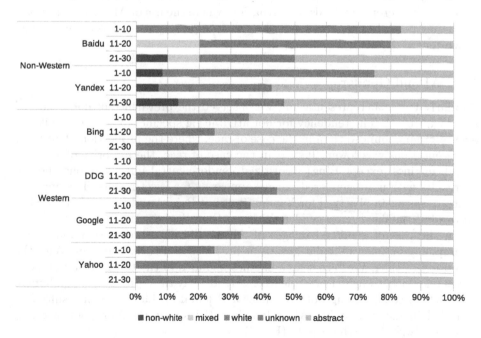

Fig. 2. Proportion of racialized representations of AI among anthropomorphized images (1–10 refers to results 1 to 10; 11–20 to results 11 to 20; 21–30 to results 21 to 30).

In those cases, when AI images have a racial component, it is almost always associated with whiteness, thus supporting earlier claims about a skewed racial portrayal of AI on search engines [14, 46]. The most common form such an association takes is the stylization of human-like entities representing AI with white materials and Caucasian face features. In some cases, it is supplemented with images of humans or part of their bodies (e.g., arms) representing developers or users of AI, most of whom are again shown as white. While the proportion of such racialized images in top 10 results for Western search engines is relatively low, their presence still promotes "White utopian imaginary" [14] of AI and enforces racial homogeneity in relation to it.

Such a skewed representation is amplified by an almost complete absence of non-white entities in image search results. Their absence is particularly striking for Western search engines, where the only form of racial diversity available are images of body parts that can not be easily related to a particular race (e.g., an arm the color of which can not be easily detected because of the way the image is lit). This exclusive focus on whiteness can be treated as a form of symbolic erasure of non-white groups not only from AI industry, but also the larger context of its use that encompasses most of contemporary societies [14].

Surprisingly, the non-Western engines, which prioritize images accentuating AI whiteness more than the Western ones, are also the only ones to include non-white or mixed AI portrayals. With the exception of two images showing AI as a black- or brown-skinned entity, these images show non-white AI developers or users. Such discrepancy leads to a situation, where the use of AI is contextualized by adding non-white contexts, but the core interpretation of AI as a "technology of whiteness" [29] is not challenged.

5.3   AI and Gender

Similarly to racial representation, we observed the prevalence of non-gendered portrayals of AI. The tendency for not attributing specific sex features to it was even more pronounced than in the case of race, where the proportion of abstract representations was lower. Just as in the case of race, the majority of Western search engines (except Bing) prioritized gender-neutral images among the top 10 results with more gendered images appearing for lower results. The opposite pattern was again observed for Yandex (but not Baidu) and Bing, where the top 10 results contained more gendered images than the later ones.

In the case of gendered images of AI, we did not observe that much of a discrepancy between different groups as in the case of racialized ones. With the exception of Bing, Western search engines included in the top 10 results images based on which it was not possible to clearly identify the entity's sex (e.g., human arms which could belong both to males and females). Later sets of results also included images presenting AI as female entities, but their proportion rarely exceeded 10% of search outputs (Fig. 3).

As in the case of racialized images, non-Western engines provided more diverse representations of AI, including both female and male entities as well as the mix of two. Unlike Western engines, where images of AI as a male entity

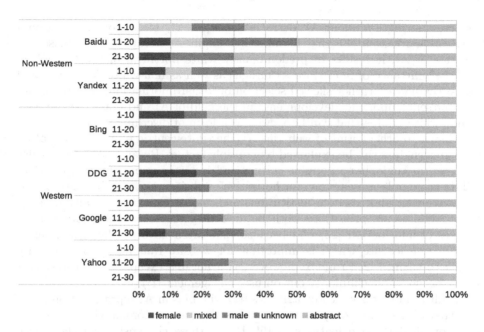

Fig. 3. Proportion of gendered representations of AI among anthropomorphized images (1–10 refers to results 1 to 10; 11–20 to results 11 to 20; 21–30 to results 21 to 30).

were almost absent, both Baidu and Yandex prioritized more masculine representation of AI. Such effect was achieved by highlighting images of both male developers and users as well as human-like robots with masculine facial features. One possible explanation of non-Western engines promoting a masculine portrayal of AI can be its different representation in popular culture. At least in the case of Russia, where Yandex originates from, a number of prominent cultural products present AI as a masculine entity (e.g., The Adventures of Electronic, Far Rainbow, Guest from the Future), whereas feminine representations are rather few.

While the aforementioned observation can be treated as evidence that search engine outputs depend on popular culture representations of AI, we did not observe any overly sexualized images of female AI despite its intense sexualization in Western popular culture. This finding indicates that cultural embeddedness of bias does not necessarily translate into its visibility in search outputs and can be attributed to more active countering of gender bias in the recent years [38].

6   Discussion

Our observations indicate that visual representation of AI on the world's most popular search engines is skewed in some racial and, to a lesser degree, gender aspects. While it is not sufficient to claim that search mechanisms used to retrieve information about AI are racially or genderly biased, our findings support earlier research [40] that found search engines reiterating social biases. In the case of AI, it results in predominantly white portrayal of the technology and the omittance of non-white AI designs as well as non-white developers and users. By offering rather skewed selection of visual information, search engines misrepresent important developments in the field of AI and erase the presence of non-white groups that can be viewed as a form of discrimination.

Similar to other forms of web bias [7], the white-centric representation of AI on search engines can be explained by multiple factors. Because of its prevalence in Western Anglophone popular culture and industry, representation of AI as White commonly appears on "authoritative" websites, such as the ones related to government and research institutions and mainstream media. Outputs from these websites are prioritized both because they are treated as more reliable sources of information [23] and because they often have the large number of backlinks, a feature which is important for website ranking on the majority of search engines [2] (Yandex, however, is a notable exception with its larger emphasis not on backlinking, but on user engagement [1]).

Additional factor which contributes to racial bias in AI representation is the fact that image search outputs are often based on text accompanying the image, but not on the image features [3,15]. Under these circumstances, the search algorithm is not necessarily able to differentiate between white and non-white representations of AI. Instead, it just retrieves images which are accompanied by certain text from the websites, the ranking of which is determined using the same criteria as text search results. Considering that racial bias in AI representation remains mainstream [14] as contrasted by gender bias (e.g., it is harder to imagine academic or government websites hosting images of sexualized AI), it results in the iteration of white-centric representations, in particular by Western search engines.

The reliance on textual cues for generating image search outputs and engine-specific ranking signals (e.g., number of backlinks and source type) can also explain differences in AI representation between Western and non-Western search engines. Unlike Western engines, where the selection of ranking signals is similar and results in reiteration of the same set of images stressing the whiteness of AI, the focus on the specific regions (i.e., China for Baidu and Russia for Yandex) together with substantial differences in ranking mechanisms (e.g., prioritization of backlinks coming from China for Baidu [2] and the reliance on different ranking signals for Yandex [1]) leads to the inclusion of more non-white representations of technology. However, if this explanation is valid, then in order to be able to deal with racial bias in a consistent manner, search engines would need either to more actively engage with actual image features (and not just text accompanying images) or expand the selection of websites prioritized for retrieving image outputs beyond currently prioritized mainstream Western websites, where white-centered AI representations are prevalent.

Overall, racial bias in the way web search mechanisms treat visual representation of AI can hardly be viewed as something that search engines invent on their own. However, they do reinforce the bias by creating a vicious cycle in which images of AI as "technology of whiteness" [29] appear on the top of search results and are more likely to be utilized by users, including educators or media practitioners. However, this reinforcement loop can be broken as shown by the substantially less biased representation of AI in terms of gender: despite the strong tendency for its femalization and subsequent sexualization in popular culture, we found relatively few gendered images of AI in the top results and none of them was sexualized.

Together with the earlier cases of addressing skewed web search outputs that were identified by the researchers (e.g., racialized gender bias [38]), our observations support the argument of Otterbacher [39] about the importance of designing new approaches for detecting bias in IR systems. In order to be addressed, bias has first to be reliably identified, but so far there is only a few IR studies that investigate the problem in a systematic way. By applying a new approach to examine bias in the context of AI, our paper highlights the importance of conducting further research to achieve better understanding of how significant are racial and gender biases in search outputs in relation to different aspects of contemporary societies, including (but not limited to) other forms of innovation.

It is also important to note several limitations of the research we conducted. First, we used very simple binary classification schematas both for race and gender features of AI portrayal. Second, our observations rely on a snapshot experiment conducted at a certain point of time, so it does not account for possible fluidity of image search results. Third, the experimental setup (i.e., the choice of the query and the infrastructure location) can also influence the observations produced.

References

1. SEO Tips on How to Optimize for Yandex. https://www.link-assistant.com/news/yandex-seo.html
2. Search Engine Differences: Google, Bing, Yandex & More. https://www.deepcrawl.com/knowledge/technical-seo-library/search-engine-differences/
3. Yandex - Technologies - Computer vision. How it works. https://yandex.com/company/technologies/vision/
4. Adams, R.: Helen A'Loy and other tales of female automata: a gendered reading of the narratives of hopes and fears of intelligent machines and artificial intelligence. AI Soc. **35**(3), 569–579 (2020)
5. Adams, R., Loideáin, N.N.: Addressing indirect discrimination and gender stereotypes in AI virtual personal assistants: the role of international human rights law. Cambridge Int. Law J. **8**(2), 241–257 (2019)
6. Araújo, C.S., Meira Jr., W., Almeida, V.: Identifying stereotypes in the online perception of physical attractiveness. In: Spiro, E., Ahn, Y.-Y. (eds.) SocInfo 2016. LNCS, vol. 10046, pp. 419–437. Springer, Cham (2016). https://doi.org/10.1007/978-3-319-47880-7_26
7. Baeza-Yates, R.: Bias on the web. Commun. ACM **61**(6), 54–61 (2018)

8. Baker, P., Potts, A.: 'Why do white people have thin lips?' Google and the perpetuation of stereotypes via auto-complete search forms. Crit. Discourse Stud. **10**(2), 187–204 (2013)
9. Bartneck, C., et al.: Robots and racism. In: Proceedings of the 2018 ACM/IEEE International Conference on Human-Robot Interaction, pp. 196–204. ACM (2018)
10. Battelle, J.: The Search: How Google and Its Rivals Rewrote the Rules of Business and Transformed Our Culture. Hachette UK (2011)
11. Blake, M.K., Hanson, S.: Rethinking innovation: context and gender. Environ. Planning A: Econ. Space **37**(4), 681–701 (2005)
12. Bleiker, R.: Visual Global Politics. Routledge (2018)
13. Bonart, M., Samokhina, A., Heisenberg, G., Schaer, P.: An investigation of biases in web search engine query suggestions. Online Inf. Rev. **44**(2), 365–381 (2019)
14. Cave, S., Dihal, K.: The whiteness of AI. Philos. Technol. **33**(4), 685–703 (2020)
15. Cui, J., Wen, F., Tang, X.: Real time google and live image search re-ranking. In: Proceedings of the 16th ACM International Conference on Multimedia, pp. 729–732 (2008)
16. DiSalvo, C., Gemperle, F.: From seduction to fulfillment: the use of anthropomorphic form in design. In: Proceedings of the 2003 International Conference on Designing Pleasurable Products and Interfaces, pp. 67–72. ACM (2003)
17. Doise, W., Mugny, G., James, A.S., Emler, N., Mackie, D.: The social development of the intellect, vol. 10. Elsevier (2013)
18. Eddo-Lodge, R.: Why I'm No Longer Talking to White People About Race. Bloomsbury Publishing (2020)
19. Epstein, R., Robertson, R.E.: The search engine manipulation effect (SEME) and its possible impact on the outcomes of elections. Proc. Natl. Acad. Sci. **112**(33), E4512–E4521 (2015)
20. Eubanks, V.: Automating Inequality: How High-Tech Tools Profile, Police, and Punish the Poor. St. Martin's Press (2018)
21. Friedman, B., Nissenbaum, H.: Bias in computer systems. ACM Trans. Inf. Syst. **14**(3), 330–347 (1996)
22. Gillespie, T.: The relevance of algorithms. In: Gillespie, T., Boczkowski, P.J., Foot, K.A. (eds.) Media Technologies, pp. 167–194. The MIT Press (2014)
23. Grind, K., Schechner, S., McMillan, R., West, J.: How google interferes with its search algorithms and changes your results. Wall Street J. **15** (2019)
24. Haim, M., Arendt, F., Scherr, S.: Abyss or shelter? On the relevance of web search engines' search results when people Google for suicide. Health Commun. **32**(2), 253–258 (2017)
25. Hannak, A., et al.: Measuring personalization of web search. In: Proceedings of the 22nd International Conference on World Wide Web, pp. 527–538. ACM (2013)
26. Heider, D.: White News: Why Local News Programs Don't Cover People of Color. Routledge (2014)
27. Hübinette, T., Tigervall, C.: To be non-white in a colour-blind society: conversations with adoptees and adoptive parents in Sweden on everyday racism. J. Intercult. Stud. **30**(4), 335–353 (2009)
28. Jiang, M.: The business and politics of search engines: a comparative study of Baidu and Google's search results of Internet events in China. New Media Soc. **16**(2), 212–233 (2014)
29. Katz, Y.: Artificial Whiteness: Politics and Ideology in Artificial Intelligence. Columbia University Press (2020)

30. Kay, M., Matuszek, C., Munson, S.A.: Unequal representation and gender stereotypes in image search results for occupations. In: Proceedings of the 33rd Annual Conference on Human Factors in Computing Systems, pp. 3819–3828. ACM (2015)
31. Kivel, P.: Uprooting Racism - 4th Edition: How White People Can Work for Racial Justice. New Society Publishers (2017)
32. Kulshrestha, J., et al.: Search bias quantification: investigating political bias in social media and web search. Inf. Retrieval J. **22**(1), 188–227 (2019)
33. Leufer, D.: Why we need to bust some myths about AI. Patterns **1**(7) (2020). https://www.ncbi.nlm.nih.gov/pmc/articles/PMC7660373/
34. Makhortykh, M., González Aguilar, J.M.: Memory, politics and emotions: internet memes and protests in Venezuela and Ukraine. Continuum **34**(3), 342–362 (2020)
35. Makhortykh, M., Urman, A., Ulloa, R.: How search engines disseminate information about COVID-19 and why they should do better. Harvard Kennedy Sch. Misinformation Rev. **1** (2020)
36. Müller, H., Despont-Gros, C., Hersh, W., Jensen, J., Lovis, C., Geissbuhler, A.: Health care professionals' image use and search behaviour. In: Proceedings of Medical Informatics Europe (MIE 2006), pp. 24–32. IOS Press (2006)
37. Nilsson, N.J.: Artificial Intelligence: A New Synthesis. Morgan Kaufmann Publishers Inc. (1998)
38. Noble, S.U.: Algorithms of Oppression: How Search Engines Reinforce Racism. New York University Press (2018)
39. Otterbacher, J.: Addressing social bias in information retrieval. In: Bellot, P., et al. (eds.) CLEF 2018. LNCS, vol. 11018, pp. 121–127. Springer, Cham (2018). https://doi.org/10.1007/978-3-319-98932-7_11
40. Otterbacher, J., Bates, J., Clough, P.: Competent men and warm women: gender stereotypes and backlash in image search results. In: Proceedings of the 2017 CHI Conference on Human Factors in Computing Systems, pp. 6620–6631. ACM (2017)
41. Otterbacher, J., Checco, A., Demartini, G., Clough, P.: Investigating user perception of gender bias in image search: the role of sexism. In: The 41st International Conference on Research & Development in Information Retrieval, pp. 933–936. ACM (2018)
42. Pan, B., Hembrooke, H., Joachims, T., Lorigo, L., Gay, G., Granka, L.: In Google we trust: users' decisions on rank, position, and relevance. J. Comput.-Mediated Commun. **12**(3), 801–823 (2007)
43. Pradel, F.: Biased Representation of Politicians in Google and Wikipedia Search? The Joint Effect of Party Identity. Gender Identity and Elections. Political Communication, pp. 1–32 (2020)
44. Schultheiß, S., Sünkler, S., Lewandowski, D.: We still trust in Google, but less than 10 years ago: an eye-tracking study. Inf. Res. **23**(3), 1–13 (2018)
45. Schwemmer, C., Knight, C., Bello-Pardo, E.D., Oklobdzija, S., Schoonvelde, M., Lockhart, J.W.: Diagnosing gender bias in image recognition systems. Socius **6**, 1–17 (2020)
46. Sparrow, R.: Do robots have race?: Race, social construction, and HRI. IEEE Robot. Autom. Mag. **27**(3), 144–150 (2020)
47. Statcounter: Search Engine Market Share Worldwide (2020). https://gs.statcounter.com/search-engine-market-share
48. Traub, M.C., Samar, T., van Ossenbruggen, J., He, J., de Vries, A., Hardman, L.: Querylog-based assessment of retrievability bias in a large newspaper corpus. In: Proceedings of the 16th ACM/IEEE-CS on Joint Conference on Digital Libraries, pp. 7–16. ACM (2016)

49. Trielli, D., Diakopoulos, N.: Partisan search behavior and Google results in the 2018 U.S. midterm elections. Inf. Commun. Soc. 1–17 (2020)
50. Unkel, J., Haim, M.: Googling Politics: Parties, Sources, and Issue Ownerships on Google in the 2017 German Federal Election Campaign. Social Science Computer Review, pp. 1–20 (2019)
51. Urman, A., Makhortykh, M., Ulloa, R.: Auditing source diversity bias in video search results using virtual agents. In: Companion Proceedings of the Web Conference 2021, pp. 232–236. ACM (2021)

Equality of Opportunity in Ranking: A Fair-Distributive Model

Elena Beretta[1,2](✉)(iD), Antonio Vetrò[1](iD), Bruno Lepri[2](iD),
and Juan Carlos De Martin[1](iD)

[1] Nexa Center for Internet and Society, DAUIN, Politecnico di Torino, Turin, Italy
{elena.beretta,antonio.vetro,demartin}@polito.it
[2] Fondazione Bruno Kessler, Povo, Italy
lepri@fbk.eu

Abstract. In this work, we define a Fair-Distributive ranking system based on Equality of Opportunity theory and fair division models. The aim is to determine the ranking order of a set of candidates maximizing utility bound to a fairness constraint. Our model extends the notion of protected attributes to a pool of individual's *circumstances*, which determine the membership to a specific *type*. The contribution of this paper are i) a Fair-Distributive Ranking System based on criteria derived from distributive justice theory and its applications in both economic and social sciences; ii) a class of fairness metrics for ranking systems based on the Equality of Opportunity theory. We test our approach on an hypothetical scenario of a selection university process. A follow up analysis shows that the Fair-Distributive Ranking System preserves an equal exposure level for both minority and majority groups, providing a minimal system utility cost.

Keywords: Fairness in rankings · Algorithmic fairness · Position bias · Algorithmic bias · Distributive justice · Equality of opportunity

1 Introduction

Ranking systems have rapidly spread in nowadays economies: despite such tools have been widely employed since decades in Information Retrieval field [21], they have recently come back at the cutting edge thanks to the explosive growth of computational power and data availability [15]. Ranking is one of the predominant forms by which both online and offline software systems present results in a wide variety of domains ranging from web search engines [19] to recommendation systems [21]. The main task of ranking systems is to find an allocation of elements to each of the n positions so that the total value obtained is maximized. The key technical principle that for decades has driven this optimization is the *Probability Ranking Principle* [23], according to which elements are ranked in descending order depending on their probability of relevance for a certain query q. Consequently, each element will have a probability of exposure given by its

© Springer Nature Switzerland AG 2021
L. Boratto et al. (Eds.): BIAS 2021, CCIS 1418, pp. 51–63, 2021.
https://doi.org/10.1007/978-3-030-78818-6_6

relevance for the query [27]. It is widely recognized that the position of an element in the ranking has a crucial influence on its exposure and its success; hence, systems with ranking algorithms, whose only task is to maximize utility, do not necessarily lead to fair or desirable scenarios [13]. In fact, a number of researches [12,32,33] have demonstrated that rankings produced in this way can lead to the over-representation of one element to the detriment of another, causing forms of algorithmic biases that in some cases can lead to serious social implications. Web search engine results that inadvertently promote stereotypes through over-representation of sensitive attributes such as gender, ethnicity and age are valid examples [1,16,30,37]. In order to mitigate and overcome biased results, researchers have proposed a number of fairness metrics [3]. However, the majority of these studies formalizes the notion of equity only in supervised machine learning systems, keeping equity in ranking systems a poorly explored ground despite the increasing influence of rankings on our society and economy. The lower attention devoted to this field is probably due to the complexity of ranking and recommendation systems, which are characterized by dynamics difficult to predict, multiple models and antithetic goals, and are difficult to evaluate due to the great sparsity (e.g., see [6,7,20]). In addition, a leading path to exploring the trade-off between the expected utility of a ranking system and its fairness has not yet been mapped out. We address these challenges through developing a multi-objective ranking system that optimizes the utility of the system and simultaneously satisfies some ethical constraints. Our model is inspired by *fair division* models [34] dealing on how to divide a set of resources among a series of individuals. The main contributions of this article are the following: first, we introduce a Fair-Distributive Ranking System combining methods of supervised machine learning and criteria derived from economics and social sciences; secondly, we define a class of fairness metrics for ranking systems based on the Equality of Opportunity theory [25]. Finally, we conduct an empirical analysis to study the trade-off between fairness and utility in ranking systems.

2   Related Work

Several recent works have addressed the issue of fairness in ranking systems. Some studies minimize the difference in representation between groups in a ranking through the concept of demographic parity, that requires members of protected groups are treated similarly to the advantaged ones or to the entire population [2,26,35,36]. In particular, Yang and Stoyanovich [35] have dealt with this issue as a multi-objective programming problem, while Celis *et al.* [8] have approached it from the perspective of the ranking results' diversification, as in [36]. More recently, Asudeh *et al.* [2] have proposed a class of fair scoring functions that associates non-negative weights to item attributes in order to compute an item score. Singh and Joachims [28] have proposed a Learning-to-Rank algorithm that optimizes the system's utility according to the merit of achieving a certain level of exposure. Lastly, some recent studies have investigated the notion of fairness through equalizing exposure; in this specific strand studies differ in the way exposure is allocated: while Biega *et al.* [4] have investigated individual fairness alongside utility, Singh and Joachims [27] have proposed an optimal probabilistic ranking to equalize exposure among groups. It is worth noting that the majority of the previous works have established equity constraints reflecting demographic parity constraints by narrowing the elements fraction for each attribute in the ranking or balancing utility with exposure merit. The methodology we propose goes beyond these parity and merit constraints for several reasons: a) the protected attributes are not a-priori established but are updated on the basis of the sample features, and b) the exposure is defined on the basis of the *effort* variable; this variable represents the real effort that the elements have made to be included in the Top-N-rank according to Roemer's Equality of Opportunity theory [25].

3   Problem Statement

In Information Retrieval the notion of utility is commonly stated as the expected ranking that maximizes the system's utility by exploiting the nth ranking r and a query q, such that $argmaxU(ranking_r|q)$, where r = 1...R (R is the rankings set); it is generally achieved through a series of utility measures in ranking system domain that leverage a mapping function β to detect the relevance of an item to each user given a certain query q, $\beta(Rel(item_i|user_u, q))$, where i = 1...I and u = 1...U (I and U are the items set and the users set). Several recent works establish a certain exposure degree to each individual or group of individuals as a fairness constraint. The exposure indicates the probability of attention that the item gets based on the query and its ranking position, and is generically calculated as $\frac{1}{\log(1+j)}$, where j is the position of the $item_i$ in the $ranking_r$. We adapt the example proposed by Singh and Joachims [27] to our scenario: suppose a group of students has to enroll at university, the decision-maker then sorts the students according to their relevance for the expressed query and draws up a certain number of rankings to evaluate the system response accuracy. Relevance is thus derived from the probability that the candidate is relevant for the query.

In this example, 8 individuals are divided into 3 groups based on ethnicity attribute. Individuals belonging to the white group have relevance 1, 0.98, 0.95, the Asians have 0.93, 0.91, 0.88, the African-Americans 0.86, 0.84. Students are sorted in ranking according to relevance. Since exposure is a measure exploiting relevance and ranking position, it is computed after sorting. As shown in Fig. 1a, Asian and African-American students, despite being placed a few positions below white ones, get a very low exposure; this means their average exposure is significantly lower compared to the white group, despite a minimal deviation in relevance. Efforts to enforce a fairness constraint on exposure, even if important, are missing the real point that is instead tied to relevance. As a matter of fact, exposure is calculated on the basis of the candidate's position, regardless of the student's traits. Consider the new ranking in Fig. 1b. In this case, a fairness constraint is applied to proportionally allocate exposure among ethnic groups; despite the constraint, the African-American minority remains in

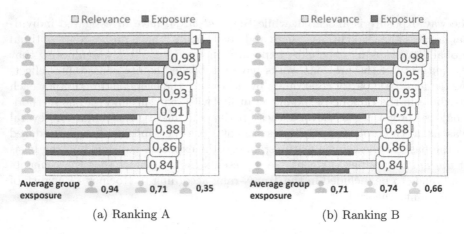

Fig. 1. Both pictures a and b revise the example of Singh and Joachims [27]. Blue: white group; green: Asian group; red: African-American group. (Color figure online)

lower positions compared to the other two groups. This problem is even more serious in case of binary relevance: assuming the decision-maker would admit to the university the first 3 students, no African-American individuals would be included in the top-3-ranking. To address the problem of fairness in rankings we suggest to marginally consider exposure and to focus on analyzing how relevance is computed and which features correlate with the query q. This means that a ranking is considered unfair if the students' relevance, hence their position, is systematically established on the basis of irrelevant features such as protected attributes.

4 A Fair-Distributive Ranking Model

Preliminary. Egalitarian theories [24] such as EOp arise from the notion of distributive justice, which recognizes that all goods should be equally distributed across society. The key principle of Roemer s Equality of Opportunity (EOp) theory is based on the assumption that the resources obtained by individuals depend on two factors: individual choices, which lie within the sphere of personal responsibility, and circumstances, which are exogenous to individual control. He claims that if inequalities in a set of individuals are caused by birth circumstances, which include variables such as gender, race, or familiar socioeconomic status and so forth, then these are morally unacceptable and must be compensated by society. The theory is therefore based on four key principles: circumstances, effort, responsibility and reward. Responsibility is a theoretical notion reflecting the effort degree that individuals invest in achieving the acts they perform. The reward is the fraction of resources that individuals belonging to a disadvantaged group get in case an inequality of opportunity occurs, and it is established by a certain policy [9,22]. According to Roemer, policies should be oriented to equalize the opportunities that different *types*, or groups of individuals, categorized in accordance with diverse circumstances, must be able to have in order to achieve a given goal. A *type* is a set of individuals sharing the same circumstances, while the set of individuals characterized by the same degree of effort is called a *tranche*. Below We provide our notion of fair ranking according to Roemer's EOp theory:

A ranking is said to be fair according to Roemer's EOp theory if all individuals belonging to different types have the same opportunity to reach high ranking position, and if relevance and exposure are given by personal responsibility and not by birth circumstances.

In order to offer a better understanding of our notation, a summary of some basic notions of EOp's theory is briefly provided:

i **Effort**: proxy indicating individual's personal responsibility. According to Roemer, effort is derived by computing the Cumulative Distribution Function of each type, and then by extracting the quantile's distribution.
ii **Types:** groups of individuals, categorized in accordance with diverse circumstances;
iii **Tranche**: the set of individuals characterized by the same degree of effort;
iv **Policy**: actions oriented to equalize type's opportunity;
v **Utility**: a measure of the system's ability to provide relevant results. In the case of ranking systems, the utility is defined as the ability to provide the best ranking according to a certain query q.

Notation. According to Roemer, individuals are fully described by a two-dimensional list: the first one is the set of circumstances beyond individuals' control denoting the population partition into a set of non-overlapping types T characterized by certain attributes; the second one expresses the traits for which individuals are fully responsible and is described by the scalar variable effort π. Given a certain query q, the Fair-Distributive Ranking Γ is the one in which the utility maximization (e.g., the best candidate selection) is a function of circumstances, degrees of effort and a policy:

$$\Gamma = argmax_{\theta \in \Theta} u^t(q|e_i(\pi), \theta) \tag{1}$$

As a corollary, exposure is allocated equally among individuals: ranking Γ is therefore the one that maximizes the area below the lowest function exp^t, i.e. the type-specific-exposure:

$$\max_{\theta \in \Theta} \int_0^1 min_t exp^t(\pi, \theta) \, d\pi \tag{2}$$

Equation 2 denotes the opportunity-equalizing policy in ranking according to EOp theory.

Fair-Distributive Ranking Criteria. Ranking Γ has to show the following properties: (i) *Ranked type fairness.* Γ is exploited by overcoming the a-priori assessment of the sensitive attributes through partitioning population in types; (ii) *Circumstances-effort based ranking.* Γ is based on a counterfactual score obtained from effort and circumstances' variables; the counterfactual score indicates which score individuals would have got if they were not belonging to their type T; and (iii) *Counterfactual-ordered ranking utility.* Γ is ordered by decreasing counterfactual score.

4.1 Ranked Type Fairness

To split the population in types we perform the conditional inference trees method proposed by Hothorn [14]; to the best of our knowledge, the only application of this algorithm in exploring inequalities has been carried out by Brunori [5] to study socio-economic differences on panel data. The algorithm exploits the permutation test theory developed by Strasser [29] to generate recurring binary partitions and recursively split the Euclidean space of the individuals' variables in convex sets of hyperplanes, overcoming the problem of overfitting and variable selection [18]. Let $P(Y|X)$ be a conditional probability distribution of the response Y given the vector of n covariates $X = X_1, \ldots, X_i$; the recursion measures correlation among Y and the X vector and performs multiple hypothesis tests to assess correlation significance. If a statistically significant correlation doesn't exist, recursion stops. Formally, types are permuted in this way:

$$T_k = \begin{cases} S_i^X & \text{if } H_0^i : P(Y|X_i) = P(Y), \\ recursion\ stops & \text{otherwise.} \end{cases} \tag{3}$$

where S_i^X is the set of x^i possible realizations.

4.2 Circumstances-Effort Based Ranking and Counterfactual-Ordered Ranking Utility

Since effort is not directly observable, we need a proxy in order to measure it. Roemer argues that it exists an effort distribution function that characterizes the entire subgroup within which the location of the individual is set and what is needed is a measure of effort that is comparable between different types. The basic assumption is that two individuals belonging to a different type t who occupy the same position in their respective distribution functions have exerted the same level of effort - and therefore of responsibility. Since, under the same circumstances, individuals who make different choices exercise different degrees of effort - and thus achieve a different outcome -, the differences in outcome within the same type are by definition determined by different degrees of effort, and therefore are not considered in the computation of the EOp. In general, Roemer states that to estimate effort it is necessary to:

  I aggregate individuals according to their circumstances;
 II compare outcome distributions;

III measure the effort that an individual has exerted through the quantile occupied in his or her type distribution.

Consequently, all the individuals positioned at the same quantile in the distribution of the respective type are by assumption characterized by the same level of effort. Hence, the counterfactual score distribution $\tilde{y}$ is computed following these steps:

1. approximate each type-score cumulative distribution $ecdf(y)$ through tenfold cross-validation on Bernstein polynomials log-likelihood: $LL_B(p_m = \sum_{i=1}^{n} \log f_B(x_j, p_m))$[1];
2. identify the degree of effort through the type-score distribution $y^k(\pi)$;
3. apply a smoothing transformation on $y^k(\pi)$ by scaling each tranche distribution (i.e., individuals have exerted same degree of effort) until individuals have the same tranche-score and then multiplying the tranche-score by each individual's score. The result of the smoothing process is a standardized distribution $\tilde{y}$ where all the unexplained inequalities are removed, i.e., only inequalities due to circumstances or degrees of effort are observed.

Inequality of opportunity is captured by applying an inequality index on the standardized distribution $\tilde{y}$. The counterfactual score $u_\pi^t(\theta)$ is then computed by assigning to individuals the fraction of inequality of their respective quantile-type-score distribution $y^k(\pi)$. Finally, individuals are ranked according to their counterfactual score in decreasing order. The ranking Γ is therefore given by:

$$\Gamma = u_\pi^t(\tilde{y}, \text{IneqIndex}(\tilde{y})) \tag{4}$$

5 Experiment

5.1 Data and Settings

We design an hypothetical scenario where high school students compete to be admitted at university (i.e. a typical scenario in several countries). Firstly, the whole students' population is simply ordered by decreasing counterfactual score (relevance is treated as not binary); then, the Fair-Distributive ranking Γ for fair-top-N-rankings is studied (as the available positions are assumed as finite, relevance is treated as binary). The conducted experiments compare three types of ranking: the first one is based on real students' test scores serving as a benchmark; the second one is based on the standardized distribution $\tilde{y}$; the last one is our ranking Γ based on counterfactual score $u_\pi^t(\theta)$. For the analysis, we employ the Student Performance Dataset [10] reporting students test scores of two Portuguese schools. Dataset contains 649 instances and 33 attributes, especially demographic ones (i.e. gender, parents' education, extra educational support).

---

[1] For a detailed explanation of Bernstein Polynomials Log Likelihood, see [5,17,38].

5.2   Metrics

We apply three types of metrics in order to fulfill both ranking and fairness constraints: i) ranking domain metrics. ii) inequality domain metrics (i.e., Gini index and Theil index), and iii) a set of metrics we propose to study our fairness constraints (i.e., Opportunity Loss/Gain Profile, Opportunity Loss/Gain Set, Unexplained Inequality Rate, Reward Profile, Reward Rate). Regarding the inequality metrics, Gini index is a statistical concentration index ranging from 0 to 1 that measures the inequality degree distribution [11]; a low or equal to zero Gini index indicates the tendency to the equidistribution and expresses perfect equality, while a high or equal to 1 value indicates the highest concentration and expresses maximum inequality. Theil index [31] is a measure of entropy to study segregation; a zero Theil value means perfect equality. Finally, we have proposed a new fairness metrics set: the Opportunity-Loss/Gain Profile and the Opportunity-Loss/Gain Set are computed to study inequality in the original distribution. They indicate which levels of score could be reached by each type with different effort degrees. The Unexplained Inequality Rate calculates the amount of fair removed inequality due to individuals' responsibility. The Reward Profile calculates the type that obtained the highest gain/loss from the re-allocation of scores - i.e. after applying fairness constraints; while the Reward Rate calculates the average re-allocation score rate for each type. All formulas are summarized in Table 1.

Table 1. Summary of inequality domain metrics and of a set of novel metrics proposed to study fairness constraints. *Notation*: F(y)= cumulative distribution function of the score, μ = mean score; R = number of types, p_i = frequency of types; y_π^t = score distribution aggregated by type and quantile; $\tilde{y}_i$= standardized score; $adj(\tilde{y}_\pi^t)$= adjusted mean-type score at each effort degree (after policy).

Metric	Formula	Input	Metrics domain
Gini index	$1 - \frac{1}{\mu} \int_0^\infty (1 - F(y))^2 dy$	All Distr.	Inequality
Theil index	$\frac{1}{N} \sum_{i=1}^{N} ln(\frac{\mu}{y_i})$	All Distr.	Inequality
Opportunity-L/G profile	$min/max(y_\pi^t - \mu(y_\pi))$	Sc.Distr.	New set of fairness measures
Opportunity-L/G set	$y_\pi^t - \mu(y_\pi)$	Sc.Distr.	New set of fairness measures
Unexplained inequality rate	$\frac{1}{N} \sum y_i - \tilde{y}_i$	Sc.Distr., Stnd.Sc.Distr.	New set of fairness measures
Reward profile	$min/max(y_\pi^t - adj(\tilde{y}_\pi^t))$	Sc.Distr., Adj Sc.Distr.	New set of fairness measures
Reward rate	$y_\pi^t - adj(\tilde{y}_\pi^t)$	Sc.Distr., Adj Sc.Distr.	New set of fairness measures

5.3   Results and Discussion

Table 2 summarizes our main results: first, we observe that the Γ ranking shows less inequality compared to benchmark ranking, as emerges from Gini's index

Table 2. Summary of results

Initial outcome						Policy outcome					
						Overall results					
Gini			0.144					0.112			
Theil			0.025					0.025			
Unexp.Ineq.			-					0.126			
						Tranche results					
		1	2	3	4	5		1	2	3	4	5
Outcome.Set	**A**	0.02	0.01	−0.04	0.04	0.04	Reward **A**	0.11	−0.11	−0.04	−0.09	−0.08
	B	0.09	0.09	0.08	0.16	0.17	**B**	0.06	−0.15	−0.12	−0.18	−0.21
	C	0.07	0.12	0.02		0.12	**C**	0.07	−0.21	−0.08	-	−0.14
	D	−0.08	−0.22	−0.07	−0.16	−0.31	**D**	−0.07	0.13	−0.01	0.09	0.28
	E	0.03	0.05	0	0.03	0	**E**	0.14	−0.21	−0.09	−0.12	−0.01
	F	−0.11	−0.06	−0.05	−0.08	−0.07	**F**	0.22	−0.05	−0.03	0.03	0.04
	G	−0.01	0.01	0.06	0.01	0.04	**G**	0.16	−.07	−0.17	−0.09	−0.09

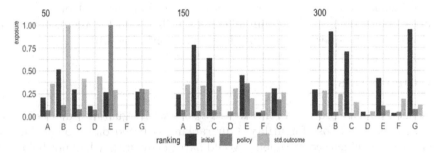

(a) Barplot of aggregate exposure for the top-50, top-150 and top-300, initial score ranking, standardized ranking and Γ ranking.

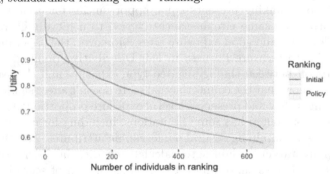

(b) Utility results on the Initial and Γ ranking in terms of relevance for a query q

Fig. 2. Exposure and relevance results

trend. Both ranking exhibit same value of Theil index, revealing entropy is similarly balanced. By observing the Outcome Set, we notice that D and F types get the lower average outcomes for all degrees of effort; this doesn't necessarily mean they are in a disadvantaged position. There are indeed multiple reasons, which do not necessarily indicate inequality, why some types systematically show a lower average outcome. We compute Gini Index on the standardized distribution to observe if there are types that systematically receive a lower outcome due to their type membership. In this way, only and exclusively inequalities caused by circumstances and effort degrees are obtained. This explains why types showing a lower average outcome are not directly compensated with higher rewards. Reward Rate is expressed as a dispersion around the quantile mean for each type, thus showing that it doesn't produce a significantly change in expected ranking utility. The aggregated exposure is computed recursively on all rankings with n+1 individuals. Analysis shows extremely disproportionate exposure values for the initial score ranking for all top-N-ranking. The Γ ranking keeps a proportionate aggregate exposure level among types for large subsets, while for smaller subsets it tends to favor individuals in groups which displays high levels of inequality (Fig. 2a). Overall, these results indicate that our approach produces a fair ranking Γ with minimal cost for utility, that we compute in terms of relevance for the query "best candidates selection" (Fig. 2b).

6   Conclusions

The method we have proposed generates a ranking with a guaranteed fair division score, with minimal cost for utility. Our ranking is based on a counterfactual score indicating which score students would have gotten if they had not belonged to different type. In this sense, the ranking is drawn up on the basis of the effort (aka, individual responsibility) that individuals have exerted to reach the initial score. As a result, our ranking presents equal opportunities for each group of individuals exhibiting the same circumstances (*types*) to achieve high ranking positions (high relevance) and good exposure rates. Moreover, the paper provides a set of new metrics to measure fairness in Fair-Distributive ranking. Finally, we study the trade-off between the aggregated type exposure and the system's utility: our analyses show that the counterfactual score doesn't affect significantly the expected ranking utility and preserves level of exposure proportionally among groups. The method presented has some limitations, including for example: the need to have a dataset containing several demographic attributes, and the need to have one or more target variables to calculate conditional inference trees (alternatively, the method is subordinate to the construction of score indices). As far as next steps are concerned, it is important to i)verify the robustness of the model (internal validity) with larger datasets (also synthetic ones) and ii) verify the external validity of the approach by applying the model on different fields of application. In the long term, our intention is to implement a ranking simulator that tests the results of different distributive justice theories.

References

1. ALRossais, N.A., Kudenko, D.: Evaluating stereotype and non-stereotype recommender systems. In: Proceedings of the 12th ACM Conference on Recommender Systems. RecSys 2018. ACM, Vancouver (2018)
2. Asudeh, A., Jagadish, H.V., Stoyanovich, J., Das, G.: Designing fair ranking schemes. In: Proceedings of the 2019 International Conference on Management of Data, SIGMOD 2019, pp. 1259–1276. Association for Computing Machinery, New York (2019). https://doi.org/10.1145/3299869.3300079
3. Barocas, S., Hardt, M., Narayanan, A.: Fairness and machine learning (2018). http://www.fairmlbook.org
4. Biega, A.J., Gummadi, K.P., Weikum, G.: Equity of attention: amortizing individual fairness in rankings. In: The 41st International ACM SIGIR Conference on Research & Development in Information Retrieval, SIGIR 2018, pp. 405–414. Association for Computing Machinery, New York (2018). https://doi.org/10.1145/3209978.3210063
5. Brunori, P., Neidhöfer, G.: The evolution of inequality of opportunity in Germany: A machine learning approach. ZEW - Centre Eur. Econ. Res. Discussion **20** (2020). https://doi.org/10.2139/ssrn.3570385
6. Burke, R.: Multisided fairness for recommendation, July 2017. http://arxiv.org/abs/1707.00093
7. Burke, R., Sonboli, N., Ordonez-Gauger, A.: Balanced neighborhoods for multisided fairness in recommendation. In: Conference on Fairness, Accountability and Transparency in Proceedings of Machine Learning Research, vol. 81, pp. 202–214. Proceedings of Machine Learning Research (PMLR), New York, 23–24 February 2018. http://proceedings.mlr.press/v81/burke18a.html
8. Celis, L.E., Straszak, D., Vishnoi, N.K.: Ranking with fairness constraints (2018)
9. Checchi, D., Peragine, V.: Inequality of opportunity in Italy. J. Econ. Inequality **8**(4), 429–450 (2010). https://doi.org/10.1007/s10888-009-9118-3
10. Cortez, P., Silva, A.: Using data mining to predict secondary school student performance. In: Brito, A., Teixeira, J. (eds.) Proceedings of 5th FUture BUsiness TEChnology Conference (FUBUTEC 2008). pp. 5–12 (2008). https://archive.ics.uci.edu/ml/datasets/Student+Performance
11. Gastwirth, J.L.: The estimation of the Lorenz curve and Gini index. Rev. Econ. Stat. **54**, 306–316 (1972)
12. Hardt, M., Price, E., Srebro, N.: Equality of opportunity in supervised learning. In: Proceedings of the 30th International Conference on Neural Information Processing Systems, NIPS 2016, pp. 3323–3331. Curran Associates Inc., Red Hook (2016)
13. Helberger, N., Karppinen, K., D'Acunto, L.: Exposure diversity as a design principle for recommender systems. Inf. Commun. Soc. **21**(2), 191–207 (2016)
14. Hothorn, T., Hornik, K., Zeileis, A.: Unbiased recursive partitioning: a conditional inference framework. J. Comput. Graph. Stat. **15**(3), 651–674 (2006)
15. Irfan, S., Babu, B.V.: Information retrieval in big data using evolutionary computation: a survey. In: 2016 International Conference on Computing. Communication and Automation (ICCCA), pp. 208–213. IEEE, New York (2016)
16. Karako, C., Manggala, P.: Using image fairness representations in diversity-based re-ranking for recommendations. In: Adjunct Publication of the 26th Conference on User Modeling, Adaptation and Personalization, UMAP 2018. pp. 23–28. ACM, Singapore (2018). https://doi.org/10.1145/3213586.3226206

17. Leblanc, A.: On estimating distribution functions using Bernstein polynomials. Ann. Inst. Stat. Math. **64**, 919–943 (2012). https://doi.org/10.1007/s10463-011-0339-4

18. Li Donni, P., Rodríguez, J.G., Rosa Dias, P.: Empirical definition of social types in the analysis of inequality of opportunity: a latent classes approach. Soc. Choice Welfare **44**(3), 673–701 (2014). https://doi.org/10.1007/s00355-014-0851-6

19. Makhijani, R., Chakrabarti, S., Struble, D., Liu, Y.: Lore: a large-scale offer recommendation engine with eligibility and capacity constraints. In: Proceedings of the 13th ACM Conference on Recommender Systems, RecSys 2019, pp. 160–168. Association for Computing Machinery, New York (2019). https://doi.org/10.1145/3298689.3347027

20. Patro, G.K., Biswas, A., Ganguly, N., Gummadi, K.P., Chakraborty, A.: Fairrec: two-sided fairness for personalized recommendations in two-sided platforms. In: Huang, Y., King, I., Liu, T., van Steen, M. (eds.) WWW 2020: The Web Conference 2020, pp. 1194–1204. ACM/IW3C2, Taipei, Taiwan (2020). https://doi.org/10.1145/3366423.3380196

21. Pei, C., et al.: Personalized re-ranking for recommendation. In: Proceedings of the 13th ACM Conference on Recommender Systems, RecSys 2019, pp. 3–11. Association for Computing Machinery, New York (2019). https://doi.org/10.1145/3298689.3347000

22. Ramos, X., Van de Gaer, D.: Approaches to inequality of opportunity: principles, measures and evidence. J. Econ. Surv. **30**, 855–883 (2016). https://doi.org/10.1111/joes.12121

23. Robertson, S.E.: The Probability Ranking Principle in IR, pp. 281–286. Morgan Kaufmann Publishers Inc., San Francisco (1997)

24. Roemer, J.E.: A pragmatic theory of responsibility for the egalitarian planner. Philos. Public Aff. **22**(2), 146–166 (1993)

25. Roemer, J.E., Trannoy, A.: Equality of opportunity. Handb. Income Distrib. **2**(2), 217–300 (2015)

26. Singh, A., Joachims, T.: Equality of opportunity in rankings (2017). https://www.k4all.org/wp-content/uploads/2017/09/WPOC2017_paper_9.pdf

27. Singh, A., Joachims, T.: Fairness of exposure in rankings. In: Proceedings of the 24th ACM SIGKDD International Conference on Knowledge Discovery & Data Mining, KDD 2018, p. 2219–2228. Association for Computing Machinery, New York (2018). https://doi.org/10.1145/3219819.3220088

28. Singh, A., Joachims, T.: Policy learning for fairness in ranking. In: Wallach, H., Larochelle, H., Beygelzimer, A., dAlché-Buc, F., Fox, E., Garnett, R. (eds.) Advances in Neural Information Processing Systems 32, pp. 5426–5436. Curran Associates Inc, New York (2019)

29. Strasser, H., Weber, C.: On the asymptotic theory of permutation statistics. Math. Methods Statist. **2**, 220–250 (1999)

30. Sweeney, L.: Discrimination in online ad delivery. Queue - Storage **11**(3), 10:10–10:29 (2013). https://doi.org/10.1145/2460276.2460278

31. Theil, H.: Statistical Decomposition Analysis: With Applications in the Social and Administrative Sciences, vol. 14. North-Holland Publishing Company, Amsterdam (1972)

32. Tsintzou, V., Pitoura, E., Tsaparas, P.: Bias disparity in recommendation systems, November 2018

33. Weinsberg, U., Bhagat, S., Ioannidis, S., Taft, N.: Blurme: inferring and obfuscating user gender based on ratings. In: Proceedings of the Sixth ACM Conference on Recommender Systems, RecSys 2012, pp. 195–202. Association for Computing Machinery, New York (2012). https://doi.org/10.1145/2365952.2365989
34. Yaari, M.E., Bar-Hillel, M.: On dividing justly. Soc. Choice Welfare **1**(1), 1–24 (1984)
35. Yang, K., Stoyanovich, J.: Measuring fairness in ranked outputs. In: Proceedings of the 29th International Conference on Scientific and Statistical Database Management. SSDBM 2017. Association for Computing Machinery, New York (2017). https://doi.org/10.1145/3085504.3085526
36. Zehlike, M., Bonchi, F., Castillo, C., Hajian, S., Megahed, M., Baeza-Yates, R.: Fa*ir: a fair top-k ranking algorithm. In: Proceedings of the 2017 ACM on Conference on Information and Knowledge Management, CIKM 2017, pp. 1569–1578. Association for Computing Machinery, New York (2017). https://doi.org/10.1145/3132847.3132938
37. Zehlike, M., Sühr, T., Castillo, C., Kitanovski, I.: Fairsearch: a tool for fairness in ranked search results. In: Companion Proceedings of the Web Conference 2020, WWW 2020, pp. 172–175. Association for Computing Machinery, New York (2020). https://doi.org/10.1145/3366424.3383534
38. Zhong, G.: Efficient and robust density estimation using Bernstein type polynomials. J. Nonparametric Stat. **28**(2), 250–271 (2016). https://doi.org/10.1080/10485252.2016.1163349

Incentives for Item Duplication Under Fair Ranking Policies

Giorgio Maria Di Nunzio, Alessandro Fabris(✉), Gianmaria Silvello,
and Gian Antonio Susto

University of Padua, Padua, Italy
{dinunzio,fabrisal,silvello,sustogia}@dei.unipd.it

Abstract. Ranking is a fundamental operation in information access systems, to filter information and direct user attention towards items deemed most relevant to them. Due to position bias, items of similar relevance may receive significantly different exposure, raising fairness concerns for item providers and motivating recent research into fair ranking. While the area has progressed dramatically over recent years, no study to date has investigated the potential problem posed by duplicated items. Duplicates and near-duplicates are common in several domains, including marketplaces and document collections available to search engines. In this work, we study the behaviour of different fair ranking policies in the presence of duplicates, quantifying the extra-exposure gained by redundant items. We find that fairness-aware ranking policies may conflict with diversity, due to their potential to incentivize duplication more than policies solely focused on relevance. This fact poses a problem for system owners who, as a result of this incentive, may have to deal with increased redundancy, which is at odds with user satisfaction. Finally, we argue that this aspect represents a blind spot in the normative reasoning underlying common fair ranking metrics, as rewarding providers who duplicate their items with increased exposure seems unfair for the remaining providers.

Keywords: Algorithmic fairness · Duplicates · Fair ranking

1 Introduction

Ranking is a central component in search engines, two-sided markets, recommender and match-making systems. These platforms act as intermediaries between providers and consumers of items of diverse nature, facilitating access to information, entertainment, accommodation, products, services, jobs and workers. The rank of an item in a result page is a strong predictor of the attention it will receive, as users devote most of their attention to the top positions in a list, and are less likely to view low-ranking items [15]. This *position bias* is at the root of fairness concerns for providers of ranked items, as comparably relevant results may receive remarkably different exposure. In the absence of countermeasures,

© Springer Nature Switzerland AG 2021
L. Boratto et al. (Eds.): BIAS 2021, CCIS 1418, pp. 64–77, 2021.
https://doi.org/10.1007/978-3-030-78818-6_7

unfair exposure can affect item providers on e-commerce websites, job-search platforms and commercial search engines, such as Amazon sellers, Airbnb hosts, job candidates on LinkedIn and owners of contents ranked by Google [6,14].

Unfair exposure can compound and increase over time, as the same query, issued multiple times to a system, is met with the same ranking. Each time the query is processed by the system, items gain a fixed, potentially unfair, level of exposure; this is a severe problem with static ranking policies, which map relevance scores to rankings in a deterministic fashion. Non-static policies, on the other hand, can respond to identical queries with different rankings, and they are more suited to equitably distribute exposure among relevant items. In recent years, fair ranking policies and measures have been proposed, which consider repetitions of the same query and encourage rotation of relevant items in the top-ranked positions [5,6,10,21,23].

While these measures and approaches are surely a sign of solid progress in the area of fair ranking, in this paper we highlight a potential blind spot in their normative reasoning: duplicates. Item duplicates and near-duplicates are not uncommon in online domains such as e-commerce websites [2] and online document collections [13]. Anecdotal evidence for this phenomenon can be found in official forums for item providers of popular marketplaces[1,2,3] and in Fig. 1. Based on the reasoning brought forth in recent works, requiring equal exposure for equally relevant items [6,10], two copies of the same item deserve more exposure (in sum) than a single copy. On the contrary, in some situations it is reasonable to postulate that multiple copies of an item deserve the same attention the item would be entitled to on its own, especially if the copies benefit the same provider.

The key contribution of this work is to analyze the tension between fairness and diversity when duplicates are not properly considered and factored into the fair ranking objective. More in detail, we show that, under different settings, common fair ranking policies reward duplicates more than static policies solely focused on relevance. We argue that this phenomenon is unfair to the providers of unique (non-duplicate) items and problematic for system owners and users as it introduces an incentive for redundancy. The rest of this paper is organized as follows. Section 2 introduces related work, covering fairness and diversity in ranking. Section 3 is the core of our study, where we formalize the problem and analyze the benefits obtained by providers through item duplication. We quantify the extra-attention earnt by duplicated items in a controlled setting, as we vary the relevance of the items available to a system, its ranking policy and the cost of duplication. Section 4 contains closing remarks and outlines directions for future work.

---

[1] https://community.withairbnb.com/t5/Hosting/Unfair-duplication-of-same-listing-to-gain-more-exposure/td-p/850319, all links accessed on 02-03-21.

[2] https://community.withairbnb.com/t5/Help/Duplicate-photos-in-listings-and-terms-of-service/td-p/1081009.

[3] https://sellercentral.amazon.com/forums/t/duplicate-search-results/445552.

Fig. 1. Amazon result page for query `controller` issued on February 19, 2021 by a Boston-based unregistered user in *incognito* browser mode. Top 4 results comprise near-duplicates in positions 1 and 3 (0-based indexing).

2   Related Work

2.1   Fairness in Ranking

Fairness in ranking requires that the items ranked by a system receive a suitable share of exposure, so that the overall allocation of user attention is considered fair according to a criterion of choice [6,21]. Fair ranking criteria depend on the specific context and normative reasoning, often inheriting and adapting notions from the machine learning fairness literature, such as independence and separation [3].

Position bias and *task repetition* are peculiar aspects of many fair ranking problems. *Position bias* refers to the propensity of users of ranking systems to concentrate on the first positions in a list of ranked items, while devoting less attention to search results presented in lower positions [15]. Common measures of accuracy in ranking, such as Expected Reciprocal Rank (ERR) [8], hinge on this property: they reward rankings where items are presented in decreasing order of relevance, so that the positions which attract most user attention are occupied by the most relevant items. These are static ranking measures, which summarize the performance of a system with respect to an information need by modeling a single user-system interaction. However, users can issue the same query multiple times, requiring a search engine to repeatedly attend to the same task (*task repetition*). Repeated queries, stemming from the same information need, are sometimes called *query impressions*.[4]

Recently, several measures of fairness in rankings have been proposed, which take into account the peculiarities of ranking problems [6,10,21]. These measures incorporate *position bias*, by suitably modeling user browsing behaviour when estimating item exposure, and consider *task repetition* by evaluating systems over multiple impressions of the same query, thus encouraging rotation of relevant items in top ranks. For example, *equity of amortized fairness* [6] considers cumulative attention and relevance of items over multiple query repetitions, and is defined as follows. "A sequence of rankings $\rho^1, \ldots, \rho^J$ offers equity of amortized attention if each subject receives cumulative attention proportional to her cumulative relevance", where the accumulation and amortization process are intended over multiple queries and impressions.

Depending on its amortization policy, measures of fairness in rankings can be (i) *cross-query* or (ii) *within-query*. (i) Cross-query measures are aimed at matching cumulative attention and relevance across different information needs [6]; this approach has the advantage of naturally weighing information needs based on their frequency and to enforce fairness over a realistic query load. On the downside, these fairness measures may end up rewarding systems that display irrelevant items in high-ranking positions. (ii) Within-query measures, on the other hand, enforce fairness over impressions of the same query [10]; this amortization policy results in one measurement for each information need and does not run the risk of rewarding systems that compensate an item's exposure across different information needs, which may result in balancing false negatives (missed exposure when relevant) with false positives (undue exposure when irrelevant).

Different approaches have been proposed to optimize ranking systems against a given fairness measure. Most of them make use of the *task repetition* property by employing stochastic ranking policies. These systems are non-deterministic since, given a set of estimated relevance scores, the resulting rankings are not necessarily fixed. A key advantage of stochastic ranking policies over deterministic ones lies in the finer granularity with which they can distribute exposure over multiple impressions of a query. Depending on whether they keep track of the unfairness accumulated by items, policies can be *stateless* or *stateful*. Stateless systems are based on drawing rankings from an ideal distribution independently [10,21,22]. This family of approaches can yield high-variance exposure for items, especially over few impressions, due to rankings being independent from one another. Moreover, they are not suitable to target cross-query measures as they would require estimating the future query load. Stateful solutions, on the other hand, keep track of the unfairness accumulated by items [6,18,23], and exploit it to build controllers or heuristics that can actively drive rankings toward solutions that increase the average cumulative fairness.

---

[4] https://fair-trec.github.io/2020/doc/guidelines-2020.pdf.

2.2 Diversity in Ranking

The diversity of items in search results is important for users of products and services that feature a ranking component [7,9,11]. In the absence of ad-hoc approaches measuring and favouring diversity, very similar items may be present in a result page [7,19]. Duplicates and near-duplicates are the most severe example of redundant results [4,9].

Redundant items are present in collections for web search [4], with repercussions on search engines that need to handle duplicates at different stages of their life cycle, including training, testing and deployment [7,12,13]. Moreover, duplicate or near-duplicate listings of items can be present in online marketplaces, such as Airbnb and Amazon [2]. Multiple listings for the same item can derive from a legitimate need to highlight slightly different conditions under which a product or service is provided, or from an adversarial attempt to increase visibility on the platform through redundancy. Especially in the latter case, duplicates are viewed unfavourably by system owners for their negative impact on user experience [1].

3 Duplicates and Fair Ranking

In this section, we illustrate the mechanism through which fairness in ranking may reward duplicates by granting multiple copies of the same item more exposure than it would obtain as a single item. Section 3.1 introduces the problem, explains its root cause and presents a basic model of duplication and its cost. Section 3.2 details the synthetic experimental setup, summarizing the key parameters of the problem and the values chosen for the present analysis. Results are reported in Sect. 3.3. The relevant notation is summarized in Table 1.

3.1 Rewarding Duplicates

If a ranking approach is purely based on the relevance of single items and unaware of their potential redundancy, two copies of the same item will receive more attention than a single copy. For example, let us consider an item u_i ranked in position $\rho_i^j = n$, receiving in turn a share of user attention a_i^j. If a copy $u_{\bar{i}}$ is created, in the absence of a ranking signal that rewards diversity, the item pair will rank in positions $\rho_i^j = n$, $\rho_{\bar{i}}^j = n + 1$ (or viceversa). As a result, under a non-singular attention model, the sum of attentions received by the item pair is greater than the original a_i^j.

The above consideration holds true regardless of notions of fairness in rankings. However, in the presence of fairness constraints, there may be a further advantage for duplicates. For example, under *equity of amortized fairness* [6], which requires cumulative exposure of items proportional to their cumulative relevance, two items of identical relevance deserve twice as much exposure as a single item.

In reality, there are several factors that make duplication "expensive" in terms of the features commonly exploited by systems for item retrieval and

Table 1. Notation employed in this work.

Symbol	Meaning
u_i	items to be ranked by system, $i \in \{1, \ldots, I\}$
$u_{\bar{i}}$	duplicate of item u_i
q_j	query impressions issued to system, $j \in \{1, \ldots, J\}$
ρ^j	ranking of items in response to query q_j
ρ_i^j	rank of item u_i in ranking ρ^j
π	a ranking policy
ρ_π	$\{\rho^1, \ldots, \rho^J\}$ sequence of rankings obtained via policy π
$u(\rho_\pi)$	utility function rewarding ranking sequence based on user satisfaction
a_i^j	attention received by item u_i in ranking ρ^j
r_i^j	relevance of item u_i for the information need expressed by q_j
k	cost of duplication, such that $r_{\bar{i}}^j = k r_i^j$, $k \in (0, 1)$
$\delta_{i+1,i}^j$	difference in relevance for adjacently ranked items (simplified to δ)
A_i	$\sum_{j=1}^J a_i^j$, i.e. cumulative attention received by item u_i
R_i	$\sum_{j=1}^J r_i^j$, i.e. cumulative relevance of item u_i over queries $\{q_1, \ldots, q_J\}$
$f(A, R)$	fairness function, defining the ideal relationship between A_i and R_i

ranking. Firstly, some of these features, such as user ratings, stem from the interaction of users with items; if an item is duplicated, its interactions with users will be distributed across its copies, presumably reducing their relevance score and lowering their rank in result pages. Moreover, a ranking system may explicitly measure the diversity of retrieved items [9] and favour rankings with low redundancy accordingly [19]. Finally, some platforms forbid duplication, in the interest of user experience, and enforce this ban with algorithms for duplicate detection and suppression procedures [1].

Therefore, we treat duplication as an expensive procedure, with a negative impact on items' relevance scores. We assume that the cost of duplicating an item only affects the new copy, while leaving the relevance of the original copy intact. We model duplication cost as a multiplicative factor $k \in (0, 1)$, reducing the relevance score of new copies of an item. In other words, if a copy $u_{\bar{i}}$ of item u_i is created, then r_i remains constant, while $r_{\bar{i}} = k r_i$. Richer models of duplication cost are surely possible (e.g. also reducing the relevance r_i of the original copy), and should be specialized depending on the application at hand.

3.2 Experimental Setup

We cast fair ranking as an unconstrained optimization problem over a ranking policy π, whose objective function is a linear combination of a utility measure and a fairness measure.

$$\mathcal{Q}(\pi) = \lambda u(\rho_\pi) + (1 - \lambda) f(R_i, A_i(\rho_\pi)), \quad \lambda \in (0, 1) \qquad (1)$$

Here $u(\cdot)$ is a function computing the utility of a sequence of rankings ρ_π for item consumers, produced by a policy π. For example, in an IR setting, $u(\cdot)$ is a proxy for the information gained by users from ρ_π. We measure the utility of a ranking (for a single impression) via normalized ERR [8], where the normalization ensures that a ranking where items are perfectly sorted by relevance has utility equal to 1, regardless of the items available for ranking and their relevance. ERR is based on a cascade browsing model, where users view search results from top to bottom, with a probability of abandoning at each position which increases with rank and relevance of examined items.[5] The overall utility $u(\rho_\pi)$ is computed as the average utility over all impressions. More in general, utility can be broadly characterized as user satisfaction, potentially including notions of diversity in rankings [9].

The objective function $\mathcal{Q}$ also comprises a function $f(\cdot)$ which combines the cumulative relevance R_i and exposure A_i of items to compute the fairness of ranking policy π toward item providers. To this end, we follow [5] by requiring that items receive a share of cumulative exposure that matches their share of cumulative relevance. More precisely, let us define the attention and relevance accumulated by item u_i over J queries as $A_i = \sum_{j=1}^{J} a_i^j$, $R_i = \sum_{j=1}^{J} r_i^j$, and let us denote as $\bar{A}_i$ and $\bar{R}_i$ their normalized versions

$$\bar{A}_i = \frac{A_i}{\sum_{i=1}^{I} A_i}; \quad \bar{R}_i = \frac{R_i}{\sum_{i=1}^{I} R_i}. \tag{2}$$

Cumulative unfairness is then quantified by the ℓ_2 norm of vector

$$\bar{A} - \bar{R} = [\bar{A}_1 - \bar{R}_1, \ldots, \bar{A}_I - \bar{R}_I] \tag{3}$$

and fairness by its negation:

$$f(A, R) = -\|\bar{A} - \bar{R}\|_2. \tag{4}$$

To quantify the attention a_i^j received by an item ranked in position ρ_i^j we use, again, the browsing model of ERR [8], so that the same user model underlies the estimates of item exposure and user utility.

We adopt a *within-query* policy for fairness amortization and focus on a single information need. Five items $(u_0, u_1, u_2, u_3, u_4)$ of relevance $r = (r_0, r_1, r_2, r_3, r_4)$ compete for attention in rankings over multiple impression of the same query. While in practice systems are required to rank large sets of items, this reduced cardinality allows us to enumerate all solutions and compute the perfect greedy solution without resorting to approximations or heuristics. We consider three relevance distributions, corresponding to different availability of relevant items and, consequently, different targets of ideal exposure. Specifically, item relevance decreases linearly from $r_0 = 1$, for the most relevant item, to $r_4 = \min(r_i^j)$ for the least relevant one, so that $r = (1, 1-\delta, 1-2\delta, 1-3\delta, 1-4\delta)$. Three values are

---

[5] Following [5], the probability of user stopping at position p, after viewing items $\{u_1, \ldots, u_p\}$ is set to $P(\text{stop}|u_1, \ldots, u_p) = \gamma^{p-1} c r_p \prod_{i=1}^{p-1}(1 - c r_i)$, $c = 0.7, \gamma = 0.5$.

tested for parameter δ, namely $\delta = 0.25$ (large relevance difference), $\delta = 0.125$ (intermediate relevance difference) and $\delta = 0.05$ (small relevance difference).

To solve the optimization problem, we test a *stateful* policy that explicitly targets the objective function (Eq. 1) by keeping track of the relevance and exposure accumulated by items up to some impression t. At step $t+1$, we exploit this information to compute the best greedy solution via enumeration. This ranking policy is compared against a *stateless* approach that exploits Placket-Luce (PL) sampling [17,20]. PL sampling is based on drawing the top-ranked item at random from a categorical distribution where the probability of drawing item u_i is equal to $r_i^j / \sum_{i=1}^{I} r_i^j$. The chosen item is then removed from the pool of candidate items, from which the second ranking item is drawn in the same way, based on ℓ_1-normalization of the relevance scores of remaining candidates. The procedure is repeated until all items are drawn.

To evaluate the effects of item duplication in systems where copies incur different relevance penalties, we let the cost of duplication take values $k = 1$ (free copy) and $k = 0.5$ (relevance of duplicate item is halved). For each combination of relevance distribution, summarized by parameter δ, and cost of duplication k, we test each policy in six different settings. In each setting a different item u_i is duplicated, and an additional setting accounts for a scenario without any duplicates.

3.3 Results

As a first step, we ensure that the stateful policy can effectively trade off relevance and fairness in the basic setting where no duplicates are present. In Fig. 2, we evaluate the impact of parameter λ on the utility and unfairness of rankings produced by the stateful policy, where unfairness is defined as the negation of function $f(\cdot)$ in Eq. 4. As a baseline, we test the PL-based policy π_{PL}, reporting median values for utility and unfairness over 1,000 repetitions, along with the 5th and 95th percentile. Each panel in Fig. 2 corresponds to a different combination of relevance difference, parametrized by δ, and number of impressions J. The top row corresponds to a less frequent query ($J = 20$) and the bottom row to a more frequent one ($J = 100$). Panels on the left depict results for a large relevance difference ($\delta = 0.25$), middle panels correspond to an intermediate relevance difference ($\delta = 0.125$) and left panels to a small one ($\delta = 0.05$).

We find that, over large relevance differences (left panels), a value $\lambda \geq 0.3$ is required to approach zero unfairness, while, for small relevance differences (right panels), $\lambda = 0.1$ is sufficient. This is expected: as relevance becomes uniform across items, even a policy marginally focused on fairness ($\lambda = 0.1$) can bring about major improvements in the distribution of attention. Moreover, for a small relevance difference, the trade-off between fairness and utility is less severe, which is also expected. When items have a similar relevance, a policy can more easily grant them a share of exposure proportional to their share of relevance, while only suffering a minor loss in terms of utility. Furthermore, the unfairness of exposure brought about by a solution purely based on relevance ($\lambda = 0$) increases as the difference in relevance for the available items become smaller. This is a desirable

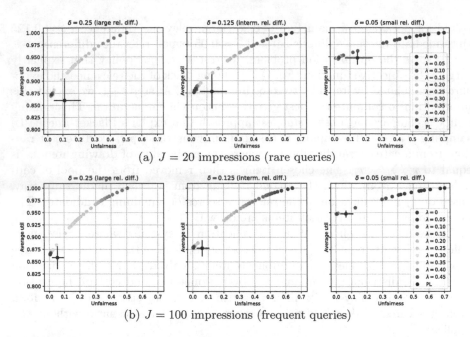

(a) $J = 20$ impressions (rare queries)

(b) $J = 100$ impressions (frequent queries)

Fig. 2. Unfairness (x axis) vs average utility (y axis) for *stateful* greedy solutions over different values of λ (downsampled and color-coded in legend). In black, summary of 1,000 Plackett-Luce repetitions, reporting median, 5th and 95th percentile for utility and unfairness. Each column corresponds to a different relevance profile for the available items, namely large relevance difference (left $-\delta = 0.25$), intermediate difference (middle $-\delta = 0.125$) and small difference (right $-\delta = 0.05$). Solutions with $\lambda > 0.5$ are omitted for better color-coding as they are all in a close neighbourhood of $\lambda = 0.5$.

property of unfairness function $u(\cdot)$. Indeed, if a small difference in relevance ($\frac{r_0}{r_4} = 1.25$) corresponds to a large difference in attention ($\frac{A_0}{A_4} > 1,000$), then the distribution of exposure stands out as particularly unfair for item u_4.

Although dominated by the stateful approach we just analyzed, the baseline PL-based policy π_{PL} consistently provides low-unfairness solutions. Unfairness is especially low for frequent queries, while for a rare query PL sampling is less likely to successfully distribute the cumulative exposure of items so that it matches their cumulative relevance. For frequent queries, the intervals spanned by the 5th and 95th percentile are narrower, signalling lower variance. PL sampling has been found to be a good baseline approach to obtain a fair policy from relevance scores under top-heavy browsing models such as the one underlying ERR [10]. Overall, our experiment confirms this finding.

To study the interaction between item duplication and equity of ranking, we firstly concentrate on a stateful greedy solution with $\lambda = 0.5$, representing a policy strongly focused on fairness. In Fig. 3, solid lines represent the distribution of cumulative attention A_i for each item u_i under a fairness-aware policy ($\lambda = 0.5$ - blue) and a policy solely focused on utility ($\lambda = 0$ - red), in the absence of

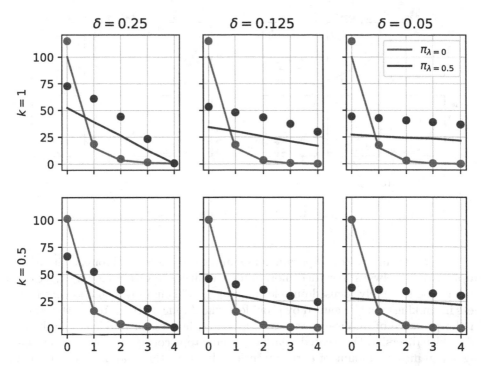

Fig. 3. Solid lines represent the attention A_i accumulated by each item (y axis) under a fairness-aware policy $\pi_{\lambda=0.5}$ (blue) or a policy solely focused on (ERR-based) utility $\pi_{\lambda=0}$ (red) in the absence of duplicates, over $J = 100$ impressions of the same query. Item indices $i \in \{0, \ldots, 4\}$ vary along the x axis. Round markers summarize the extra-attention one item would obtain if duplicated. Each column corresponds to a different relevance profile for the available items, namely large relevance difference (left $-\delta = 0.25$), intermediate difference (middle $-\delta = 0.125$) and small difference (right $-\delta = 0.05$). Each row corresponds to a different relevance multiplier for duplicates, namely $k = 1$ (top) and $k = 0.5$ (bottom). (Color figure Online)

duplicates. The query of interest is repeated for $J = 100$ impressions. Each column corresponds to a different value of δ, which determines large difference (left panels), intermediate difference (middle panels) and small difference (right panels) in relevance for items u_i. Interestingly, cumulative attention under policy $\pi_{\lambda=0.5}$ ends up resembling the distribution of relevance r_i^j for items u_i, i.e. a linear distribution with variable steepness. Policy $\pi_{\lambda=0}$, on the other hand, is not affected by the distribution of relevance.

Each round marker at position $x = i$ represents the sum of the attentions $(A_i + A_{\bar{i}})$ received by item u_i and its copy $u_{\bar{i}}$, if said item was duplicated (while remaining items are not). In other words, compared against solid lines of the same color, round markers summarize the extra-attention one item would obtain if duplicated. Different rows in Fig. 3 correspond to a different relevance multiplier for duplicates, namely $k = 1$ (top) and $k = 0.5$ (bottom).

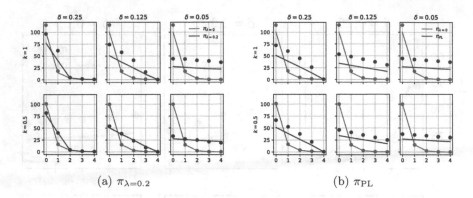

Fig. 4. Same analysis as Fig. 3 with different ranking policies.

For every combination of parameters k and δ considered and for each item u_i, duplicates are always rewarded more under a fairness-aware policy $\pi_{\lambda=0.5}$ than under a policy solely focused on relevance $\pi_{\lambda=0}$. This finding suggests that fairness in rankings may be gamed by providers who duplicate their items. Moreover, in the presence of duplicates or near-duplicates, fairness of rankings may be at odds with diversity. Duplicated items, especially top-scoring ones, end up obtaining a significant amount of extra-attention. In turn, this may incentivize item providers to duplicate their listings. If redundancy in candidate items increases, it becomes harder for a ranking system to achieve diverse rankings, with potential repercussions on user satisfaction [11] and perception [16]. As expected, however, the benefits of duplication become smaller as its cost increases (bottom panels).

Figure 4a summarizes the same analysis for $\lambda = 0.2$, which corresponds to a more balanced ranking policy. In general, policy $\pi_{\lambda=0.2}$ is more similar to $\pi_{\lambda=0}$, i.e. it is more focused on relevance and rewards duplicates less than $\pi_{\lambda=0.5}$. The most relevant items still obtain a sizeable benefit from duplication, especially when the copying process does not affect item relevance (top panels). Finally, we evaluate the extent to which a policy based on PL sampling rewards duplicates. Figure 4b reports the extra-attention obtained by duplicated items under π_{PL}. These results are similar to those obtained under policy $\pi_{\lambda=0.5}$ in Fig. 3, showing that duplicates are likely to receive a sizeable extra-exposure also under the stateless PL-based policy. This finding is not surprising given that, in order for $\pi_{\lambda=0.5}$ and π_{PL} to achieve similarly low unfairness for frequent queries (Fig. 2b), they must distribute item exposure in a similar fashion.

4   Conclusions

In this work we have shown that duplicates are a potential blind spot in the normative reasoning underlying common fair ranking criteria. On one hand, fairness-aware ranking policies, both stateful and stateless, may be at odds with diversity due to their potential to incentivize duplicates more than policies solely focused on relevance. This can be an issue for system owners, as diversity of search results is often associated with user satisfaction [11]. On the other hand, allowing providers who duplicate their items to benefit from extra-exposure seems unfair for the remaining providers. Finally, system users (item consumers) may end up being exposed to redundant items in low-diversity search results; this would be especially critical in situations where items convey opinion.

While technical solutions for near-duplicate detection and removal are certainly available [1,7], they may not always be viable, as nearly identical listings can be posted in accordance with system regulation, e.g. to stress slight differences in products. Control over near-duplicates is even weaker in web page collections indexed by search engines. Therefore, it is important to consider the entities and subjects who benefit from exposure of an item and factor them into the normative reasoning underlying a fair ranking objective. While in marketplaces beneficiaries of exposure are more easily identifiable, for document collections the situation is surely nuanced, including for instance the writer, publisher and subject of a document.

Future work should comprise a more detailed study, including cross-query measures, considering different user browsing models and richer models for duplication and its cost. Moreover, it will be interesting to systematically assess the relationship between provider-side fairness and diversity of search results in the presence of duplicates, and the extent to which these desirable objectives are in conflict with one another.

Acknowledgements. We thank anonymous reviewers for their thoughtful and helpful comments.

References

1. Amazon: Potential duplicates. https://sellercentral.amazon.com/gp/help/external/G202105450. Accessed 12 June 2020
2. Amazon: Split different products into different pages. https://sellercentral.amazon.com/gp/help/external/help.html?itemID=201950610. Accessed 12 June 2020
3. Barocas, S., Hardt, M., Narayanan, A.: Fairness and Machine Learning. fairmlbook.org (2019). http://www.fairmlbook.org
4. Bernstein, Y., Zobel, J.: Redundant documents and search effectiveness. In: Proceedings of the 14th ACM International Conference on Information and Knowledge Management, pp. 736–743. CIKM 2005, ACM, New York, NY, USA (2005)
5. Biega, A.J., Diaz, F., Ekstrand, M.D., Kohlmeier, S.: Overview of the trec 2019 fair ranking track. In: The Twenty-Eighth Text REtrieval Conference (TREC 2019) Proceedings (2019)

6. Biega, A.J., Gummadi, K.P., Weikum, G.: Equity of attention: amortizing individual fairness in rankings. In: The 41st International ACM SIGIR Conference on Research & Development in Information Retrieval, pp. 405–414. SIGIR 2018, ACM, New York, NY, USA (2018)
7. Broder, A.Z.: Identifying and filtering near-duplicate documents. In: Giancarlo, R., Sankoff, D. (eds.) CPM 2000. LNCS, vol. 1848, pp. 1–10. Springer, Heidelberg (2000). https://doi.org/10.1007/3-540-45123-4_1
8. Chapelle, O., Metlzer, D., Zhang, Y., Grinspan, P.: Expected reciprocal rank for graded relevance. In: Proceedings of the 18th ACM Conference on Information and Knowledge Management, pp. 621–630. CIKM 2009, ACM, New York, NY, USA (2009)
9. Clarke, C.L., Kolla, M., Cormack, G.V., Vechtomova, O., Ashkan, A., Büttcher, S., MacKinnon, I.: Novelty and diversity in information retrieval evaluation. In: Proceedings of the 31st Annual International ACM SIGIR Conference on Research and Development in Information Retrieval, pp. 659–666. SIGIR 2008, ACM, New York, NY, USA (2008)
10. Diaz, F., Mitra, B., Ekstrand, M.D., Biega, A.J., Carterette, B.: Evaluating stochastic rankings with expected exposure. In: Proceedings of the 29th ACM International Conference on Information & Knowledge Management, pp. 275–284. CIKM 2020, ACM, New York, NY, USA (2020)
11. Ekstrand, M.D., Harper, F.M., Willemsen, M.C., Konstan, J.A.: User perception of differences in recommender algorithms. In: Proceedings of the 8th ACM Conference on Recommender Systems, pp. 161–168. RecSys 2014, ACM, New York, NY, USA (2014)
12. Fröbe, M., Bevendorff, J., Reimer, J.H., Potthast, M., Hagen, M.: Sampling bias due to near-duplicates in learning to rank. In: Proceedings of the 43rd International ACM SIGIR Conference on Research and Development in Information Retrieval, pp. 1997–2000. SIGIR 2020, ACM, New York, NY, USA (2020)
13. Fröbe, M., Bittner, J.P., Potthast, M., Hagen, M.: The effect of content-equivalent near-duplicates on the evaluation of search engines. In: Jose, J.M., et al. (eds.) Advances in Information Retrieval, pp. 12–19. Springer International Publishing, Cham (2020)
14. Geyik, S.C., Ambler, S., Kenthapadi, K.: Fairness-aware ranking in search & recommendation systems with application to linkedin talent search. In: Proceedings of the 25th ACM SIGKDD International Conference on Knowledge Discovery & Data Mining, pp. 2221–2231. KDD 2019, ACM, New York, NY, USA (2019)
15. Joachims, T., Radlinski, F.: Search engines that learn from implicit feedback. Computer **40**(8), 34–40 (2007)
16. Kay, M., Matuszek, C., Munson, S.A.: Unequal representation and gender stereotypes in image search results for occupations. In: Proceedings of the 33rd Annual ACM Conference on Human Factors in Computing Systems, pp. 3819–3828. CHI 2015, Association for Computing Machinery, New York, NY, USA (2015)
17. Luce, R.D.: Individual Choice Behavior. Wiley, Hoboken (1959)
18. Morik, M., Singh, A., Hong, J., Joachims, T.: Controlling fairness and bias in dynamic learning-to-rank. In: Proceedings of the 43rd International ACM SIGIR Conference on Research and Development in Information Retrieval, pp. 429–438. SIGIR 2020, ACM, New York, NY, USA (2020)
19. Nishimura, N., Tanahashi, K., Suganuma, K., Miyama, M.J., Ohzeki, M.: Item listing optimization for e-commerce websites based on diversity. Front. Comput. Sci. **1**, 2 (2019)

20. Plackett, R.L.: The analysis of permutations. J. Roy. Stat. Soc. Ser. C (Appl. Stat.) **24**(2), 193–202 (1975)
21. Singh, A., Joachims, T.: Fairness of exposure in rankings. In: Proceedings of the 24th ACM SIGKDD International Conference on Knowledge Discovery & Data Mining, pp. 2219–2228. KDD 2018, ACM, New York, NY, USA (2018)
22. Singh, A., Joachims, T.: Policy learning for fairness in ranking. In: Wallach, H., Larochelle, H., Beygelzimer, A., dAlché-Buc, F., Fox, E., Garnett, R. (eds.) Advances in Neural Information Processing Systems, vol. 32, pp. 5426–5436. Curran Associates, Inc., Red Hook (2019)
23. Thonet, T., Renders, J.M.: Multi-grouping robust fair ranking. In: Proceedings of the 43rd International ACM SIGIR Conference on Research and Development in Information Retrieval, pp. 2077–2080. SIGIR 2020, ACM, New York, NY, USA (2020)

Quantification of the Impact
of Popularity Bias in Multi-stakeholder
and Time-Aware Environments

Francisco Guíñez$^{(\boxtimes)}$, Javier Ruiz , and María Ignacia Sánchez

Pontificia Universidad Católica, Santiago, Chile
{fhguinez,jiruiz2,mcsanchez}@uc.cl

Abstract. Popularity bias is one of the main biases present in recommendation algorithms, which means most popular items are over-
recommended by the algorithms, while items with less interactions are
invisible. In this paper we analyze the impact of the popularity bias
over time for different stakeholders considering different recommendation
algorithms. The datasets used were Last.FM-1B and KASANDR, while
the algorithms compared were ALS and BPR, with Most Popular and
random recommendations used as a baseline. The main contribution of
this paper provides a new way of measuring popularity in a variable way
over time and analyzes which algorithms maintain a popularity bias over
time that negatively impacts stakeholders. The analysis of the unfairness
metrics shows that the popularity bias is not static over time and that
the ALS algorithm obtains more stable results with less unfairness than
BPR among different groups of stakeholders.

Keywords: Popularity bias · Popularity bias over time ·
Stakeholders · Multi-stakeholders · Time-aware

1 Introduction

Popularity bias is one of the main biases present in recommendation algorithms
[1]. This consists in the fact that the most popular items are over-recommended
by the algorithms, while items with less interactions are invisible [19]. This generates a rich-get-richer effect [24], in which recommendations increase the popularity of already popular items and do not give the less popular ones a chance to
emerge. In general, efforts to decrease this bias have been placed on those who
consume these recommendations, i.e., the users. However, in platforms where
there are multiple stakeholder groups, it is important to consider what impact
each one has, otherwise some of these groups may have incentives to stop using
the platform. In order to make good and useful recommendations to users, it
is important that the recommender system takes into consideration the novelty
and diversity of these recommendations [13]. For example, if Netflix made only
popular recommendations due to the bias of its algorithm, only the directors of
the most popular movies would win. In turn, those who would be most interested

L. Boratto et al. (Eds.): BIAS 2021, CCIS 1418, pp. 78–91, 2021.
https://doi.org/10.1007/978-3-030-78818-6_8

in the platform would be those users who have more popular tastes. This would hurt those directors and users who create/consume less popular movies, which would eventually give them incentives to leave the platform.

Within this context, it is also important to consider the time in which an item is popular as a variable. That is, items that are popular today may not be popular tomorrow. Thus, users who at one time had popular tastes may eventually become users with less common tastes; and similarly, suppliers may go from being unpopular to becoming popular. While metrics have been constructed to measure the impact of popularity bias, they have not considered the time dimension of interactions.

Thus, the main contributions of this paper are:

1. Propose a way to measure the popularity of the items but considering the dynamics of time. This will also allow us to catalogue stakeholders in dynamic groups of popularity over time.
2. Perform a popularity bias analysis over time, considering the state of the art metrics on the subject, which measure the impact of the popularity bias on users and providers.

2   Related Work

If we examine the related work, it is possible to identify three main areas of research: Recommendations for multiple stakeholders, analysis of time-aware recommendations, and the presence of bias and injustice in multiple contexts.

2.1   Multistakeholders

As described above, a stakeholder is defined as a person or group of people interested in a business who are directly affected by the decisions made in it. Thus, within the context of recommendation, considering multiple stakeholders implies making recommendations taking into account the differentiated interests between the different groups and considering the needs of each one [14]. The research in this subject arises after the academy has historically focused on the interests of the end user when proposing recommending models, but the complexity of these made it necessary to recognize that they serve multiple objectives [2,15], various models have been proposed in this direction in the last decade [23,26,32,37].

Specifically, an interesting multiple approach is presented in [1], where, based on a music dataset, the quality of recommendations for both end users and composing artists are considered, in addition to subdividing these groups according to their popularity in high, medium and low.

This field of research is related to the search for new and more diverse evaluation metrics for recommending systems, because of the need to evaluate groups as well as individuals [22].

2.2 Time-Aware Recommendations

Over the years, this topic has been approached from two main perspectives, which are independent and complementary [18]. On the one hand, we have the notion that the popularity of an item may change over time, and occurs intrinsically in every context, but is also influenced by external events. Examples of this perspective are the prediction of values on a timeline through before and after interactions [36] and the incorporation of time-dependent weights that decrease the importance of old items [6,17].

On the other hand, there is the temporal evolution of the users; the way they interact with their environment is not constant and therefore their tastes or opinions vary depending on the temporal context [12,33]. In particular, this has motivated research for models with a time dimension. Among them, for example: models aware of the day of the week [5], models aware of the time of the day [35] and models where the importance of the interactions is penalized according to how many newer interactions with the same item the user has [25].

2.3 Bias and Unfairness

Finally, it is important to mention that both the presence of multiple stakeholders and the time dimension are sources of bias and injustice when making recommendations [7].

When we recognize stakeholder groups differentiated by popularity, it is common to keep in mind a popularity bias that is unfair to groups describing unpopular segments [4]. In addition, popularity bias has been shown to impact the evaluation of recommender systems [8,21], being important to know the objective of the recommendation to measure the real impact. In [9] various algorithms are compared in a context that needs to consider both precision and diversity of the results, so algorithms that compensate for popularity bias perform well.

There have been efforts to measure this injustice by means of knowledge graphs [16] and considering the efficiency of pareto [34], while other works have analyzed the implications that unfair models have on people [3,20]. Also, [10] proposes two ways of measuring bias, one aimed at giving equal exposure to all items and the other aimed at giving exposure according to the actual popularity of the item.

Likewise, not considering the notions of temporal evolution described in the Sect. 2.2 almost always implies the presence of a time bias that is impossible to measure [33]. Therefore, in the literature we see methods such as the one proposed in [18] which counteracts this bias by means of penalizers proportional to the measured bias, or [11] that uses variational autoencoders.

3 Datasets

In order to carry out the desired study, we used two datasets: 'LFM-1B' [28], which has the reproductions made by users to different songs in Last.FM site, and

KASANDR-train_de [30], which has records of e-commerce sales. Both datasets were pre-processed in order to adapt the amount of information to the available computing capacity. After the pre-processing, we obtained the Last.FM dataset with 316,666 interactions between a user and a specific album. Meanwhile, for KASANDR, we obtained a dataset with 520,196 interactions between a user and a specific item.

The resulting dataset of Last.fm was divided into 6 parts, each of which had interactions up to a certain point in time. The first part had interactions occurring until the end of the sixth month of 2011, the second until the end of the seventh month of 2011, the third until the end of the eighth month of 2011, and so on. Meanwhile for KASANDR, since this dataset only contains data for 14 days, the resulting dataset was divided into 6 parts, each of them separated by two days starting from day 5. A summary of the matrix of interactions associated with both datasets can be seen in the Table 1.

For simplicity, we will call the subdivision of these datasets "periods". In the case of Last.fm each period will be monthly, while in KASANDR each period will be once every two days. For each periodic dataset, a division of 80% was made for training and 20% for testing.

Table 1. Summary of interaction matrices

Last.FM dataset						
Month	7	8	9	10	11	12
# of interactions	124,869	151,657	179,953	209,423	242,800	316,666
# of users	9,573	11,101	12,631	14,093	15,716	19,129
# of suppliers (artists)	18,202	20,799	23,360	25,752	28,355	33,638
# of items (albums)	26,583	31,003	35,385	39,551	44,050	53,636
KASANDR dataset						
Day	5	7	9	11	13	15
# of interactions	184,620	251,395	326,053	390,456	462,196	522,196
# of users	9,526	12,371	15,092	17,345	19,806	24,936
# of suppliers (sellers)	620	634	643	651	659	665
# of items (products)	103,832	132,540	162,656	186,415	213,906	228,537

4 Proposed Method

Intuitively, when we talk about the popularity of a song for example, we consider that it becomes popular when many users start listening to it. Thus, most works in the area consider the number of interactions of an item as a key factor to define its popularity.

On the other hand, from a mathematical perspective, when we are facing a continuous change in time, it is natural to model the problem as a derivative, understood as the ratio of instantaneous change of a variable [31]. Common examples of the application of the derivative concept are the change of motion in time, which translates into speed, and the change of speed in time, which translates into acceleration.

Having said this and considering the state of the art, given that the objective of this work is to measure the popularity bias considering the existence of a time variable, we propose a new way of measuring the popularity of an item, which interprets popularity as the ratio of instantaneous change related to the number of interactions that an item achieves in time. Having this popularity value for each item, we will proceed to classify the set of items into three subgroups of items: populars ($\mathcal{H}^t$), moderately popular ($\mathcal{M}^t$) and of low popularity ($\mathcal{T}^t$). A similar procedure will also be carried out to group users and suppliers as stakeholders.

4.1 Time Popularity Metrics

We will define N_i^t as the number of interactions achieved by the item i until a period of time t. For example, for an item i, $N_i^{2018} = 1000$ will imply that until 2018 the item has achieved a number of 1000 interactions. This variable is discrete, and easily obtainable through the datasets. In our case (and as described in Sect. 3) for Last.FM dataset $t \in \{7, \ldots, 12\}$ are monthly periods from July to December in 2011. For KASANDR dataset $t \in \{5, 7, 9, 11, 13, 15\}$ are daily periods from June 2016.

Our interest will be in approximating N_i^t with a soft function $N_i(t)$ such that $N_i(t) = N_i^t$ for all period t. There are many methods of approximation of functions with different degrees of accuracy, however, since the main focus of this project is an analysis at the bias level, a polynomial adjustment was chosen, which proves to be effective and fast without sacrificing too much accuracy. We emphasize the importance of maintaining a low computational cost in this work, since in certain cases it is necessary to adjust large amounts of data. For this purpose, the library *statsmodels* was used [29], which contains what is needed to create a non-linear model based on dataframes in a simple way, and allows for performing a polynomial regression using least squares. Another benefit of this library is that it allows for adjusting the degree d of the polynomial with which the regression is sought, which will allow to obtain coefficients to model different variants of the function when required. In this case, it was considered that $d = 3$ gave an error small enough for this context.

Once the coefficients of this regression are obtained, the function $N_i(t)$ adjusts to the variable N_i^t with an error of ε_i, which will be used to build the item popularity function:

$$\text{Pop}_i(t) = \frac{\partial}{\partial t} N_i(t) \tag{1}$$

This popularity function will allow to calculate the popularity of an item at any instant of time, since the popularity is represented as the ratio of instantaneous change related to the number of interactions that an item achieves in time.

To illustrate this, we will take as example the album *21* from Adele, which was released on January 24, 2011. Figure 1a shows the discrete acumulated inter-actions N_i^t and its aproximation $N_i(t)$ using $d = 5$ to illustrate. On the other side, Fig. 1b shows the popularity of this item in time. Altough the number of interactions increase monotonely in time (Fig. 1a) from which we could say that the popularity of this item is constant, Fig. 1b shows that this is not necessarily true since the popularity changes over time. Every album has variations in the speed of growth of its interactions, no matter how small they are. Our popularity function detects these variations, which can be seen in Fig. 1b with a zoomed Y axis. The better the adjustment of $N_i(t)$, the better modeled the popularity function will be.

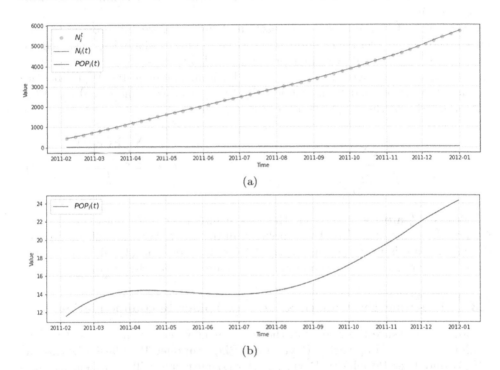

(a)

(b)

Fig. 1. N_i^t, $N_i(t)$ and $\text{Pop}_i(t)$ illustration for the album item *21* from Adele.

It should be noted that, depending on the dataset, other measures of pop-ularity could be proposed. For example, instead of considering the number of interactions accumulated by an item N_i^t, you could consider the number of user interactions achieved by this item B_i^t. That is, for each user, a 1 is added to the variable B_i^t if an interaction was made with the item i until the period t. Other approaches could be to divide these variables by the number of total users, so as to capture the growth of the item within a specific context. All these variants were implemented and tested, but their results were similar to (1), so the latter was finally chosen given its low computational time compared to the others.

Sequential recommendations will be made. In particular, recommendations will be generated in each period using as periods those defined in Sect. 3.

4.2 Dynamic Grouping of Items and Stakeholders

Once these popularity functions $\text{POP}_i(t)$ for all i items have been obtained, the dynamic grouping of items and stakeholders (users and suppliers) is carried out. To make this grouping in the items, as in [1], we used the Pareto Principle [27]. Given a period of time t, the items are ordered from most to least popular according to $\text{POP}_i(t)$. The first 20% of these items will represent group $\mathcal{H}^t$. The last 20% of the items will belong to the $\mathcal{T}^t$ group. The remaining items will belong to $\mathcal{M}^t$.

With regard to the grouping of users and suppliers, we will proceed to calculate the simple average of popularity of the items that have been listened to or created, respectively. A similar procedure will then be carried out for grouping, using the same percentages of cuts as for item grouping. Let $\text{W}_u(t)$ be the average level of popularity interactions by the user u over time t, and $\text{P}_a(t)$ be the popularity of the supplier a over time t, then:

$$\text{W}_u(t) = \frac{\sum\limits_{i \in E_u^t} \text{POP}_i(t)}{|E_u^t|} \qquad (2) \qquad \qquad \text{P}_a(t) = \frac{\sum\limits_{i \in C_a^t} \text{POP}_i(t)}{|C_a^t|} \qquad (3)$$

Where E_u^t are the items that the user u interacted with until time t, and C_a^t are the items offered by the supplier a until time t. We will call the groups derived from this procedure as $\mathcal{U}_1^t, \mathcal{U}_2^t, \mathcal{U}_3^t$ for the users and $\mathcal{A}_1^t, \mathcal{A}_2^t, \mathcal{A}_3^t$ for the suppliers, where the larger the number, the more popular the group.

4.3 Measuring the Unfairness of Stakeholder Recommendations

In order to measure the impact of the recommendations on the different stakeholders, the Item Popularity Deviation (IPD), Supplier Popularity Deviation (SPD) and User Popularity Deviation (UPD) measures will be taken, as proposed by [1][1], but adapted to a version that considers temporality. On the other hand, to measure the coverage of items that do not belong to the popular group, the well-known metrics of Aggregate Diversity (Agg-Div) and Long Tail Coverage (LC) will be used, in addition to the metric Average Percentage of Long-tail Items (APL) proposed by [1]. That being said, the following variables are defined:

- ℓ_u^t: List of item recommendations delivered by an algorithm to a user u in time t.
- L^t: Set of recommended items in the time period t.

---

[1] With respect to UPD, a small modification in the way it is calculated will be considered, but it follows the same idea proposed by [1].

- $V(i)$: Function that returns the supplier of the item i
- $\mathcal{U}^t = \{\mathcal{U}_1^t, \mathcal{U}_2^t, \mathcal{U}_3^t\}$: Set with the popularity groups of users for a time t.
- U^t: Group of all users on the platform, up to the time t.
- $\mathcal{A}^t = \{\mathcal{A}_1^t, \mathcal{A}_2^t, \mathcal{A}_3^t\}$: Sets with the popularity groups of suppliers for a time t.
- $\mathcal{I}^t = \{\mathcal{H}^t, \mathcal{M}^t, \mathcal{T}^t\}$: Set with the popularity groups of the items for a time t.
- E_u^t: List of items that user u interacted with before time t.
- n: Number of recommendations.

$$APL = \frac{1}{|U^t|} \sum_{u \in U^t} \frac{|\{i, i \in (\ell_u^t \cap (\mathcal{M}^t \cup \mathcal{T}^t))\}|}{|\ell_u^t|} \qquad (4)$$

$$UPD = \frac{\sum_{g \in \mathcal{U}^t} |UPD(g)|}{|\mathcal{U}^t|} \qquad (6)$$

$$SPD = \frac{\sum_{s \in \mathcal{A}^t} |SPD(s)|}{|\mathcal{A}^t|} \qquad (5)$$

$$IPD = \frac{\sum_{c \in \mathcal{I}^t} |IPD(c)|}{|\mathcal{I}^t|} \qquad (7)$$

Here, we calculate $SPD(s)$ and $IPD(c)$ as proposed in [1], with the difference that the popularity groups, instead of being defined statically by the number of interactions, were defined according to the proposed new popularity metric, which considers a time-varying subdivision. In addition, we also considered the variables associated with the recommendations given to a user and the interactions of a user in a variable way in time. On the other hand, we considered a slight variation of the formula for $UPD(g)$ with respect to what was proposed by [1], but it was decided to maintain the same idea proposed to calculate SPD and IPD and to average over the user popularity groups the subtraction between the proportion of recommendations achieved by a group and the proportion of interactions achieved by that same group, that is:

$$UPD(g) = qu(g) - pu(g) \qquad (8)$$

$$qu(q) = \frac{\sum_{u \in U^t} \sum_{j \in \ell_u^t} \mathbb{1}(V(j) \in s)}{n \times |U^t|} \qquad (9)$$

$$pu(g) = \frac{\sum_{u \in U^t} \sum_{j \in E_u^t} \mathbb{1}(V(j) \in s)}{|E_u^t|} \qquad (10)$$

For these last three metrics, lower values mean that there is a smaller average difference between the proportion of the recommended and the proportion of the actual interactions achieved per popularity group, so the algorithm would be fair to the different popularity groups.

5   Experimented Recommender Systems

In order to find an ideal configuration for the recommendation algorithms and to enable them to do their job better, different combinations of values for their hyperparameters were tested on a cross validation of four folds.

The hyperparameters studied, both for ALS and BPR, were the number of latent factors (50, 100 and 200) and the regularization parameter (0.01 and 0.1). In addition, the learning rate was varied for BPR (0.001, 0.01 and 0.1).

First, for Last.FM dataset, the decision was made to make 5 recommendations per user, since a smaller number does not allow us to adequately analyze the capacity of the algorithms to recommend less popular items due to most popular options monopolize all the recommendations. On the other hand, a higher number of recommendations would not be representative of the context to be studied, since very few users have interacted with more than 5 different items, adding noise to the metrics.

Second, in the case of KASANDR dataset, we decided to make 5 recommendations also based on what was said in [30].

Then, for each specific hyperparameter configuration, MAP@5 and nDCG@5 were calculated for each period. Finally, the average of the metrics for each set of parameters was obtained in order to select the one that delivers a higher value.

For Last.FM dataset, the chosen parameters for ALS were 50 latent factors and 0.1 as a regularization parameter. With this configuration higher values were obtained in both MAP@5 and nDCG@5. Meanwhile for BPR, the chosen parameters were 100 latent factors, 0.01 as a regularization parameter and 0.01 as a learning rate parameter.

For KASANDR dataset, the chosen parameters for ALS were 200 latent factors and 0.1 as a regularization parameter, with higher values obtained in MAP@5 and nDCG@5. Meanwhile for BPR, the chosen parameters were 200 latent factors, 0.01 as a regularization parameter and 0.001 as a learning rate parameter.

6   Results

Once the best hyperparameter configurations were defined, recommendations were made for each user in each monthly (Last.FM) and daily (KASANDR) dataset, resulting in six groups of recommendations for each one. Then, for these recommendations the unfairness was measured using the metrics described in Sect. 4.3. In addition, recommendations were made with the Most Popular and Random algorithms to have a baseline of values for the studied metrics, since the first algorithm should deliver the highest values of popularity bias, while the second should illustrate a moderate unfairness. It is important to note that Random should not have completely fair values, since it negatively affects the recommendations of the most popular items. The results obtained can be reviewed in Fig. 2 and 3.

As displayed in both Figures, except for Agg-div and LC, which tend to be more linear, all the metrics have uneven variations as they move forward in time, showing that the bias is not static, that is, it can both increase and decrease over time.

In addition, the ALS recommendation algorithm manages to overcome BPR in Agg-div, LC, IPD, SPD and UPD metrics in most of the epochs for both

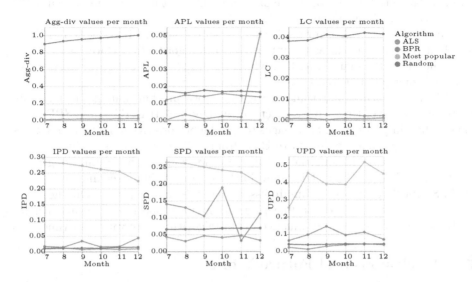

Fig. 2. Unfairness metric results for Last.FM dataset

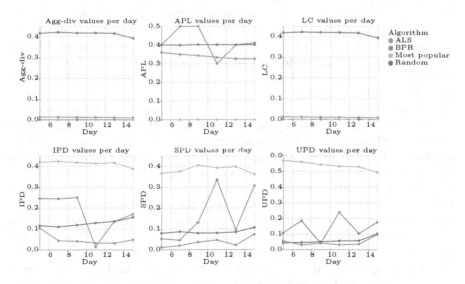

Fig. 3. Unfairness metric results for KASANDR dataset

dataset. Moreover, for APL metric, the best algorithm depends on the epoch and the dataset. This performance of ALS means that it is less unfair than BPR when recommending unpopular items.

Another aspect worth noting is that, when it comes to IPD, SPD and UPD, which are metrics that measure unfairness, both algorithms perform much better than the Most Popular algorithm, which naturally turns out to be very unfair in prioritizing popular items.

It is interesting to note that ALS is the algorithm that manages to maintain better metrics over time with respect to Agg-Div, LC, IPD, APL and SPD. This means that, in general, ALS manages to give higher priority in recommendations to less popular items compared to BPR from a time-aware perspective.

With respect to the unfairness of recommendations among popularity groups, the UPD, SPD and IPD metrics show fairly constant values over time in the case of ALS, which means that unfairness is maintained constantly. On the other hand, these metrics have non-linear variations from one month to another for BPR, which shows that the injustice of this algorithm may vary over time.

7   Conclusions and Future Work

As the objective of this work was to explore and make a first approach to the analysis of popularity bias in algorithms considering a temporal dimension, it would be interesting to address the following tasks in the future:

- Due to the computational demands of the number of items, we decided to abstract the problem to monthly and daily time points, which translates into an adjustment error that could be important. Thus, in the future the adjustment of each function $N_i(t)$ could be better and more accurate. For example, a greater number of points could be considered to obtain a better adjustment, or an adjustment error of $\varepsilon_i = \varepsilon \ \forall i$ could be set and the number of degrees of the polynomial d_i could be increased until achieving a value less than or equal to this error.
- Given that the focus was on temporal analysis of popularity bias, temporary recommendations were made using a basic algorithm. In the future, more sophisticated and less costly methods could be used in making them. Furthermore, it would be interesting to analyze how other algorithms besides ALS and BPR behave with respect to their temporal popularity bias.
- On the other hand, it would be interesting to analyze in detail the possibilities provided by the item popularity metric based on the derivative. By pre-computing the popularity of the items over time, it is possible to know at any time which items belong to the groups $\mathcal{H}^t$, $\mathcal{M}^t$ and $\mathcal{T}^t$. With this it is possible to build an algorithm that allows rewarding recommendations from less popular groups. Naturally, in order to control this benefit, an adjustment parameter α would be required, which would allow weighting the importance given to this aspect. It would be interesting to analyze how such a metric behaves in contrast to conventional metrics to measure coverage and variability of recommendations.

The results presented in Sect. 6 demonstrated that the popularity bias is not static in time. This highlights the need to build time-conscious recommendations, since timeless analyses do not give a complete picture of the problem to be addressed.

A dataset of musical interactions and e-commerce interactions were used as object of study, with which recommendations were made considering a sequence of instants in time. With the results obtained, we concluded that ALS is less unfair than BPR when recommending unpopular items, since ALS is able to maintain lower and more consistent metrics of injustice over time.

The main difficulties arose from the high computational cost of estimating the popularity functions for each item, which was overcome by subsampling the information. This decision did not greatly affect the results of this research and a similar analysis can be carried out in the future with better hardware.

References

1. Abdollahpouri, H.: Popularity bias in recommendation: a multi-stakeholder perspective. Ph.D. thesis (2020). https://doi.org/10.13140/RG.2.2.18789.63202
2. Abdollahpouri, H., et al.: Multistakeholder recommendation: survey and research directions. User Model. User-Adap. Inter. **30**(1), 127–158 (2020)
3. Abdollahpouri, H., Mansoury, M., Burke, R., Mobasher, B.: The impact of popularity bias on fairness and calibration in recommendation. arXiv e-prints arXiv:1910.05755 (2019)
4. Abdollahpouri, H., Mansoury, M., Burke, R., Mobasher, B.: The unfairness of popularity bias in recommendation, August 2019
5. Adomavicius, G., Tuzhilin, A.: Context-aware recommender systems. In: Ricci, F., Rokach, L., Shapira, B., Kantor, P.B. (eds.) Recommender Systems Handbook, pp. 217–253. Springer, Boston, MA (2011). https://doi.org/10.1007/978-0-387-85820-3_7
6. Anelli, V.W., Di Noia, T., Di Sciascio, E., Ragone, A., Trotta, J.: Local popularity and time in top-N recommendation. In: Azzopardi, L., Stein, B., Fuhr, N., Mayr, P., Hauff, C., Hiemstra, D. (eds.) ECIR 2019. LNCS, vol. 11437, pp. 861–868. Springer, Cham (2019). https://doi.org/10.1007/978-3-030-15712-8_63
7. Baeza-Yates, R.: Bias in search and recommender systems. In: Fourteenth ACM Conference on Recommender Systems, p. 2 (2020)
8. Bellogín, A., Castells, P., Cantador, I.: Statistical biases in information retrieval metrics for recommender systems. Inf. Retrieval J. **20**(6), 604–634 (2017)
9. Boratto, L., Fenu, G., Marras, M.: The effect of algorithmic bias on recommender systems for massive open online courses. In: Azzopardi, L., Stein, B., Fuhr, N., Mayr, P., Hauff, C., Hiemstra, D. (eds.) ECIR 2019. LNCS, vol. 11437, pp. 457–472. Springer, Cham (2019). https://doi.org/10.1007/978-3-030-15712-8_30
10. Boratto, L., Fenu, G., Marras, M.: Connecting user and item perspectives in popularity debiasing for collaborative recommendation. Inf. Process. Manage. **58**(1) (2021). https://doi.org/10.1016/j.ipm.2020.102387
11. Borges, R., Stefanidis, K.: On mitigating popularity bias in recommendations via variational autoencoders (2021)
12. Campos, P.G., Díez, F., Cantador, I.: Time-aware recommender systems: a comprehensive survey and analysis of existing evaluation protocols. User Model. User-Adap. Inter. **24**(1–2), 67–119 (2014)

13. Castells, P., Hurley, N.J., Vargas, S.: Novelty and diversity in recommender systems. In: Ricci, F., Rokach, L., Shapira, B. (eds.) Recommender Systems Handbook, pp. 881–918. Springer, Boston (2015). https://doi.org/10.1007/978-1-4899-7637-6_26
14. Chelliah, M., Zheng, Y., Sarkar, S.: Recommendation for multi-stakeholders and through neural review mining. In: Proceedings of the 28th ACM International Conference on Information and Knowledge Management, pp. 2979–2981 (2019)
15. Ekstrand, M.D., et al.: All the cool kids, how do they fit in?: popularity and demographic biases in recommender evaluation and effectiveness. In: Friedler, S.A., Wilson, C. (eds.) Proceedings of the 1st Conference on Fairness, Accountability and Transparency. Proceedings of Machine Learning Research, vol. 81, pp. 172–186. PMLR, New York, 23–24 February 2018. http://proceedings.mlr.press/v81/ekstrand18b.html
16. Fu, Z., et al.: Fairness-aware explainable recommendation over knowledge graphs. arXiv preprint arXiv:2006.02046 (2020)
17. Garg, D., Gupta, P., Malhotra, P., Vig, L., Shroff, G.: Sequence and time aware neighborhood for session-based recommendations: STAN. In: Proceedings of the 42nd International ACM SIGIR Conference on Research and Development in Information Retrieval, pp. 1069–1072 (2019)
18. Koren, Y.: Collaborative filtering with temporal dynamics. In: Proceedings of the 15th ACM SIGKDD International Conference on Knowledge Discovery and Data Mining, pp. 447–456 (2009)
19. Kowald, D., Schedl, M., Lex, E.: The unfairness of popularity bias in music recommendation: a reproducibility study. In: Jose, J.M., et al. (eds.) ECIR 2020. LNCS, vol. 12036, pp. 35–42. Springer, Cham (2020). https://doi.org/10.1007/978-3-030-45442-5_5
20. Liu, W., Guo, J., Sonboli, N., Burke, R., Zhang, S.: Personalized fairness-aware re-ranking for microlending. In: Proceedings of the 13th ACM Conference on Recommender Systems, pp. 467–471 (2019)
21. Mena-Maldonado, E., Cañamares, R., Castells, P., Ren, Y., Sanderson, M.: Agreement and disagreement between true and false-positive metrics in recommender systems evaluation. In: Proceedings of the 43rd International ACM SIGIR Conference on Research and Development in Information Retrieval, pp. 841–850 (2020)
22. Morik, M., Singh, A., Hong, J., Joachims, T.: Controlling fairness and bias in dynamic learning-to-rank. arXiv preprint arXiv:2005.14713 (2020)
23. Nguyen, P., Dines, J., Krasnodebski, J.: A multi-objective learning to re-rank approach to optimize online marketplaces for multiple stakeholders. arXiv preprint arXiv:1708.00651 (2017)
24. Nikolov, D., Lalmas, M., Flammini, A., Menczer, F.: Quantifying biases in online information exposure. J. Am. Soc. Inf. Sci. **70**(3), 218–229 (2019). https://doi.org/10.1002/asi.24121
25. Pavlovski, M., et al.: Time-aware user embeddings as a service. In: Proceedings of the 26th ACM SIGKDD International Conference on Knowledge Discovery & Data Mining, pp. 3194–3202 (2020)
26. Rodriguez, M., Posse, C., Zhang, E.: Multiple objective optimization in recommender systems. In: Proceedings of the Sixth ACM Conference on Recommender Systems, pp. 11–18 (2012)
27. Sanders, R.: The pareto principle: its use and abuse. J. Serv. Mark. **1**, 37–40 (1987). https://doi.org/10.1108/eb024706
28. Schedl, M.: The LFM-1B dataset for music retrieval and recommendation. In: ICMR (2016). https://doi.org/10.1145/2911996.2912004

29. Seabold, S., Perktold, J.: Statsmodels: econometric and statistical modeling with python. In: 9th Python in Science Conference (2010)
30. Sidana, S., Laclau, C., Amini, M.R., Vandelle, G., Bois-Crettez, A.: KASANDR: a large-scale dataset with implicit feedback for recommendation. In: Proceedings of the 40th International ACM SIGIR Conference on Research and Development in Information Retrieval, pp. 1245–1248 (2017)
31. Stewart, J.: Calculus: Early Transcendentals. Cengage Learning (2010)
32. Wang, S., Gong, M., Li, H., Yang, J.: Multi-objective optimization for long tail recommendation. Knowl.-Based Syst. **104**, 145–155 (2016)
33. Xiang, L., Yang, Q.: Time-dependent models in collaborative filtering based recommender system. In: 2009 IEEE/WIC/ACM International Joint Conference on Web Intelligence and Intelligent Agent Technology. vol. 1, pp. 450–457. IEEE (2009)
34. Xiao, L., Min, Z., Yongfeng, Z., Zhaoquan, G., Yiqun, L., Shaoping, M.: Fairness-aware group recommendation with pareto-efficiency. In: Proceedings of the Eleventh ACM Conference on Recommender Systems, pp. 107–115 (2017)
35. Yuan, Q., Cong, G., Ma, Z., Sun, A., Thalmann, N.: Time-aware point-of-interest recommendation. In: Proceedings of the 36nd International ACM SIGIR Conference on Research and Development in Information Retrieval, pp. 363–372 (2013)
36. Zhang, Y., Zheng, Z., Lyu, M.R.: WSPred: a time-aware personalized qos prediction framework for web services. In: 2011 IEEE 22nd International Symposium on Software Reliability Engineering, pp. 210–219 (2011)
37. Zheng, Y., Pu, A.: Utility-based multi-stakeholder recommendations by multi-objective optimization. In: 2018 IEEE/WIC/ACM International Conference on Web Intelligence (WI), pp. 128–135. IEEE (2018)

When Is a Recommendation Model Wrong? A Model-Agnostic Tree-Based Approach to Detecting Biases in Recommendations

Joanna Misztal-Radecka[1,2]([✉]) [ID] and Bipin Indurkhya[3] [ID]

[1] AGH University of Science and Technology, Kraków, Poland
misztalradecka@agh.edu.pl
[2] Ringier Axel Springer Polska, Warsaw, Poland
[3] Jagiellonian University, Kraków, Poland
bipin.indurkhya@uj.edu.pl

Abstract. Most of the recommendation algorithms are tuned to optimize the global objective function. However, the distribution of error may differ dramatically among different combinations of attributes, and such design of algorithms may lead to propagating the hidden data biases. In this work, we propose a model-agnostic technique to detect the combinations of user and item attributes correlated with unequal treatment by the recommender. Our results on a popular movie dataset show that the proposed technique can detect hidden biases for different popular recommendation algorithms. The debiasing techniques may be applied for improving the performance of the discriminated cases.

Keywords: Recommender systems · System fairness · Bias detection

1 Introduction

Recommendation systems are typically optimized to improve a global objective function, such as the error between the real and predicted user action. However, these approaches result in optimization for the mainstream trends while minority preference groups, as well as those interested in niche products, are not represented well. Given a lack of understanding of the dataset characteristics and insufficient diversity of represented individuals, such approaches inevitably lead to amplifying hidden data biases and existing disparities. While the problem of system fairness has recently attracted much research interest, most of the works are based on analyzing a single dimension selected a-priori, such as a sensitive user attribute or a protected category of products. However, it is not clear how to identify which groups should be protected, and different types of recommendation algorithms are prone to different vulnerabilities.

Moreover, bias is often caused by certain combinations of circumstances rather than a single feature. For instance, a recommender may propagate a gender bias from the training data by under-estimating the preferences of female

© Springer Nature Switzerland AG 2021
L. Boratto et al. (Eds.): BIAS 2021, CCIS 1418, pp. 92–105, 2021.
https://doi.org/10.1007/978-3-030-78818-6_9

students for technical courses [30]. Another challenge for recommendation systems is to consider temporal shifts of interests, which may be due to seasonality. For example, a news recommendation system may consider that certain football-related articles were popular last week, and may assign similar articles appearing this week high probability scores. However, the popularity could be due to a match that was taking place, and so the probabilities for this week will be overestimated. There are several other situations when the suggested recommendations do not work out well, for example when some people have unusual tastes or there is a scarcity of feedback [1,8]. In all such situations, it may be difficult to identify the protected attributes a-priori. We address this problem in our research by identifying the particular circumstances when a recommender system's predictions are wrong. More precisely, this paper makes the following contributions:

1. A model-agnostic approach is proposed to detect any systematic recommendation bias. Our method is based on a post-hoc tree-based model, and, in contrast to other existing works on recommendation fairness, it identifies combinations of attributes for which the recommendations are significantly worse than in other cases.
2. We show that our proposed method can detect different types of biases by analyzing the detected systematic errors of collaborative filtering algorithms for a public dataset of movie recommendations. Moreover, we demonstrate that the biases detected for the feature combinations are more severe than for single attributes.

Our approach is based on a well-established tree-based technique, while its novelty lies in applying this method to detect the algorithmic bias in the predictions of a recommendation model.

The rest of this paper is organized as follows. Section 2 summarizes the current challenges of recommendation systems and the state of the art in the field of algorithmic fairness and explainability. The research problem is articulated in Sect. 3 and the proposed approach is described in Sect. 4. The experimental evaluation is presented in Sect. 5. Finally, we summarize the conclusions and future work directions in Sect. 6.

2 Background and Related Work

In this section, the main challenges of the current recommendation systems are discussed, and an overview of the related work concerning recommendation fairness and generating explanations for recommendation algorithms is presented.

Current Challenges of Recommendation Systems

Current recommendation systems face many tough problems when dealing with real-world data, thereby degrading their performance in various situations. For instance, data sparsity is a critical problem for many online recommender systems, as often there is not enough information to make predictions for a given user or a new item. The cold-start problem is especially troublesome for collaborative filtering (CF) approaches, which recommend items to a user based on the ratings of other users who have similar tastes.

Moreover, data collected from the web is prone to different types of biases related to user demography, nationality, and language [3,6,15,19,29]. More generally, a small number of influential users may end up having a massive impact on the recommendations of other users [12]. Moreover, the *grey and black sheep* users have unusual tastes and so have no or few similar users have, therefore the CF methods fail to find adequate recommendations for them [23,27]. Two other types of biases [3] are the *presentation* and the *position* biases, which are related to how particular items are displayed to a user on a website: better-positioned products have a higher probability of being selected than those that are not so prominently visible. Moreover, as noticed by [22], offline recommender systems face many challenges in dynamic domains such as online services due to user interest shift and dynamic popularity trends [2,7]. It has been found that user preferences are not constant but are influenced by temporal factors such as the time of the day, the day of the week, or the season.

All these situations can lead to generating irrelevant recommendations due to systematic biases and disparities. In our research, we aim to automatically detect such disparities to enable taking corrective actions.

Recommendation Fairness and Explainability

The problem of algorithmic fairness has recently attracted much research interest and researchers have distinguished its different aspects [4,10,11,13,30]. In [25], the evaluation metric for recommendations is aggregated according to the groups defined by the user attributes to detect if an algorithm makes more relevant recommendations for users belonging to some specific groups. The discrimination with respect to sensitive attributes and social bias has also been studied in [30] and the authors proposed a modification of the learning objective by adding a fairness term. In [5], the authors show that a recommender tuned to improve a global prediction objective leaves many items badly modeled and thus underserved. They propose a *focused learning* approach to learn additional models to improve the recommendation quality for a specified subset of items.

However, in most of these approaches, fairness evaluation is limited to a single pre-defined attribute (such as a demography feature or an item category). In our work, we consider disparity related to a combination of factors, and aim at generating these combinations automatically. We use a tree-based model for explaining the model errors; thus, our approach may be formally characterized as an *Explanation Through Interpretable Model* [16]. Similar approaches were previously applied for building explainable recommenders [26,28,31]; however, we apply a post-hoc model for explaining the bias of any recommendation model rather than its output. In [26], a tree-based model is trained on a set of interpretable labels to provide explanations for a black-box learning-to-rank algorithm on web search. Though our works also applies a tree-based post-hoc model, we aim at approximating the model errors, whereas [26] focuses on evaluating how well the post-hoc model approximates the original ranking. Thus, we use a similar model to solve a different type problem, and therefore these approaches are not comparable.

3   Problem Definition

The recommendation algorithms are usually trained to predict the score for a user-item pair, where the target may be given explicitly (user-item rating values, for example) or specified implicitly (a purchase or a click, for example). As pointed out in the previous section, these predictions may be inaccurate for various reasons, depending on the domain, the data characteristics and the algorithm at hand. Moreover, the disparities may be caused by a complex combinations of factors rather than a single dimension. Hence, our goal in this research is to identify those situations where many systematic recommendation errors occur regularly.

In most standard recommendation algorithms, the model parameters are adjusted based on a global optimization function. For instance, for the popular model-based matrix factorization (MF) collaborative filtering algorithms, learning is performed by minimizing a global objective function, which is defined as the sum of the differences between the real r and the predicted $\hat{r}$ ratings in the training set for all the data samples. Hence, the model weights are adjusted to optimize the predictions for the majority of the cases or the most impactful instances. As shown by [5], this leads to underfitting for some unusual situations such as specific interest groups and niche products, and results in a long-tailed distribution of the prediction errors.

Another example of unequal error distribution is the standard k-Nearest Neighbors (KNN) collaborative filtering algorithm. In this case, the predicted rating is estimated based on the similarity between the user or the item vectors. Hence these predictions may be inaccurate for users who have a low similarity to others (*grey sheep*), or those with very few ratings (the *cold-start* problem).

Moreover, when tuning the model hyper-parameters (such as the number of neighbors for KNN or the vector size for MF), the performance of the model on the validation set is estimated with an average error measure, such as absolute or squared error of all the examples. Though the optimization is performed globally, the model may underperform in certain situations, such as for particular types of users or items. As the average error does not carry any information about the metric's distribution, these hidden biases may remain unnoticed.

In this research, our goal is to detect those situations where the recommender introduces such systematic biases: that is, when the average error for some combinations of metadata is significantly higher than for the other cases. To define this problem more formally, let $r_{u,i} \in R$ be a rating of a user u for an item i, $x^{ui} = x_1^{ui}, \ldots, x_K^{ui}, x^{ui} \in X$ are the attributes associated with this rating (a vector of user and item features) and $\hat{r}_{u,i}$ is the model's prediction for this rating. Then, $T_k = \{k_1, \ldots k_N\}$ is a set of possible values for an attribute x_k (for instance, for feature $genre$ the possible values are $T_{genre} = \{crime, comedy, thriller\}$, and so on). Next, we define the subset of instances:

$$X_{k_n, l_m, \ldots} = X_{k_n} \cap X_{l_m} \cap \ldots = \{x^{ui} : x_k^{ui} = k_n \wedge x_l^{ui} = l_m \wedge \ldots\}, X_{k_n, l_m, \ldots} \subset X$$

$$X_{\sim k_n, l_m, \ldots} = X \setminus X_{k_n, l_m, \ldots}$$

Then, $e(r_{u,i}, \hat{r_{u,i}}) \geq 0$ is the error between the real and predicted ratings for user u and item i. We consider an error function which has non-negative values and does not necessarily have a normal distribution. The average error for ratings with attributes from $X_{k_n, l_m, \ldots}$ is denoted by:

$$\overline{e}_{X_{k_n, l_m, \ldots}} = \sum_{n=1}^{N} \frac{e(r_{u,i}, \hat{r}_{u,i})}{N}, x^{ui} \in X_{k_n, l_m, \ldots}$$

We want to detect the combinations of user and item attributes such that the average error for each of these combinations is significantly higher than for the other cases:

$$\{(k_n, l_m, \ldots) : \overline{e}_{X_{k_n, l_m, \ldots}} > \overline{e}_{X_{\sim k_n, l_m, \ldots}}\}$$

For instance, if the prediction error is higher for female users and thriller movies, this set may contain a combination $(gender_{female}, genre_{thriller})$. We are interested in detecting such situations for both the training error (when the model underfits for some combinations of features such as the cold start problem or the *grey sheep)* and the test set (if the model was fitted on the train set and the characteristics of the new data differ from the training set, for instance, due to the interest shift or seasonality).

4   Proposed Approach

To identify those situations where the recommender results are systematically biased, we split the instances for which the error is significantly higher than for the remaining group. We fit a Chi-square Automatic Interaction Detection (CHAID) tree for regression, which is a well-established statistical method proposed by Gordon V. Kass in 1980. We fit the tree model with the inputs of x^{ui} as independent variables and the target $e(r_{u,i}, \hat{r}_{u,i})$ as the predicted dependent variable. In each iteration, the CHAID algorithm cycles through all attributes k, and the pairs of values $k_j, k_l \in T_k$ with no significant difference ($p > \alpha_{merge}$) in error distribution are merged into one category $k_{j,l}$. Then, the next tree split is performed on the attribute k with the most significant difference (the smallest adjusted p-value), concerning the predicted error value. This procedure is repeated recursively until no further splits can be made ($p > \alpha_{split}$ for all nodes or the max tree depth was achieved).

Since errors are continuous values that do not have a normal distribution, the median Levene's test [9] is used for assigning the statistical significance of particular splits by evaluating the homogeneity of their variances. It tests the null hypothesis that the population variances are equal. If the resulting p-value is less than the significance level α, the obtained variance differences are unlikely to have occurred in random samples taken from a population with equal variances, and the null hypothesis is rejected. We note that other statistical tests would have been possible if more assumptions about the error distribution could be made. For example, F-test could be applied for normally distributed metrics, or chi-square test could be applied for categorical outputs.

5   Experimental Validation

The goal of the experiments is to validate if the proposed method is capable of detecting more severe disparities than those detected for the single attributes that are usually used for the recommendations fairness evaluation. To this end, we conducted experiments on the popular MovieLens 100K recommendation dataset consisting of ratings from 943 users for 1682 items along with their metadata attributes. The dataset contains users who rated at least 20 movies and for whom there is complete demographic information. Each movie can be assigned to multiple genres (from 19 categories) and its production year is provided. For a detailed statistics of the dataset, we refer to [17]. First, synthetic recommendation predictions with a set of pre-defined biases were generated, and then the results were analyzed for standard collaborative filtering algorithms. In both the cases, mean absolute error (MAE) of the predicted ratings was used.

5.1   Simulating Biased Recommendations

First, to generate an illustrative example of the bias detection process, we simulated predictions from a biased recommender, and analyzed the detected disparities. The synthetic outputs were generated by adding random Gaussian noise to the real target values from the test set: $\hat{r}_{u,i} = r_{u,i} + \epsilon, \epsilon \sim \mathcal{N}(\mu, \sigma)$, where the distribution parameters of this noise determine the error characteristics. A perfect theoretical predictor has $\mu = 0, \sigma = 0$ (outputs the real ratings in all cases). The value of μ defines how much the predicted ratings are different from the true value, while σ determines how the results vary among the samples set. If μ and σ are equal for all subsets of samples, the recommender is considered fair. We consider here the following simulated cases with different types of systematic biases that correspond to the fairness objectives defined by [30]:

1. *Value unfairness* (Fig. 1A)—the predictions for certain situations are systematically underestimated: $\mu_b < 0$. In this example, the predictions for female users and thriller movies are systematically lower than the real ratings, which leads to a higher error on the test set ($\sigma = 0.1$ for all cases).

$$\mu = \begin{cases} -0.5 & \text{if } gender = F \text{ and } genre = thriller \\ 0 & \text{otherwise} \end{cases}$$

2. *Absolute unfairness* (Fig. 1B)—the prediction accuracy is lower for certain combination of attributes (the model underfits for some situations): $\sigma_b > \sigma$. In this example, the estimations for a category of old crime movies are less accurate and $\mu = 0$ for all cases.

$$\sigma = \begin{cases} 1.5 \text{ if } genre = crime \text{ and } year = old \\ 0.8 \text{ otherwise} \end{cases}$$

In both these cases, the mean absolute error of the samples from the biased groups is higher than for the remaining instances. We use Kernel Density Estimate (KDE) to visualize the distribution of the error metric for the detected tree nodes as a continuous probability density curve. The distribution for each node is normalized separately such that the area under each of the density curves sums to 1.

Figure 1 shows the detected bias trees for both the above cases and corresponding error distributions for each of the branches. In the first example (Fig. 1A), the average error on the whole dataset is 0.192 (value in the tree root). The first split is performed based on the thriller genre (error 0.307 for thrillers and 0.159 for others), and the second split is based on the user's gender (0.801 for female and 0.159 for male users). The average values and distributions of errors for non-thrillers and thrillers for male users are equal, and the attributes corresponding to the significant biases were correctly identified. Similarly, in the second example (Fig. 1B), the split is first performed for the crime movies (MAE 0.76 vs. 0.638), and then the ratings are divided depending on the movie production year, with the highest error detected for the oldest movies (1.157). In both these examples, the average error of the whole sample clearly does not reflect these differences.

5.2   Detecting Biases for Collaborative Filtering Algorithms

Next, to evaluate practical applications of our proposed method, we applied it for detecting biases for five different collaborative filtering recommendation algorithms: Slope One [21], k-nearest neighbors (KNN), Co-Clustering [14], Non-Negative Matrix Factorization (NMF) [20] and Singular Value Decomposition (SVD) [24]. To ensure that our results can be reproduced, we used publicly available open-source implementation of the CF algorithms [18].

Each of the selected recommendation algorithms was trained to predict ratings from the training set. We used a 5-fold cross-validation procedure for selecting the hyper-parameters of each recommendation model with the parameter grid defined in Table 1, and a 20% hold-out test set. First, the hyper-parameters are selected on the cross-validated training set, and then the model is re-trained on the whole training set. We report the recommender results for the training and the test sets with respect to global MAE, and then we compare the results for the detected tree leaves representing the combinations of user-item attributes as well as the activity features. Finally, the distribution of error for each of the detected subsets and the most extreme leaf values (maximum and minimum average errors) are analyzed.

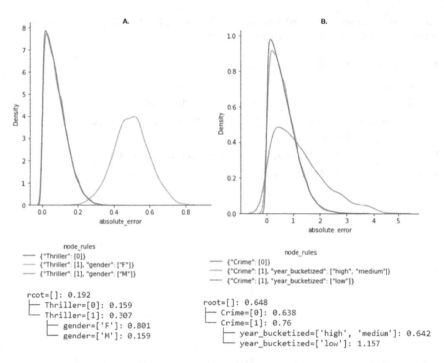

Fig. 1. Examples of the distribution and conditions of the detected recommendation biases for the simulated cases: (A) A recommender makes systematically lower predictions of thriller movie ratings for female users (lower μ of the generated rating distribution). (B) A recommender makes systematically inaccurate predictions for old crime movies (higher σ of the generated ratings distribution). The probability density (Y axis) of the absolute error of the model (X axis) is estimated with KDE.

The following user and item features are used to search for potential biases:

- User attributes—gender, age,
- Item attributes—genre, production year,
- Activity-based features—number of rated items for a user (activity), number of users with a rating for an item (popularity).

The continuous variables are discretized into three equal-sized buckets based on the sample quantiles. We set $\alpha = 0.01$ (for both the merge and the split conditions) to detect significant differences in error distribution. To avoid over-fitting or selecting too specific rules that would be hard to interpret, the minimum number of samples in a leaf node is set to 100.

Results. First, the maximum and minimum detected values of error in leaves for different node depths are compared. As presented in Fig. 2, the detected minimum and maximum values are more extreme at higher depths of the tree. This indicates that our proposed method can detect more severe disparities than

Table 1. Recommendation algorithms with corresponding hyper-parameter grids. Parameters in bold are selected by the grid search.

Algorithm	Hyper-parameter grid
Slope one	—
KNN	K: [10, 20, **50**, 100], user-based: [**true**, false]
Co-clustering	n user clusters: [**5**, 10, 20, 50, 100], n item clusters: [5, 10, 20, **50**, 100]
NMF	n factors: [**10**, 20, 50, 100], biased: [**true**, false]
SVD	n factors: [10, **20**, 50, 100], biased: [**true**, false]

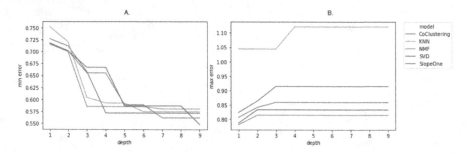

Fig. 2. Minimum (A) and maximum (B) test-error values at different tree levels for the compared CF algorithms.

the single-attribute approaches that are most often used for detecting algorithmic biases.

While the minimum leaf error is smaller at higher tree depths, the maximum detected leaf error increases for the first 2 or 4 levels and then remains constant. This may mean that either the further splits did not result in any significant differences, or the detected samples were too small. Hence, in further analysis we limit the depth of trees to 3 levels.

The results for the compared recommendation algorithms in terms of global MAE and detected biased leaves are presented in Table 2 and Fig. 3. For all the models, the highest test error was identified for a combination of user, item and activity-based features. This observation supports the conclusion that our proposed approach identifies the roots of discrimination more accurately than the analysis based on one type of attributes. We observe that while Slope One and SVD yield the smallest error on the test set, SVD and Co-Clustering show the least tendency to discriminate particular feature combinations. Co-Clustering has the least difference between the largest (0.851) and the smallest (0.611) test error in leaves with a standard deviation of 0.078. On the contrary, KNN has the least error on the training set and the largest error on the test set. An analysis of error distribution in leaves shows that it overfits only for some feature combinations: the difference between the largest (0.797) and the smallest (0.283) leaf error on the training set. The largest differences are detected for the

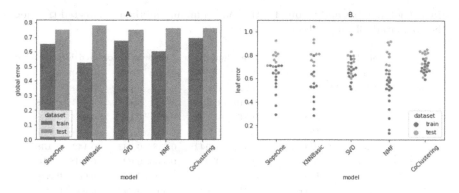

Fig. 3. (A) Global MAE for the training and the test sets for different recommendation algorithms. (B) MAE aggregated for each leaf in the bias-detection tree.

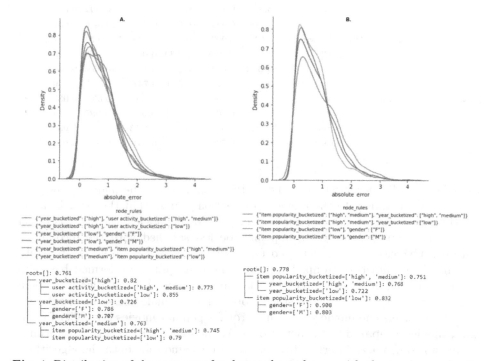

Fig. 4. Distribution of the test error for detected tree leaves with the maximum depth limited to 2, and tree structures for the two CF algorithms—(A) NMF, (B) KNN. The probability density (Y axis) of the absolute error of the model (X axis) is estimated with KDE.

combination of all features. Similarly, Fig. 3 shows that NMF clearly overfits for some attribute combinations as the error for these leaves is close to zero.

Figure 4 shows the constructed bias trees (with the maximum depth limited to 2 for better readability) and the test error distributions for each detected leaf

Table 2. Global MAE and results for the maximum and minimum detected tree nodes for the compared CF algorithms.

Model	Global error		Tree	Max leaf error		Min leaf error		Std leaves errors	
	Train	Test	Attributes	Train	Test	Train	Test	Train	Test
Slope one	0.653	**0.749**	Activity	0.710	0.851	0.335	0.725	**0.138**	0.054
			All	0.710	**0.924**	**0.291**	**0.640**	0.133	**0.078**
			Item	**0.752**	0.902	0.487	**0.640**	0.082	0.074
			User	0.712	0.799	0.630	0.730	0.035	0.036
KNN	**0.525**	0.778	Activity	0.671	**1.044**	0.318	0.733	0.142	**0.138**
			All	**0.797**	**1.044**	**0.283**	0.622	**0.148**	0.121
			Item	0.666	0.910	0.330	**0.571**	0.087	0.099
			User	0.649	0.968	0.498	0.743	0.055	0.090
Co-clustering	0.694	0.764	Activity	0.700	0.825	0.691	0.745	0.006	0.037
			All	0.770	**0.851**	**0.594**	**0.611**	0.049	**0.078**
			Item	**0.897**	0.824	**0.594**	0.678	**0.092**	0.057
			User	0.776	0.804	0.668	0.751	0.043	0.037
NMF	0.604	0.761	Activity	0.648	0.907	0.163	0.733	**0.171**	0.077
			All	0.673	**0.918**	**0.134**	**0.642**	0.162	**0.100**
			Item	**0.679**	0.804	0.519	0.654	0.056	0.063
			User	0.650	0.825	0.554	0.747	0.035	0.040
SVD	0.674	0.750	Activity	0.738	0.796	0.663	0.730	0.032	0.035
			All	**0.792**	**0.977**	**0.512**	**0.603**	**0.080**	**0.104**
			Item	0.782	0.870	**0.512**	**0.603**	0.073	0.083
			User	0.746	0.797	0.650	0.731	0.037	0.030

for NMF and KNN models. For the NMF recommender, the main difference is detected with respect to the movies' production year so that the error is larger for the latest movies and less active users. For older movies, the error is larger for female users; hence, this group may be less satisfied with the recommendations. The least error is detected for older movies and male users—possibly, the model overfits this group. For KNN, the first split is performed based on the item popularity. More precisely, the largest error is for the least frequent items (indicating the item cold-start problem) and female users. The next level of split considers the movie year—the error for popular movies is smaller for the older movies compared to the newer ones. While some attributes that determine significant differences in error distribution are common for both the algorithms (for instance, the item popularity and the user gender), it can also be seen that the reasons for discrimination are different. In particular, the user-based KNN approach seems to be particularly sensitive for the item popularity bias and the cold-start problem, while some types of items and users are not modeled well by NMF.

6   Conclusions and Future Work

From the results presented in this paper we can conclude that while different recommendation algorithms may yield comparable results when averaged globally, the distribution of error may differ dramatically for different combinations of attributes. Hence, the globally-optimized approaches may result in severe disparities and unfair functioning of recommender systems. To address this problem, we presented a model-agnostic approach to detecting possible biases and disparities in the recommendation systems that may result from a combination of user and item attributes. The results on a real-world movie recommendation dataset show that our proposed method can identify severe disparities for certain feature combinations that are missed by the single-attribute approaches most often used for analyzing the recommender fairness.

In the future, we plan to incorporate debiasing techniques in our approach, such as *focused learning* [5] or fairness objective [30]. Moreover, we plan to apply our method to enhance the design process of hybrid approaches to better address the diversity of users and items. We are also experimenting with other algorithms and datasets from different domains to analyze potential algorithmic biases in various other recommendation settings. Finally, we plan to incorporate additional attributes such as the recommendation context to identify other types of biases such as presentation and position bias.

References

1. Abdollahpouri, H., Mansoury, M., Burke, R., Mobasher, B.: The connection between popularity bias, calibration, and fairness in recommendation. In: Fourteenth ACM Conference on Recommender Systems, pp. 726–731. RecSys 2020, Association for Computing Machinery, New York (2020). https://doi.org/10.1145/3383313.3418487
2. Anclli, V.W., Di Noia, T., Di Sciascio, E., Ragone, A., Trotta, J.: Local popularity and time in top-n recommendation. In: Azzopardi, L., Stein, B., Fuhr, N., Mayr, P., Hauff, C., Hiemstra, D. (eds.) Adv. Inf. Retrieval, pp. 861–868. Springer International Publishing, Cham (2019)
3. Baeza-Yates, R.: Bias on the web. Communications of the ACM 61, 54–61 (2018). https://doi.org/10.1145/3209581
4. Barocas, S., Hardt, M., Narayanan, A.: Fairness and Machine Learning (2019). http://www.fairmlbook.org
5. Beutel, A., Chi, E.H., Cheng, Z., Pham, H., Anderson, J.: Beyond globally optimal: focused learning for improved recommendations. In: Proceedings of the 26th International Conference on World Wide Web, pp. 203–212. WWW 2017, International World Wide Web Conferences Steering Committee, Republic and Canton of Geneva, CHE (2017). https://doi.org/10.1145/3038912.3052713
6. Bolukbasi, T., Chang, K.W., Zou, J.Y., Saligrama, V., Kalai, A.T.: Man is to computer programmer as woman is to homemaker? debiasing word embeddings. In: Lee, D.D., Sugiyama, M., Luxburg, U.V., Guyon, I., Garnett, R. (eds.) Advances in Neural Information Processing Systems 29, pp. 4349–4357. Curran Associates, Inc. (2016)
7. Boratto, L., Fenu, G., Marras, M.: The effect of algorithmic bias on recommender systems for massive open online courses. In: Azzopardi, L., Stein, B., Fuhr, N., Mayr, P., Hauff, C., Hiemstra, D. (eds.) Adv. Inf. Retrieval, pp. 457–472. Springer International Publishing, Cham (2019)

8. Boratto, L., Fenu, G., Marras, M.: Connecting user and item perspectives in popularity debiasing for collaborative recommendation. Inf. Proc. Manage. **58**(1), 102387 (2021). https://www.sciencedirect.com/science/article/pii/S0306457320308827

9. Brown, M.B., Forsythe, A.B.: Robust tests for the equality of variances. J. Am. Stat. Assoc. **69**(346), 364–367 (1974). https://doi.org/10.1080/01621459.1974.10482955. https://www.tandfonline.com/doi/abs/10.1080/01621459.1974.10482955

10. Burke, R., Sonboli, N., Ordonez-Gauger, A.: Balanced neighborhoods for multi-sided fairness in recommendation. In: Friedler, S.A., Wilson, C. (eds.) Proceedings of the 1st Conference on Fairness, Accountability and Transparency. Proceedings of Machine Learning Research, vol. 81, pp. 202–214. PMLR, New York, NY, USA, 23–24 Feb 2018. http://proceedings.mlr.press/v81/burke18a.html

11. Deldjoo, Y., Anelli, V.W., Zamani, H., Bellogin, A., Di Noia, T.: Recommender systems fairness evaluation via generalized cross entropy. In: Proceedings of the 2019 ACM RecSys Workshop on Recommendation in Multistakeholder Environments (RMSE) (2019)

12. Eskandanian, F., Sonboli, N., Mobasher, B.: Power of the few: analyzing the impact of influential users in collaborative recommender systems. In: Proceedings of the 27th ACM Conference on User Modeling, Adaptation and Personalization, pp. 225–233. UMAP 2019, Association for Computing Machinery, New York, NY, USA (2019). https://doi.org/10.1145/3320435.3320464

13. Gajane, P., Pechenizkiy, M.: On formalizing fairness in prediction with machine learning (2017)

14. George, T., Merugu, S.: A scalable collaborative filtering framework based on co-clustering. In: Proceedings of the Fifth IEEE International Conference on Data Mining, pp. 625–628. ICDM 2005, IEEE Computer Society, USA (2005). https://doi.org/10.1109/ICDM.2005.14

15. Graells-Garrido, E., Lalmas, M., Menczer, F.: First women, second sex: Gender bias in wikipedia. CoRR abs/1502.02341 (2015). http://arxiv.org/abs/1502.02341

16. Guidotti, R., Monreale, A., Turini, F., Pedreschi, D., Giannotti, F.: A survey of methods for explaining black box models. CoRR abs/1802.01933 (2018). http://arxiv.org/abs/1802.01933

17. Harper, F.M., Konstan, J.A.: The movielens datasets: history and context. ACM Trans. Interact. Intell. Syst. **5**(4), 1–19 (2015). http://doi.acm.org/10.1145/2827872

18. Hug, N.: Surprise: a python library for recommender systems. J. Open Source Softw. **5**(52), 2174 (2020). https://doi.org/10.21105/joss.02174

19. Islam, A.C., Bryson, J.J., Narayanan, A.: Semantics derived automatically from language corpora necessarily contain human biases. CoRR abs/1608.07187 (2016). http://arxiv.org/abs/1608.07187

20. Lee, D.D., Seung, H.S.: Learning the parts of objects by nonnegative matrix factorization. Nature **401**, 788–791 (1999)

21. Li, J., Sun, L., Wang, J.: A slope one collaborative filtering recommendation algorithm using uncertain neighbors optimizing. In: Wang, L., Jiang, J., Lu, J., Hong, L., Liu, B. (eds.) Web-Age Inf. Manage., pp. 160–166. Springer, Berlin Heidelberg, Berlin, Heidelberg (2012). https://doi.org/10.1007/978-3-642-28635-3_15

22. Li, L., Wang, D., Li, T., Knox, D., Padmanabhan, B.: Scene: A scalable two-stage personalized news recommendation system. In: Proceedings of the 34th International ACM SIGIR Conference on Research and Development in Information Retrieval. pp. 125–134. SIGIR 2011, ACM, New York, NY, USA (2011). https://doi.org/10.1145/2009916.2009937
23. McCrae, J., Piatek, A., Langley, A.: Collaborative filtering (2004). http://www.imperialviolet.org
24. Salakhutdinov, R., Mnih, A.: Probabilistic matrix factorization. In: Advances in Neural Information Processing Systems, vol. 20 (2008)
25. Sánchez, P., Bellogín, A.: Attribute-based evaluation for recommender systems: Incorporating user and item attributes in evaluation metrics. In: Proceedings of the 13th ACM Conference on Recommender Systems, pp. 378–382. RecSys 2019, Association for Computing Machinery, New York, NY, USA (2019). https://doi.org/10.1145/3298689.3347049
26. Singh, J., Anand, A.: Posthoc interpretability of learning to rank models using secondary training data. CoRR abs/1806.11330 (2018). http://arxiv.org/abs/1806.11330
27. Su, X., Khoshgoftaar, T.M.: A survey of collaborative filtering techniques. Adv. in Artif. Intell. **2009** (2009). https://doi.org/10.1155/2009/421425
28. Tintarev, Nava, Masthoff, Judith: Designing and evaluating explanations for recommender systems. In: Ricci, Francesco, Rokach, Lior, Shapira, Bracha, Kantor, Paul B. (eds.) Recommender Systems Handbook, pp. 479–510. Springer, Boston, MA (2011). https://doi.org/10.1007/978-0-387-85820-3_15
29. Tsintzou, V., Pitoura, E., Tsaparas, P.: Bias disparity in recommendation systems. CoRR abs/1811.01461 (2018). http://arxiv.org/abs/1811.01461
30. Yao, S., Huang, B.: Beyond parity: Fairness objectives for collaborative filtering. In: Guyon, I., Luxburg, U.V., Bengio, S., Wallach, H., Fergus, R., Vishwanathan, S., Garnett, R. (eds.) Advances in Neural Information Processing Systems 30, pp. 2921–2930. Curran Associates, Inc. (2017)
31. Zhang, Y., Chen, X.: Explainable recommendation: A survey and new perspectives. CoRR abs/1804.11192 (2018). http://arxiv.org/abs/1804.11192

Examining Video Recommendation Bias on YouTube

Baris Kirdemir[⊠], Joseph Kready, Esther Mead, Muhammad Nihal Hussain,
and Nitin Agarwal

COSMOS Research Center, UA, Little Rock, AR, USA
{bkirdemir,jkready,elmead,mnhussain,nxagarwal}@ualr.edu

Abstract. In recent years, a growing number of journalistic and scholarly publications have paid particular attention to the broad societal impact of YouTube's video recommendation system. Significantly, the YouTube algorithm's alleged contributions to the formation of echo-chambers, filter-bubbles, polarization, radicalization, disinformation, and malicious use of information are among the top concerns. On top of the given issues, potential biases of the recommendation system in favor of a small number of videos, content producers, or channels would further exacerbate the magnitude of the problem, especially if a systematic understanding of the inherent nature and characteristics of the algorithm is lacking. In this study, we investigate the structure of recommendation networks and probabilistic distributions of the node-centric influence of recommended videos. Adopting a stochastic approach, we observe PageRank distributions over a diverse set of recommendation graphs we collected and built based on eight different real-world scenarios. In total, we analyzed 803,210 recommendations made by YouTube's recommendation algorithm, based on specific search queries and seed datasets from previous studies. As a result, we demonstrate the existence of a structural, systemic, and inherent tendency to impose bias by YouTube's video recommendation system in favor of a tiny fraction of videos in each scenario. We believe that this work sets the stage for further research in creating predictive modeling techniques that reduce bias in video recommendation systems and make algorithms fairer. The implementation of such attempts aims to reduce their potential harmful social and ethical impacts and increase public trust in these social systems.

Keywords: Recommender bias · YouTube algorithm · PageRank

1 Introduction

YouTube is among the most popular social media platforms. It is a common source of news consumption. The platform is one of the most popular hubs of content production, monetization, and cross-platform dissemination. Nevertheless, YouTube is not exempt from the dynamics that lead to the generation, dissemination, and wide-scale consumption of misinformation, disinformation, hate speech, and many other content types with ramifications for individuals and society. As a result, the platform has been subject to public debate in recent years, receiving journalistic and scholarly attention.

© Springer Nature Switzerland AG 2021
L. Boratto et al. (Eds.): BIAS 2021, CCIS 1418, pp. 106–116, 2021.
https://doi.org/10.1007/978-3-030-78818-6_10

Among the subjects of the ongoing debate are the potential roles played by YouTube's recommendation, personalization, and ranking algorithms in the spread and influence of harmful content, as well as the formation of echo-chambers and polarization [9, 12, 14, 17–20]. However, most of the evidence of the alleged effects is anecdotal and is often acquired through journalistic investigations. Although the number and scope of the systematic scholarly studies gradually increase, currently, the literature lacks an established understanding of whether the YouTube algorithm exacerbates the given set of problems.

This study aims to explore whether the YouTube recommendation algorithm produces biased results regardless of personalization, user entry point, or the topical and categorical differences between the videos watched. Such an approach would enable generalized assessments and measurement of the emergent bias of recommendations. Despite recent studies on different aspects of the problem, the current literature lacks comprehensive and systematic evaluations of whether the video recommendation system on the platform tends to be biased in favor of a small number of videos in generalizable ways. Besides, if bias exists, how should it be characterized?

This study aims to approach the problem from a graphical probabilistic perspective, focusing on the recommendation graph structures and node-centric probabilistic distributions. We operationalize our approach using PageRank computations and studying the structural properties of recommendation graphs vis-à-vis the PageRank values' distribution. We contend that exploration and characterization of emergent algorithmic biases in YouTube's video recommendation system using the mentioned graph analysis approach would significantly contribute to the relevant literature. In particular, node-centric probabilistic analysis of potential emergent biases in recommender systems will be applicable in the fairness of recommender systems, patterns of content consumption, information diffusion, echo-chamber formation, and other significant problems. By evaluating the structural tendencies of bias in YouTube recommendation graphs, we aim to contribute to the given interdisciplinary area regarding implicit and structural biases, feedback loops, and complex networks across social media platforms.

This work continues as follows. Section 2 includes a brief review of the recent literature on research problems associated with the YouTube algorithm and graph analytical approaches to evaluate and characterize recommendation systems. Section 3 describes our data collection approach and the underlying rationale for the diversification of datasets. A short introduction to the operationalization and PageRank computations are described further along with the main findings in Sect. 4. As demonstrated in multiple steps, the results show an emergent structural bias exacerbating the probability of being viewed for a small fraction of the videos in the empirical recommendation graphs. Further, we briefly discuss the potential implications, qualitative interpretations, and limitations of the study.

This paper aims to examine the following primary research questions:

1. Does the YouTube recommendation system produce biased video recommendations in favor of a small number of items?
2. Is it possible to detect, in generalizable ways, the presence of a structural recommendation bias on YouTube without any personalization and by excluding the user-specific data being provided to the algorithm?

3. Can bias be observed through the structure of recommendation networks and distributions of node-centric influence metrics?
4. Does the behavior of the recommender system on YouTube change vis-à-vis emergent bias in different use-case scenarios? For example, do distributions of recommendations change due to how a user enters the platform and starts consuming the content, language of the content, or on topical terms?

2 Related Work

This section will present a discussion of recent and relevant literature on the YouTube recommendation algorithm and associated set of problems, the use of graph analytical approaches to detect and evaluate bias in recommender systems, and the relevant foundational concepts about bias in search and recommendation. It will also introduce the rationale, overall approach, and the methods we employed in this study.

Several studies examined YouTube's video recommendation, search, and personalization systems in recent years. One of the most frequent themes in recent literature has been the radicalization of content and users, examining whether recommendations lead people to more radicalized or extreme content over time. Others examined potential biases in recommended videos regarding demographic factors such as gender, socioeconomic status, and political affiliation. Besides, a few recent studies suggest that bias in YouTube's recommendations can be understood and characterized through topological analysis of recommendation networks. Broadly, the analysis, evaluation, characterization, and mitigation of bias in search and recommendation systems constitute a growing interdisciplinary literature. Popularity bias and feedback loops have been associated with unfair recommendations in group and individual levels, impacting the user experience as well as "*diversity, novelty, and relevance*" of recommended items [21].

2.1 YouTube Algorithm, Radicalization, Misinformation

In recent years, multiple studies have examined whether YouTube recommendations would be associated with a radicalization process on the platform. Ribeiro et al. [17] suggest that users are exposed to increasingly extreme content if they had previously viewed conspiracy theory videos. Ledwich and Zaitsev [14], relying on categorizing the political content in terms of their position on the spectrum from left to right, suggested that the YouTube algorithm does not promote radical or far-right content. Instead, they claim that the algorithm consistently leads users towards channels in the mainstream or moderately left categories [14]. Both studies utilized a manual channel categorization process and annotated channels based on their position on the political spectrum. Hussein et al. [12] analyzed non-political misinformation topics. They claimed that the algorithm promotes conspiracies about specific topics like chemtrails, flat earth, the moon landing, and limits vaccination conspiracies.

Faddoul et al. [9] developed a classifier to automatically detect conspiracy theory videos on YouTube and focus on the "rabbit hole" effect. They suggested a projected reduction in conspiratorial recommendations over time after YouTube's announcement to limit radical content [22]. Still, the authors also argue that this alone does not prove that the "problem of radicalization on YouTube" has become (or will become) obsolete [9]. Roth et al. [19] focus on the concept of "filter bubbles" or "confinement" effect that allegedly exists on the YouTube platform and measure view diversity. Using a random walk strategy, they focus on confinement dynamics and analyze the video recommendation system's workings. The researchers found that recommendations tended to lead to topical confinement, which seemed "to be organized around sets of videos that garner the highest audience" [19].

While most studies in the domain focused on YouTube's algorithm and its impact on viewers, Buntain et al. [6] looked at the cross-platform aspect and analyzed videos of conspiracy theories hosted on YouTube and shared across social media platforms (Twitter and Reddit) in the eight months following YouTube's announcement of their attempts to proactively curtail such content.

2.2 Network Analysis Approaches and Topology of YouTube Recommendations

Recent literature suggests that network analysis approaches may enable examining latent characteristics and the impact of YouTube's recommendation algorithm. Typically, graphs represent videos, channels, pre-defined content categories, or inferred classes of videos as nodes, while recommendations constitute edges. Both in "node-centric" [19] and "user-centric" (personalization) [12] research settings, the basic structure and topology of the recommendation graph are used in the operationalization of concepts such as bias, fairness, confinement, filter bubbles, echo-chambers, polarization, and radicalization, often being captured through multiple hops of graph crawling or in longitudinal terms.

Roth et al. [19] examined confinement and potential formation of filter-bubbles on YouTube as a result of the recommendation algorithm. They follow a research protocol that is based on a platform-level and node-centric design, similar to our approach, arguing that "characterizing a possible confinement on this recommendation landscape constitutes a primary step toward characterizing confinement as a whole" [19]. They run a random walk model on a "recursively crawled" recommendation network and measure entropy to represent diversity. Adding the number of nodes in the graph as a metric demonstrates a negative correlation between confinement and diversity, and sometimes recommendation graphs become more confined than other instances. They also show the formation of confinement in "topical or temporal terms" and in relation to "view counts" of recommended videos [19].

Le Merrer and Trédan [13] suggest that a useful way to analyze "successive" recommendations is network analysis. As a potential application case to their definitions, they propose that such an approach can lead to the "detection" of recommendation biases explicitly induced by the *"service provider."* They demonstrate an application of their practice on YouTube recommendations. Although Le Merrer and Trédan [13] approaches the YouTube recommendation bias from a moderately different perspective from ours and focuses on biases explicitly introduced by platforms, their contention that graph topologies would show various features in biased and unbiased settings remains relevant. Finally, their experiments reveal that the distribution of path lengths in the graph becomes "more compact" when "biased edges" are introduced, resembling well-known features of small-world networks [13].

2.3 Bias in Search and Recommendation

Search and recommendation systems are increasingly intertwined. Current search and recommendation algorithms rely on historical data, user data, personalization, and a few other information sources [5]. Overall, detection and mitigation of bias in "*automated decisions*" are growing interdisciplinary research areas [21]. Biases emanating from the historical data or emergent properties of the recommendation systems may sometimes exacerbate societal problems. Thus, evaluation of video recommendation biases on YouTube relates to the overarching interdisciplinary effort to understand, characterize, and prevent bias and fairness issues in search and recommendation systems. As one of the more complex case studies, an enhanced understanding of the mechanics and structural properties of bias on YouTube would provide significant insights to information retrieval research and other relevant disciplines.

One of the specific research themes in search and recommendation systems is the "popularity bias." In general, fairness, accuracy, or coverage problems arise when popular items are ranked higher and recommended more, especially when this tendency creates a feedback loop where popular items become more popular, so it is recommended even more frequently over time. Abdollahpouri et al. [1] focuses on the problem and suggests a "learning-to-rank" algorithm that includes less popular items to recommendations, with a specific demonstration of protecting accuracy while enhancing the coverage of recommendations.

Bias also relates to potential inefficiencies in the evaluation of recommendation performance, accuracy, and effectiveness. Bellogín et al. [3] examine "statistical biases" in "metrics for recommender systems," with a particular focus on the biases that distort the evaluation of the performance of recommender systems. In a novel and experimental research design, they contribute to understanding popularity bias, especially by focusing on potential ways to improve recommender systems' evaluation. Beutel et al. [4] focus on the recommender systems as pairwise applications and propose a series of metrics to assess fairness risks in real-world applications. Beutel et al. also offer a method for "*unbiased measurements of recommender system ranking fairness.*"

Verma et al. [21] survey relevant papers from several conferences about fairness in search and recommendation systems and evaluate 22 recent papers that propose new fairness metrics and models for various application cases. They categorize the proposed methods and recent literature in five different categories, including "*non-personalized recommendation setting, crowd-sourced recommendation setting, personalized recommendation setting, online advertisements, and marketplace,*" while also emphasizing the distinction between three aspects of fairness and its evaluation: "*diversity, novelty, and relevance*" [21].

As mentioned above, there has been a growing focus on radicalization, extremism, misinformation, and other societal issues concerning how the YouTube algorithm leads its users vis-à-vis such problematic content. Nevertheless, the evaluation of video recommendation bias on YouTube should extend beyond such specific problem areas and start with the platform's search and recommendation systems' structural and inherent characteristics. Referring to the broad survey and classification of Verma et al. [21], understanding recommendation bias on YouTube may relate to dimensions of diversity, novelty, and relevance of recommendations. On the other hand, YouTube presents a non-trivial case study to understand and evaluate the recommendation system, primarily due to the constant evolution of historical data, repetitive updates of the algorithm, and challenges in acquiring sufficient, diversified, and meaningful datasets for research. This study proposes a graph analysis approach and focuses on distributions of PageRank scores of videos in recursively crawled recommendation networks. This study's primary objective is to examine whether the platform tends to impose bias in favor of a small set of videos in real-world scenarios and whether those algorithmic tendencies can be generalized. We contend that for systematic prediction, detection, and mitigation of such problems on YouTube and similar platforms, understanding the recommender system's structural properties and emergent behavioral patterns is a requirement, which would potentially precede future models and mitigation efforts.

3 Data and Methods

Our approach is based on the assumption that we should first capture the recommendation algorithm's general behavioral patterns as they tend to apply to a diverse set of conditions across the entire platform. In our opinion personalization plays a role in the evolution of recommendations to a specific logged-in user. The platform also utilizes the user's web traces through cookies. Nevertheless, a system-level, structural analysis that pays special attention to the node-specific probabilistic computations may help to understand the examined system's inherent properties. Therefore, we posit that we can fairly examine recommendation algorithm bias by excluding the user personalization aspect of the YouTube platform.

3.1 Data Collection and Seed Lists

Data collection was conducted using the YouTube Tracker tool[1] [15] and the YouTube Data API [11]. Videos were retrieved based on a keyword search or by using a list of seed videos as starting points. We then used lists of "related videos" and collected the details about other videos recommended by the YouTube algorithm. These videos would typically appear on YouTube under the "Up Next" heading or in the list of the recommended videos. We determined that two consecutive hops of crawling would enable a sizable amount of data for each experiment while also allowing us to diversify our collection (Table 1).

3.2 Bias Evaluation Through Graph Topology and PageRank Distributions

The analysis phase starts with building the recommendation graphs for each dataset we acquired by drawing edges between "parent videos" and "recommended videos." To explore and evaluate potential biases in video recommendations, we utilized a probabilistic approach focusing on the nodes potentially gaining influence over the rest of the graph due to the recommendations. We extracted the PageRank scores acquired by each node in the recommendation graph and explored PageRank [16] distributions of each

---

[1] YouTube Tracker (2020), https://vtracker.host.ualr.edu, COSMOS, UALR.

Table 1. Short description of seed data, entry points, and total number of collected recommendations in each experiment.

Seed video source	Language	Total number of recommendations
A sample of YouTube video URLs found on Twitter via search queries "COVID 19 hoax" and "COVID 19 weapon"	English	119,094
YouTube search query "covid hoax"	Mixed	126,548
YouTube search query "koronavirus biyolojik"	Turkish	123,986
A sample of YouTube links collected from Twitter and Facebook in relation to COVID-19	Turkish	77,286
A sample of misinformation videos relating to elections in Canada (acquired from Galeano et al. [10])	English	70,200
YouTube search query "Canada election Trudeau"	English	71,290
YouTube search query "Turkiye Rusya NATO"	Turkish	115,723
A sample of YouTube video URLs collected from Twitter and Facebook in relation to geopolitical events involving Turkey, Russia, and NATO	Turkish	99,083

recommendation graph. The PageRank algorithm enables us to demonstrate the probabilities of being visited for each video in a realistic random walk scenario. Besides, the PageRank metric allows use of a "damping factor" value, which defines a probability for the random walker to jump to a random node instead of strictly following the graph connections during the entire walk. Furthermore, we compared graphs we built in terms of language-based, topical, and seed source categories to see potential variances between PageRank probability distributions and curves of biases that favor small fractions of video items.

4 Experiment Results

Examination of in-degree and PageRank values for each graph confirm the skewed distribution of recommendations, with tiny fractions of nodes receiving a vast number of connections. Figure 1 shows an example of the PageRank distributions. We observed a similar shape of distribution in all of the corresponding experiments. Nevertheless, an exploratory comparison of slopes show differences between different recommendation graphs we experimented with. They also indicate transitions in how distributions of cumulative PageRank and in-degree probabilities change within a single graph.

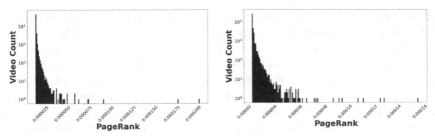

Fig. 1. Distribution of PageRank values in the recommendation graphs 1 (left) and 2 (right). We observe similar results in all recommendation graphs. The count of videos is represented in log scale on the y-axis.

Further, we plot the complementary cumulative distribution functions (CCDF) for each recommendation graph. Briefly, CCDF shows a variable's probability (PageRank in our case) being above a particular value. It is previously documented as an effective technique to explore the scale-free characteristics of real-world networks. We confirm our previous assertion that one of the core structural features of each graph is an emergent bias that favors a small fraction of recommended videos. Also, CCDF plots show power-law characteristics, although the exponent value and the portion that fits the likely power-law line vary between different graphs. Therefore, despite a remarkable confirmation of emergent bias as a common property, characterization seems to depend on various other dynamics, including patterns of the user behavior or content consumed in a basic session. In accordance with the mentioned experiment results, we found that YouTube's recommendation algorithm tends to favor a small set of items over others (research question 1) and the item-based bias can be detected without the inclusion of personalization factors (research question 2). The PageRank based analysis of the recommendation network structures reveal the probabilistic disparity between recommended items (research question 3). On the other hand, the variance of bias across different recommendation graphs should be investigated further (research question 4) (Fig. 2).

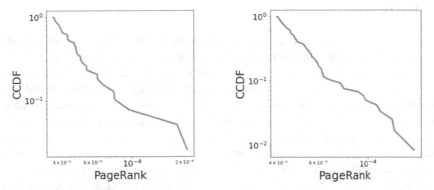

Fig. 2. Complementary Cumulative Distribution Function (CCDF) Plots of PageRank Scores in each Recommendation Graphs 1 (left) and 2 (right).

To explore the variance between different recommendation graphs and their structural features based on PageRank or in-degree distributions, we compared how the given CCDF distributions fit the power-law based on the maximum likelihood estimation developed by Clauset, Shalizi, and Newman [7]. We used a Python implementation [2] of the log-likelihood functions that enable comparative computations suitable for our purpose. We observed power-law fits and CCDF distributions having some variance, especially in terms of the exponent and how well the distributions fit the power law. For example, the recommendation graph for dataset 7 seems to fit a likely power-law almost perfectly, while the curve of the recommendation graph for dataset 8 has only a partial fit that stops approximately after the mid-point on the plot. Furthermore, the CCDF slopes of recommendation graphs 5 and 6 diverge from the power-law lines at smaller PageRank values than other graphs (Fig. 3).

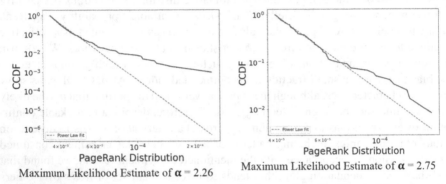

Fig. 3. The variance of PageRank probability distributions and log-likelihood of their power-law fits on CCDF plots. Examples show variance between different recommendation graphs 2 (left) and 5 (right).

5   Conclusion

This study aimed to discover, explore, and understand the potential, emergent, and inherent characteristics of bias in YouTube's video recommendations. Despite the black-box features and closed inner-workings of the algorithm itself, our approach enabled identifying recommendation bias in the studied system. Using probabilistic distributions and the PageRank algorithm to operationalize our stochastic approach, we were able to demonstrate the resulting influence of a small number of videos over the entire network.

We collected distinct datasets and explored the structural properties as well as node-centric features of the recommendation graphs. In all experiments, the bias of the recommendation algorithm in favor of a small fraction of videos seems to emerge as a basic, scale-free characteristic that is evident on the topological level. In particular, cumulative probability distributions of PageRank values demonstrate that a few videos turn out to be far more likely to be visited by a user following the recommended items with some randomness included. The experiments also show that the shape, skewness, and proportion of the bias varies between different use case scenarios. The variance of bias in different recommendation graphs should be subject to further investigations.

We also prioritized the robustness of our evaluation and characterization of bias. Primarily we relied on a diversified data collection and increased the quantity of experiments conducted under realistic scenarios and expected sources of behavioral variance in the studied system. The resulting indicators of such variance between different recommendation networks point to further investigations in the future. In the subsequent phases of this effort, we aim to produce models that can help predict and understand the behavioral patterns that lead to the documented bias and its variations.

Acknowledgements. This research is funded in part by the U.S. National Science Foundation (OIA-1946391, OIA-1920920, IIS-1636933, ACI-1429160, and IIS-1110868), U.S. Office of Naval Research (N00014-10-1-0091, N00014-14-1-0489, N00014-15-P-1187, N00014-16-1-2016, N00014-16-1-2412, N00014-17-1-2675, N00014-17-1-2605, N68335-19-C-0359, N00014-19-1-2336, N68335-20-C-0540, N00014-21-1-2121), U.S. Air Force Research Lab, U.S. Army Research Office (W911NF-17-S-0002, W911NF-16-1-0189), U.S. Defense Advanced Research Projects Agency (W31P4Q-17-C-0059), Arkansas Research Alliance, the Jerry L. Maulden/Entergy Endowment at the University of Arkansas at Little Rock, and the Australian Department of Defense Strategic Policy Grants Program (SPGP) (award number: 2020-106-094). Any opinions, findings, and conclusions or recommendations expressed in this material are those of the authors and do not necessarily reflect the views of the funding organizations. The researchers gratefully acknowledge the support. The researchers also thank MaryEtta Morris for helping with proofreading and improving the paper.

References

1. Abdollahpouri, H., Burke, R., Mobasher, B.: Controlling popularity bias in learning-to-rank recommendation. In: Proceedings of the Eleventh ACM Conference on Recommender Systems (RecSys 2017), pp 42–46 (2020)
2. Alstott, J., Bullmore, E., Plenz, D.: Power-law: a Python package for analysis of heavy-tailed distributions. PloS One **9**(1), e85777 (2014)
3. Bellogín, A., Castells, P., Cantador, I.: Statistical biases in information retrieval metrics for recommender systems. Inf. Retriev. J. **20**(6), 606–634 (2017). https://doi.org/10.1007/s10791-017-9312-z
4. Beutel, A., et al.: Fairness in recommendation ranking through pairwise comparisons. In: Proceedings of the 25th ACM SIGKDD International Conference on Knowledge Discovery & Data Mining (KDD 2019), pp. 2212–2220 (2019)
5. Boratto, L., Marras, M., Faralli, S., and Stilo, G.: International workshop on algorithmic bias in search and recommendation (Bias 2020). In: Jose, J. et al. (eds.) Advances in Information Retrieval. ECIR 2020. Lecture Notes in Computer Science. Springer (2020)
6. Buntain, C., Bonneau, R., Nagler, J., Tucker, J.A.: YouTube Recommendations and Effects on Sharing Across Online Social Platforms (2020). arXiv preprint arXiv:2003.00970
7. Clauset, A., Shalizi, C.R., Newman, M.E.: Power law distributions in empirical data. SIAM Rev. **51**(4), 661–703 (2009)
8. Davidson, J., et al.: The YouTube video recommendation system. In: Proceedings of the fourth ACM Conference on Recommender systems, pp. 293–296, September 2010

9. Faddoul, M., Chaslot, G., Farid, H.: A Longitudinal Analysis of YouTube's Promotion of Conspiracy Videos (2020). arXiv preprint arXiv:2003.03318

10. Galeano, K., Galeano, L., Mead, E., Spann, B., Kready, J., Agarwal, N.: The role of YouTube during the 2019 Canadian federal election: a multi-method analysis of online discourse and information actors, Fall 2020, no. 2, pp. 1–22. Queen's University, Canada (2020). Journal of Future Conflict

11. Google Developers: YouTube Data API, Google (2020). https://developers.google.com/youtube/v3

12. Hussein, E., Juneja, P., Mitra, T.: Measuring misinformation in video search platforms: an audit study on YouTube. Proc. ACM Hum.-Comput. Interact. **4**(CSCW1), 1–27 (2020)

13. Le Merrer, E., Trédan, G.: The topological face of recommendation. In: International Conference on Complex Networks and their Applications, pp. 897–908. Springer, Cham (2017).https://doi.org/10.1007/978-3-319-72150-7_72

14. Ledwich, M., Zaitsev, A.: Algorithmic extremism: Examining YouTube's rabbit hole of radicalization. First Monday (2020)

15. Marcoux, T., Agarwal, N., Erol, R., Obadimu, A., Hussain, M.: Analyzing Cyber Influence Campaigns on YouTube using YouTubeTracker. Lecture Notes in Social Networks, Springer. Forthcoming (2018)

16. Page, L., Brin, S., Motwani, R., Winograd, T.: The PageRank Citation Ranking: Bringing Order to the Web. Stanford InfoLab (1999)

17. Ribeiro, M.H., Ottoni, R., West, R., Almeida, V.A., Meira Jr., W.: Auditing radicalization pathways on YouTube. In: Proceedings of the 2020 Conference on Fairness, Accountability, and Transparency, pp. 131–141 (2020)

18. Roose, K.: The making of a YouTube Radical. The New York Times (2019)

19. Roth, C., Mazières, A., Menezes, T.: Tubes and bubbles topological confinement of YouTube recommendations. PloS One **15**(4), e0231703 (2020)

20. Tufekci, Z.: YouTube, the Great Radicalizer. The New York Times, vol. 10, p. 2018 (2018)

21. Verma, S., Gao, R., Shah, C.: Facets of fairness in search and recommendation. In: Borratto, L., Faralli, S., Marras, M., Stilo, G. (eds.) Bias and Social Aspects in Search and Recommendation, First International Workshop, BIAS 2020, Lisbon, Portugal, April 14, Proceedings. Communications in Computer and Information Science, vol. 1245, pp. 1–11 (2020). https://doi.org/10.1007/978-3-030-52485-2_1

22. Wakabayashi, D.: YouTube Moves to Make Conspiracy Videos Harder to Find. The New York Times, 25 Jan 2019. https://www.nytimes.com/2019/01/25/technology/youtube-conspiracy-theory-videos.html

23. Zhou, R., Khemmarat, S., Gao, L.: The impact of YouTube recommendation system on video views. In: Proceedings of the 10th ACM SIGCOMM Conference on Internet Measurement, pp. 404–410, November 2010

24. Zhou, R., Khemmarat, S., Gao, L., Wan, J., Zhang, J.: How YouTube videos are discovered and its impact on video views. Multimed. Tools Appl. **75**(10), 6035–6058 (2016). https://doi.org/10.1007/s11042-015-3206-0

An Information-Theoretic Measure for Enabling Category Exemptions with an Application to Filter Bubbles

Chenyu Jiang[1], Bowen Wu[2(✉)], Sanghamitra Dutta[3], and Pulkit Grover[3]

[1] The University of Hong Kong, Pok Fu Lam, Hong Kong
cyjiang@cs.hku.hk
[2] ETH Zurich, Ramistrasse 101, 8006 Zürich, Switzerland
wubo@student.ethz.ch
[3] Carnegie Mellon University, 5000 Forbes Avenue, Pittsburgh, PA 15213, USA
{sanghamd,pgrover}@andrew.cmu.edu

Abstract. Filter bubbles can have undesirable consequences on society by limiting user recommendations to those that already conform to their own beliefs rather than a diversity of opinions. In this work, we consider the problem of enabling users to choose which filter bubbles they want to be in and which ones they want to eliminate. We propose a method of eliminating filter bubbles in user-selected topics by unbiasing them with respect to a certain attribute, e.g., political inclination while exempting biases in the remaining topics/categories. We note that an attempt to make all the recommendations free of biases without any provision for exemptions can be highly restrictive. E.g., a user might be invested in a particular topic, e.g., climate change, and want to be in a filter bubble that motivates them. For other topics, however, the user might want to avoid filter bubbles and learn from all sides of the debate. We first propose a set of desirable properties to quantify bias in recommendations with topic exemptions, and then arrive at a simple information-theoretic measure – Value-based Conditional Mutual Information (VCMI) – that satisfies our proposed desirable properties. Next, we also demonstrate how one can use this measure in practice to train models that eliminate biases in recommendations while exempting certain biases based on preferred topics/categories. We consider two datasets: (i) a completely synthetic dataset; and (ii) a dataset that we create based on the publicly available Twitter News Sharing User Behaviour dataset.

Keywords: Filter bubble · Recommendation system · Personalization · Algorithmic fairness · Information theory

1 Introduction

Personalized recommendation systems (e.g. news feeds, social media feeds, product or video recommendations) often obsessively maximize a utility metric

---

C. Jiang and B. Wu—Equal Contribution.

© Springer Nature Switzerland AG 2021
L. Boratto et al. (Eds.): BIAS 2021, CCIS 1418, pp. 117–129, 2021.
https://doi.org/10.1007/978-3-030-78818-6_11

related to revenue generated, e.g., click-through rate (CTR) [30], hovering time, etc. However, one of the major potential perils of personalization is that it significantly influences users' opinions by entrapping them in *filter bubbles*[1] [6,7,29]. Filter bubbles refer to a state of intellectual isolation caused due to an Internet users' exposure to content that reinforces their beliefs rather than a diverse set of opinions and viewpoints [28,29].

We are interested in eliminating filter bubbles pertaining to a user's biases about belief-based attributes (denoted by Z), such as political inclination, social opinions, etc. However, an attempt to make the recommendations entirely independent of Z may be too restrictive for maintaining high utility metrics (e.g. CTR) that these platforms aim to maximize. In this work, we take the viewpoint that the users, if aware, will carefully choose which filter bubbles to participate in and which ones to eliminate. For example, a user invested in a certain category, such as climate change, may *want* to be in a filter bubble that preserves their belief-based attributes, motivates them, and enables them to forge relationships to make social change. On the other hand, the same user attempting to learn about another category, such as healthcare, may want to learn from all perspectives of the debate, and hence may want to reduce the bias of the recommender system for other categories. Thus, the platform should enable the users to choose "content-categories" in which they prefer to be in intellectual bubbles and exempt bias.

In this work, we propose a novel method of quantifying nonexempt-category-specific bias in personalized recommendation systems, and then leverage this measure to selectively reduce bias only in the categories that are not exempted by the user. We assume that an article of online content (subsequently, "an article") can belong simultaneously to several categories. If any one of these categories is exempted, then it is desirable that the bias in that article is exempted. The exempt categories could be, e.g., news from a preferred source (e.g. New York Times or Fox News), or news corresponding to a category of interest (e.g. climate change, religion, or healthcare). In the process, by being selective about categories in which bias is exempted, we succeed in preserving (in toy and real-data examples; see Sect. 4), to an extent (that depends on the fraction of categories exempted by the user), some bias in the personalization of recommendation. Our work strikes a balance between the competing goals of maximizing utility metrics for personalization and reducing bias to reduce effects of filter bubbles (related to work in algorithmic fairness; see "Related Work" below). This offers an alternative to adopting an approach of entirely anonymizing personalized search history [11] (e.g. using anonymous windows), which significantly hurt the utility of personalization.

---

[1] Acknowledging our limited visibility into recommender systems used in practice, we note that this work is not pointing fingers at any political party, news channel, or industrial recommender systems. We believe there is room for improvement in the existing design of recommender systems, and this needs to be pursued in collaboration with industry to redesign today's recommender systems.

Our main contributions in this work are as follows:

- We identify a societal problem, namely, the problem of eliminating filter bubbles while allowing the user to exempt category-specific biases, that is particularly relevant in today's world with the growing use of personalization.
- We propose a set of three desirable properties for a measure of nonexempt-category-specific bias with respect to a belief-based attribute, namely, *select bias elimination, select bias preservation* and *nonobligatory overall independence*.
- Our desirable properties help us arrive at a simple information-theoretic measure – *Value-based Conditional Mutual Information (VCMI)* – that quantifies the nonexempt-category-specific bias with respect to a belief-based attribute. VCMI is given by: $I(Z; \widehat{Y} | C_{ex} = 0)$, where Z is the belief-based attribute, $\widehat{Y}$ is the output of the recommender system, e.g., whether to show the article or not and C_{ex} denotes whether the article belongs to an exempt category or not: $C_{ex} = 1$ when the article belongs to an exempt category, and 0 otherwise. The measure is deceptively simple: we discuss use-cases to compare the applicability of this measure with other seemingly similar measures in Sect. 3.1.
- Lastly, we show how to use VCMI as a regularizer with a utility-based cost function during training of a recommendation system and compare it with (i) no bias-related regularizer; (ii) mutual information (MI) regularizer; and (iii) conditional mutual information (CMI) regularizer. Our results consider two datasets (i) a completely synthetic dataset; and (ii) a dataset that we create based on the publicly available Twitter News Sharing User Behaviour dataset [10]. For both settings, we are able to demonstrate that our proposed method removes biases from nonexempt categories, while having a substantially smaller effect on the bias in exempt categories as compared to MI and CMI.

Limitations and Criticism of Our Approach: (i) We do not discuss *how* the categorization is performed. Instead, we simply assume that there are several known categories in which articles fall. Nevertheless, in our case study, we use a simple natural language processing (NLP) based approach to arrive at categories. In general though, a good characterization of categories for news, articles, etc. may require more sophisticated methods or special system design, which is beyond the scope of this work. (ii) We assume that an entity, e.g., the user, can make judicious decisions on which bubbles to be in, which might be optimistic and deserves further sociological study. Further, we assume that the platform can enable them to arrive at such decisions. This might require a rethink of how recommender platforms are designed. For example, instead of simply choosing "like" or "unlike", a reader might suggest "allow bias" to certain articles, and "disallow bias" to certain others, to inform the recommender system of when the biases are allowed. (iii) It has been acknowledged that individual's choices may sometimes play a stronger role than algorithmic ranking in limiting the user to filter-bubbles [3,21].

2   Related Work

The concept of context-specific independence (i.e., $Z \perp \hat{Y} | C_{ex} = 0$) in Bayesian networks [5] dates back to 1996. Also, closely related to this idea is recent work on fairness under exemptions [2,14,16,23,24,31] where the goal is to perform fair classification with respect to protected attributes, e.g., gender, race etc., while exempting bias due to some critical or explanatory features (also called "resolving variables"), e.g., qualifications in hiring, choice of department in college admissions [24], annual income in loan applications. For example, in [2,16], the authors use the related measure $I(Z; \hat{Y} | X_c)$, where X_c is the set of exempt features. While our work shares conceptual similarities with these aforementioned works, our novelty lies in using these ideas to propose a measure for a different problem, that is particularly relevant in today's societal context. Compared to the works on fairness, our exemption is *value-based*, i.e., the bias needs to be exempted *only when the article falls in certain categories* (further clarified in Sect. 3.1) while preserving the bias in other categories. This means that the *realization* of categories is important here. The measure should not average over all realizations of categories, as is done in $I(Z; \hat{Y} | X_c)$, e.g., one may want a loan-decision to be conditionally independent of Z given a feature income that is critical to the decision.

The problem of filter bubbles also shares connection with some other works fair personalization [13], and fair ranking [12] which also strike a trade-off between a utility metric and fairness. However, these works do not allow for category exemptions. Future work will examine the use of a fairness criterion derived from value-based conditioning in these scenarios to allow for category exemptions.

Several measures have been proposed to correct bias in recommender systems. Collaborative filtering and ranking, sometimes used together, are the main settings for this line of work. [34] generalizes the statistical parity and equal opportunity to apply in personalized ranking systems. Similarly, [4] proposes two measures item statistical parity and item equal opportunity. The former aims at achieving uniform distribution of recommended items regardless of item popularity, whereas the latter focuses on retaining item popularity distribution faithfully. [17] defines bias as the predictability of the protected attribute given recommendation results in a collaborative filtering context. Similar to our work, [27] zooms in to the recommendation bias of an *individual* user. It evaluates how diverse the recommendation results are by computing the content diversity defined by pairwise item distances. Our work defines and solves a different problem in a different setting however we believe the same problem can also be redefined in a meaningful way for the collaborative filtering- or rank-based systems.

Another line of work focuses on "diversity" [9], i.e., diversifying recommendation results to burst filter bubbles. Our work aims to achieve this by providing the users a more fain-grained control over the bubbles that they would like to keep, and the ones that they want to not be in. Another approach uses "calibration" [33], which reflects faithfully and proportionally a user's likes/dislikes.

For example, if a user has watched 70% romance movies and 30% action movies, then the recommendation list of movies should comply to the same ratio of two genres. These works focus on faithful preservation of the bias in the user's online history. As we will show later, our work can be interpreted as a combination of diversity and calibration, each of which is achieved in a different category. Diversity is for breaking the filter bubble, whereas calibration is for preserving wanted bias. Our technique achieves both of them simultaneously via a single regularizer.

Several existing tools e.g., Ghostery [32], DuckDuckGo [11] use anonymization to protect the user's privacy, search history, preferences, etc. from being used in personalization. In contrast to these approaches, our proposed redesign of recommender systems does not prevent personalization, but debiases the recommendation (measured by VCMI) while trading off between utility and unwanted bias. Alternate softwares [7], e.g., Balancer, Scoopinion, Wobble, etc. track and inform the user about their online activity, and make them aware of their filter bubbles. There are also softwares [7] such as *ConsiderIt*, *Opinion Space*, *Reflect* etc. that adopt the viewpoint of "deliberative democracy," and gently nudge the user to read the views or articles offering a different opinion. Instead of proposing a new app or platform, our work proposes a solution which can be adopted by existing platforms. Nevertheless, adoption of this solution might, as a side-effect, increase user awareness of filter bubbles by having them make choices of exempt categories.

3 Problem Setup and Main Results

Problem Setup: For every article (i.e., data-point), Z is the belief-based attribute whose bias is of interest, X is the set of all features, Y is the true label, and $\widehat{Y}$ is the prediction output derived from X. Categories are (possibly overlapping) sets that contain articles. A subset of categories are labeled "exempt". A feature C_{ex} denotes if the article is in any exempt category: $C_{ex} = 1$ if it is in any exempt category, and 0 otherwise. Our **goal** is to find a measure that quantifies the nonexempt-category-based bias in $\widehat{Y}$ with respect to Z, while exempting the bias if $C_{ex} = 1$.

Desirable Properties: We propose the following desirable properties for a measure of nonexempt-category-based bias.

1. Select Bias Elimination: The measure is 0 if and only if the recommendations are independent of Z when the article does not fall in the exempt category, i.e., $\Pr(\widehat{Y} = y | Z = z, C_{ex} = 0) = \Pr(\widehat{Y} = y | Z = z', C_{ex} = 0)$ for all z, z', y.

2. Select Bias Preservation: The measure may be 0 even if the recommendations are not independent of Z when the article does falls in the exempt category, i.e., $\Pr(\widehat{Y} = y | Z = z, C_{ex} = 1) \neq \Pr(\widehat{Y} = y | Z = z', C_{ex} = 1)$ for any z, z', y. E.g., if $\widehat{Y} = N_0$ when $C_{ex} = 0$, and $\widehat{Y} = Z + N_1$ when $C_{ex} = 1$, where Z, N_1, N_0, C_{ex} are i.i.d. Bern(1/2).

3. Nonobligatory Overall Independence: The measure may NOT be 0 even when $\widehat{Y}$ and Z are independent, e.g., if $\widehat{Y} = Z$ when $C_{ex} = 0$ and $\widehat{Y} = 1 - Z$ when $C_{ex} = 1$, where Z, C_{ex} are i.i.d. Bern(1/2).

Our Proposed Measure: Our proposed measure of nonexempt bias, that satisfies all the three desirable properties, is Value-based Conditional Mutual Information (VCMI), given by: $I(Z; \widehat{Y}|C_{ex} = 0)$.

Notice that, VCMI $= 0$ if and only if $\Pr(\widehat{Y} = y|C_{ex} = 0, Z = z) = \Pr(\widehat{Y} = y|C_{ex} = 0, Z = z')$ for all z, z', y VCMI quantifies the dependence between Z and $\widehat{Y}$ conditioned on the fact that the article does not belong to the exempt category, i.e., $C_{ex} = 0$. Minimizing this measure implies that Z and $\widehat{Y}$ approach independence but only when $C_{ex} = 0$.

Relationship of VCMI to Conditional Mutual Information (CMI) and Mutual Information (MI): VCMI is closely related to two other measures: Mutual Information [15], MI $= I(Z; \widehat{Y})$, used for fairness broadly [22], and Conditional Mutual Information, used for fairness under feature exemptions [2,16]. For simplicity, suppose Z is binary. When MI $= 0$, we have $\Pr(\widehat{Y} = y|Z = 1) = \Pr(\widehat{Y} = y|Z = 0)$. This is equivalent to statistical parity [1,22]. However, this measure does not allow any exemptions. To allow exemptions, a relevant measure (interpreted in our setting) is: CMI $= I(Z; \widehat{Y}|C_{ex})$. When CMI $= 0$, we have $\Pr(Y = y|C_{ex} = x, Z = 1) = \Pr(Y = y|C_{ex} = x, Z = 0)$ for $x = 0, 1$. This is equivalent to conditional statistical parity [14]. Note that, CMI can be decomposed as follows: CMI $= \sum_{x \in \{0,1\}} \Pr(C_{ex} = x) I(Z; \widehat{Y}|C_{ex} = x)$. CMI is a convex combination of VCMI at different values of C_{ex}. If we partition the datapoints into groups according to their C_{ex} value, then CMI attempts to eliminate the dependence between Z and $\widehat{Y}$ in *every* group. However, VCMI attempts to eliminate this dependence only for $C_{ex} = 0$.

3.1   Thought Experiments to Understand When to Use VCMI, CMI or MI

In this section, we discuss three scenarios that clarify which measure is more appropriate among VCMI, CMI and MI. Let Z be a binary random variable denoting, e.g., the political slant of the article, e.g., left ($Z = 0$) or right ($Z = 1$).

When is VCMI More Appropriate? Suppose Alice is interested in climate change. She wants articles on climate change to be recommended irrespective of their political stance (i.e., bias is exempted). However, for all other articles, i.e., articles that do not belong to this category, she wants to avoid being isolated in filter bubbles of any particular political stance. Here, the use of MI as a regularizer would recommend her articles that are neutral in their political stance. This can even lead to a significant reduction of articles on climate change, particularly if they all have a similar political stance (strong correlation with Z). Even CMI can lead to a reduction in articles on climate change because the recommender is also minimizing $I(Z; \widehat{Y}|C_{ex} = 1)$ and not only $I(Z; \widehat{Y}|C_{ex} = 0)$. If almost every article on climate change is strongly correlated with Z, the recommender might prevent most of those articles to minimize $I(Z; \widehat{Y}|C_{ex} = 1)$. Here, VCMI is more appropriate as it only minimizes $I(Z; \widehat{Y}|C_{ex} = 0)$, debiasing articles that are not about climate change.

When is CMI More Appropriate? Suppose Alice likes a particular biased news-source, say, Foobar news, and wants unbiased articles (from Foobar news or outside), but also wants to continue to receive articles from this source (i.e., does not want debiasing to lower the likelihood of recommendation of articles from Foobar news). Using MI here could, as in Scenario I, significantly reduce articles from Foobar news since articles in Foobar news are strongly correlated with Z. What is needed here is debiasing *while exempting the bias arising from other features for* **both** *cases: whether the article is from Foobar news or not*. This is subtly different from Scenario I, where only when the article is in the exempt category is the bias exempted. CMI is more appropriate for this scenario because it minimizes the conditional bias for articles, conditioned on them belonging, and not belonging, to Foobar news. As for VCMI, it would only minimize the bias in articles not from Foobar news, exempting the bias in the articles from Foobar news.

When is MI More Appropriate? Suppose Alice wants *all* her recommendations to be neutral with respect to the political stance irrespective of the source or the category. Here, MI is the most appropriate. In our proposed redesign of recommendation systems, MI could be the default regularizer, and users can add exemptions as they see fit.

4   Experimental Evaluation

Integrate VCMI into Training: We propose two ways of integrating the VCMI measure into machine learning training.

- **sVCMI:** Single model with VCMI regularizer for all articles irrespective of whether they are exempt or not.
- **dVCMI.** Two separate models for exempt and nonexempt articles; VCMI regularizer only in the latter model.

One might think that there is little difference between above two. After all, with sufficient complexity, sVCMI can emulate dVCMI. The implicit assumption here is that the number of parameters in each of them is limited, so that they can be trained without a very large dataset (as is the case in our Twitter dataset). This limited dataset case is where we see the largest distinction between the two in our experimental evaluation.

We will train classifiers whose outputs indicate the likelihood (between 0 and 1) of recommendation of the article. We use binary cross-entropy as our *loss function*, and train five models: (i) **Vanilla**: without regularizer; (ii) **MI**: MI regularizer; (iii) **CMI**: CMI regularizer; (iv) **sVCMI**: VCMI regularizer; and (v) **dVCMI**: Two MLPs for exempt and nonexempt data respectively and apply VCMI regularizer to the later one.

Estimation of VCMI and CMI: For simplicity, inspired from related work [16], we use $\widetilde{I}(Z;\widehat{Y}) = -\frac{1}{2}\log(1 - \rho_{Z,\widehat{Y}}^2)$ to approximate MI, where $\rho_{Z,\widehat{Y}}$ is the Pearson correlation [18] between Z and $\widehat{Y}$. The approximation is exact when Z and $\widehat{Y}$ are jointly Gaussian. Similarly, CMI can be estimated as

$$\widetilde{I}(Z;\widehat{Y}|C_{ex}) = \sum_{x\in\{0,1\}} \Pr(C_{ex}=x)\widetilde{I}(Z;\widehat{Y}|C_{ex}=x)$$

$$= -\frac{1}{2} \sum_{x\in\{0,1\}} \Pr(C_{ex}=x)\log(1 - \rho_{Z,\widehat{Y}|C_{ex}=x}^2)$$

and VCMI is

$$\widetilde{I}(Z;\widehat{Y}|C_{ex}=0) = -\frac{1}{2}\log(1 - \rho_{Z,\widehat{Y}|C_{ex}=0}^2).$$

4.1 Study on Synthetic Data (Toy Example)

This toy example simulates a simple news feed system. Each article's feature vector has the following fields: (a) C_{g1}: intensity towards a particular political viewpoint; (b) C_{g2}: length; (c) C_{g3}: "freshness" (e.g. recency and departure from recent articles); and (d) C_{ex}: whether the article belongs to the exempt category: healthcare. Z is the political stance of the article. Let these variables be distributed as: $Z \sim \text{Bern}(0.5)$, $C_{ex} \sim \text{Bern}(0.8)$, $C_{g1} = Z + N$, $N \sim \mathcal{N}(0, 0.05)$, $C_{g2} \sim \mathcal{N}(0.5, 1)$, and $C_{g3} \sim \mathcal{N}(0, 3)$, where $\mathcal{N}(\mu, \sigma^2)$ is a Gaussian distribution with mean μ and variance σ^2. $Z, C_{ex}, C_{g2}, C_{g3}, N$ are mutually independent. Moreover, we have a noise term $noise \sim \mathcal{N}(0, 1.5)$. A score S, representing the user's interest towards an article, is $S = C_{g1} + C_{g3} + noise$ if $C_{ex} = 0$ and $S = C_{g1} + C_{g2} + noise$ otherwise. We assume that the true binary label $Y = \text{sgn}(S - 0.5)$, where $\text{sgn}(x) = 1$ if $x > 0$ and 0 otherwise.

Experimental Setup: We choose a Multi-Layer Perceptron (MLP) with two hidden layers as our classifier. The model output, $\widehat{Y}$ gives a continuous value between 0 and 1. The five MLP models are trained on $90,000$ samples drawn from the distributions and each is trained for 50 epochs with batch size being 256. The models are evaluated on the remaining $10,000$ samples from the same distributions. We tried different choices of the regularizer constant λ and all of them ($\lambda = 0.5, 1, 2$) gave similar results described below. Thus, in this toy example, we set $\lambda = 1$.

Experimental Findings: The category-specific biases $I(Z;\widehat{Y}|C_{ex} = 0/1)$ on the test set is shown in Fig. 1 for the five different models. It is desirable to have low nonexempt bias $I(Z;\widehat{Y}|C_{ex} = 0)$, while preserving $I(Z;\widehat{Y}|C_{ex} = 1)$, e.g., maintaining a value as close to the Vanilla model as possible. In Fig. 1 (top), all models decrease $I(Z;\widehat{Y}|C_{ex} = 0)$ below Vanilla, but sVCMI has the most reduction. In Fig. 1 (bottom), while CMI and MI decrease $I(Z;\widehat{Y}|C_{ex} = 1)$, sVCMI and dVCMI are preserving the bias in exempt categories. To have a better idea on how the distribution of the prediction score $\widehat{Y}$ changes, we also report

Jensen-Shannon (JS) distance [25] as a numerical measure of similarity between two distributions in Fig. 2. We discretize $\widehat{Y}$'s domain into 50 bins, obtain the histogram and compute all numerical values based on the normalized discretization. Figure 2 (top) shows that the JS distance between $\Pr(\widehat{Y}|Z = 0)$ and $\Pr(\widehat{Y}|Z = 1)$ in the nonexempt category is smaller than the Vanilla model for all the other models. Figure 2 (bottom) shows that JS distance between $\Pr(\widehat{Y}|Z = 0)$ and $\Pr(\widehat{Y}|Z = 1)$ are almost the same as the Vanilla model for sVCMI or dVCMI, while MI and CMI dramatically decrease the JS distance. These results show that our methods (sVCMI and dVCMI) effectively manage to make $\widehat{Y}$ independent of Z in nonexempt category, while preserving their dependence in exempt category. We also report the AUC [8] in Fig. 3. MI and CMI have significantly worse AUC, while sVCMI and dVCMI have only slightly lower AUC than Vanilla.

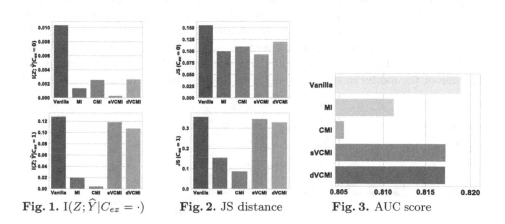

Fig. 1. $I(Z; \widehat{Y}|C_{ex} = \cdot)$ **Fig. 2.** JS distance   **Fig. 3.** AUC score

Left: Bias in nonexempt and exempt category (**toy example**). MI, CMI, sVCMI, and dVCMI, all eliminate the bias in nonexempt category. For the exempt category, sVCMI and dVCMI preserve the bias, but MI and CMI do not. **Middle:** JS distance between the distributions of $\Pr(\widehat{Y}|Z = 0)$ and $\Pr(\widehat{Y}|Z = 1)$ in nonexempt and exempt category. Using this different distance measure, the conclusion is similar. **Right:** AUC for different models in the **toy example**. Because sVCMI and dVCMI preserve the dependency between Z and $\widehat{Y}$ in exempt categories, they are able to retain higher AUC.

4.2   Case Study on a Dataset Created from Real Data

Next, we conduct a case study in a news recommendation scenario. At the outset, we note that this is a simplistic analysis, with the goal of examining benefits of VCMI over MI and CMI, rather than a full-fledged practical implementation.

Dataset Construction: We created our dataset based on the Twitter News Sharing User Behavior dataset [10], which contains 37,106 entries of users' information and their retweeted news articles ($330,575$ articles in total). We label each news article as left or right slant using the method in [10], and specify the news category of each article using an LSTM based model [26]. Assuming that retweeting means an user is interested in the article, we use collaborative filtering implemented in Implicit [19] to generate the ground truth labels (to recommend or not). We study the user in the later experiment who have the largest number of real ground-truth before the collaborative filtering.

Created Dataset Description: Each article is represented by a feature vector with the following fields: (a) Categories: multi-hot encoding of news categories; (b) Article length; (c) Source: one-hot encoding of the publisher of the news; (d) Publication time. Each piece of news is also associated with a political view, left, right or neutral. This attribute is only used when calculating our regularizers and is not included in the input features. The true labels are binary.

Experimental Setup: We predict whether the user will be interested an article. We use a MLP with two hidden layers (32 neurons per layer) as the classifier. Evaluation metrics and other parameters are the same as in the toy example. The dataset is randomly split into training and test sets with a ratio of 7:3. The models were trained for 200 epochs using $\lambda = 0.25$. We collected statistics for 32 runs of the model to mitigate effects of random initialization.

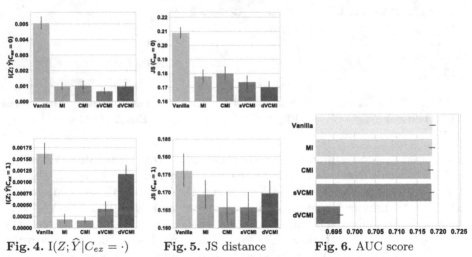

Fig. 4. $I(Z; \widehat{Y}|C_{ex} = \cdot)$ **Fig. 5.** JS distance   **Fig. 6.** AUC score

Left: Bias in nonexempt and exempt category (**case study**). Error bars indicate 95% confidence interval in all following figures. sVCMI and dVCMI better preserve $I(Z; \widehat{Y}|C_{ex} = 1)$, and reduce $I(Z; \widehat{Y}|C_{ex} = 0)$. dVCMI is better at preserving the exempt bias than sVCMI. **Middle:** JS distance between $\Pr(\widehat{Y}|Z = 0)$ and $\Pr(\widehat{Y}|Z = 1)$ in nonexempt and exempt category. sVCMI again cannot well preserve the JS distance in exempt group. **Right:** AUC for different models in the **case study**. The AUC is maintained for all models, but dVCMI takes a small hit, potentially because of data insufficiency induced by the two network approach.

Experimental Findings: We observe similar benefits of sVCMI and dVCMI (see Fig. 4) on $I(Z; \widehat{Y}|C_{ex} = 0/1)$. CMI reduces $I(Z; \widehat{Y}|C_{ex} = 0)$ and $I(Z; \widehat{Y}|C_{ex} = 1)$ significantly while sVCMI and dVCMI partially preserve $I(Z; \widehat{Y}|C_{ex} = 1)$. Compared to the toy example though, dVCMI preserves $I(Z; \widehat{Y}|C_{ex} = 1)$ better than sVCMI in the exempt category. Similar effect can be seen in the JS distance (Fig. 5), possibly due to the limited expressivity of a single network. We also note that when choosing a large λ value, the effect of CMI and sVCMI on the distribution becomes unpredictable. The AUC of the models are shown in Fig. 6. We observe no significant reduction in AUC except for dVCMI. It might be due to insufficient data for training of two separate models because this is not observed in the toy example where data is abundant, or since dVCMI reduces the JS distance for the nonexempt category the most.

5   Conclusion and Discussions

In this work, we identify the problem of allowing users to choose which filter bubbles to stay in and which ones to eliminate in recommendation systems. We propose to selectively eliminate bias towards belief-based attributes (e.g. political inclination) in certain user-chosen content-categories, while preserving such bias in others. We arrive at a simple information-theoretic measure, VCMI, for quantifying such bias. It aims to reduce dependence of Z on $\widehat{Y}$ given $C_{ex} = 0$, while maintaining, as much as possible, the accuracy as well as dependence of Z on $\widehat{Y}$ given $C_{ex} = 1$. While our experiment and case studies on the synthetic and created datasets suggest that VCMI is able to attain this goal, some notable issues remain: (i) CMI can sometimes lower $I(Z; \widehat{Y}|C_{ex} = 0)$ below that done by VCMI; (ii) VCMI may sometimes lower $I(Z; \widehat{Y}|C_{ex} = 1)$ as well, possibly due to limitations of MLP-based models and the ability to affect conditional joint distributions without affecting the overall joint distribution. We leave a comprehensive evaluation to future work. Future works may also explore the following: (i) More reliable dataset: Given the novelty of this problem, we could also not find any off-the-shelf dataset to test our measure. To conduct further study, we need labeled data from real world applications, e.g., Facebook news feed system. Nevertheless, we hope that this connection between fairness measures and filter bubbles receives further attention from the community. (ii) Alternative estimation techniques for VCMI building on [20] and the references therein. (iii) Practical applicability, e.g., by improving upon the method of selecting exempt categories or belief-based attributes that is more applicable to unsupervised or semi-supervised settings. These shortcomings need to be addressed before the method can indeed be deployed in a real world setup.

References

1. Agarwal, A., Beygelzimer, A., Dudík, M., Langford, J., Wallach, H.: A reductions approach to fair classification. arXiv preprint arXiv:1803.02453 (2018)
2. Anonymous: Conditional debiasing for neural networks (2019)
3. Bakshy, E., Messing, S., Adamic, L.A.: Exposure to ideologically diverse news and opinion on Facebook. Science **348**(6239), 1130–1132 (2015)
4. Boratto, L., Fenu, G., Marras, M.: Connecting user and item perspectives in popularity debiasing for collaborative recommendation. Inf. Process. Manag. **58**(1) (2021). https://doi.org/10.1016/j.ipm.2020.102387. https://www.sciencedirect.com/science/article/pii/S0306457320308827
5. Boutilier, C., Friedman, N., Goldszmidt, M., Koller, D.: Context-specific independence in Bayesian networks. In: Proceedings of the Twelfth International Conference on Uncertainty in Artificial Intelligence, UAI 1996, pp. 115–123. Morgan Kaufmann Publishers Inc., San Francisco (1996)
6. Bozdag, E.: Bias in algorithmic filtering and personalization. Ethics Inf. Technol. **15**(3), 209–227 (2013)
7. Bozdag, E., van den Hoven, J.: Breaking the filter bubble: democracy and design. Ethics Inf. Technol. **17**(4), 249–265 (2015)
8. Bradley, A.P.: The use of the area under the roc curve in the evaluation of machine learning algorithms. Pattern Recogn. **30**(7), 1145–1159 (1997). https://doi.org/10.1016/S0031-3203(96)00142-2
9. Bradley, K., Smyth, B.: Improving recommendation diversity. In: Proceedings of the Twelfth Irish Conference on Artificial Intelligence and Cognitive Science, Maynooth, Ireland, pp. 85–94. Citeseer (2001)
10. Brena, G., Brambilla, M., Ceri, S., Di Giovanni, M., Pierri, F., Ramponi, G.: News sharing user behaviour on twitter: a comprehensive data collection of news articles and social interactions. In: Proceedings of the International AAAI Conference on Web and Social Media, vol. 13, no. 01, pp. 592–597, July 2019. https://www.aaai.org/ojs/index.php/ICWSM/article/view/3256
11. Buys, J.: Duckduckgo: a new search engine built from open source. GigaOM OStatic blog (2010)
12. Celis, L.E., Straszak, D., Vishnoi, N.K.: Ranking with fairness constraints. arXiv preprint arXiv:1704.06840 (2017)
13. Celis, L.E., Vishnoi, N.K.: Fair personalization. arXiv preprint arXiv:1707.02260 (2017)
14. Corbett-Davies, S., Pierson, E., Feller, A., Goel, S., Huq, A.: Algorithmic decision making and the cost of fairness. In: Proceedings of the 23rd ACM SIGKDD International Conference on Knowledge Discovery and Data Mining, KDD 2017, pp. 797–806. ACM, New York (2017). https://doi.org/10.1145/3097983.3098095. http://doi.acm.org/10.1145/3097983.3098095
15. Cover, T.M., Thomas, J.A.: Elements of Information Theory. Wiley, Hoboken (2012)
16. Dutta, S., Venkatesh, P., Mardziel, P., Datta, A., Grover, P.: An information-theoretic quantification of discrimination with exempt features. In: Association for the Advancement of Artificial Intelligence (2020)
17. Edizel, B., Bonchi, F., Hajian, S., Panisson, A., Tassa, T.: FaiRecSys: mitigating algorithmic bias in recommender systems. Int. J. Data Sci. Anal. **9**(2), 197–213 (2020)

18. Edwards, A.L.: The Correlation Coefficient, chap. 4, pp. 33–46. W. H. Freeman (1976)
19. Frederickson, B.: Implicit (2019). https://github.com/benfred/implicit
20. Gao, W., Kannan, S., Oh, S., Viswanath, P.: Estimating mutual information for discrete-continuous mixtures. In: Advances in Neural Information Processing Systems, pp. 5986–5997 (2017)
21. Garrett, R.K.: The "echo chamber" distraction: disinformation campaigns are the problem, not audience fragmentation (2017)
22. Ghassami, A., Khodadadian, S., Kiyavash, N.: Fairness in supervised learning: an information theoretic approach. In: 2018 IEEE International Symposium on Information Theory (ISIT), pp. 176–180. IEEE (2018)
23. Kamiran, F., Žliobaitė, I., Calders, T.: Quantifying explainable discrimination and removing illegal discrimination in automated decision making. Knowl. Inf. Syst. **35**(3), 613–644 (2013)
24. Kilbertus, N., Rojas-Carulla, M., Parascandolo, G., Hardt, M., Janzing, D., Schölkopf, B.: Avoiding discrimination through causal reasoning. In: Proceedings of the 31st International Conference on Neural Information Processing Systems, NIPS 2017, pp. 656–666. Curran Associates Inc., USA (2017). http://dl.acm.org/citation.cfm?id=3294771.3294834
25. Lin, J.: Divergence measures based on the Shannon entropy. IEEE Trans. Inf. Theory **37**(1), 145–151 (1991)
26. Misra, R.: News category dataset (2018). https://www.kaggle.com/rmisra/news-category-dataset/
27. Nguyen, T.T., Hui, P.M., Harper, F.M., Terveen, L., Konstan, J.A.: Exploring the filter bubble: the effect of using recommender systems on content diversity. In: Proceedings of the 23rd International Conference on World Wide Web, WWW 2014, pp. 677–686. Association for Computing Machinery, New York (2014). https://doi.org/10.1145/2566486.2568012
28. O'Callaghan, D., Greene, D., Conway, M., Carthy, J., Cunningham, P.: Down the (white) rabbit hole: the extreme right and online recommender systems. Soc. Sci. Comput. Rev. **33**(4), 459–478 (2015)
29. Pariser, E.: The Filter Bubble: What the Internet is Hiding from You. Penguin UK (2011)
30. Richardson, M., Dominowska, E., Ragno, R.: Predicting clicks: estimating the click-through rate for new ads. In: Proceedings of the 16th International Conference on World Wide Web, pp. 521–530. ACM (2007)
31. Salimi, B., Rodriguez, L., Howe, B., Suciu, D.: Interventional fairness: causal database repair for algorithmic fairness. In: Proceedings of the 2019 International Conference on Management of Data, SIGMOD 2019, pp. 793–810. ACM, New York (2019). https://doi.org/10.1145/3299869.3319901
32. Signanini, J., McDermott, B.: Ghostery (2014). https://www.ghostery.com/
33. Steck, H.: Calibrated recommendations. In: Proceedings of the 12th ACM Conference on Recommender Systems, RecSys 2018, pp. 154–162. Association for Computing Machinery, New York (2018). https://doi.org/10.1145/3240323.3240372
34. Zhu, Z., Wang, J., Caverlee, J.: Measuring and mitigating item under-recommendation bias in personalized ranking systems. In: Proceedings of the 43rd International ACM SIGIR Conference on Research and Development in Information Retrieval, SIGIR 2020, pp. 449–458. Association for Computing Machinery, New York (2020). https://doi.org/10.1145/3397271.3401177

Perception-Aware Bias Detection
for Query Suggestions

Fabian Haak[(✉)] and Philipp Schaer

TH Köln – University of Applied Sciences, Cologne, Germany
{fabian.haak,philipp.schaer}@th-koeln.de

Abstract. Bias in web search has been in the spotlight of bias detection research for quite a while. At the same time, little attention has been paid to query suggestions in this regard. Awareness of the problem of biased query suggestions has been raised. Likewise, there is a rising need for automatic bias detection approaches. This paper adds on the bias detection pipeline for bias detection in query suggestions of person-related search developed by Bonart et al. [2]. The sparseness and lack of contextual metadata of query suggestions make them a difficult subject for bias detection. Furthermore, query suggestions are perceived very briefly and subliminally. To overcome these issues, perception-aware metrics are introduced. Consequently, the enhanced pipeline is able to better detect systematic topical bias in search engine query suggestions for person-related searches. The results of an analysis performed with the developed pipeline confirm this assumption. Due to the perception-aware bias detection metrics, findings produced by the pipeline can be assumed to reflect bias that users would discern.

Keywords: Bias detection · Query suggestions · Online search · Bias quantification · Natural language processing

1 Introduction

Fairness in online search and bias detection are important topics in information retrieval research. Consequently, there are many approaches for detecting bias in search results. Little research and few methodological approaches exist for bias detection in query suggestions. Query suggestions are an important aspect of online information retrieval via search engines and significantly impact what people search for [17]. Due to the sparseness of query suggestions (no author, no sources, no publishing platform, less text) and context-dependency, bias detection of query suggestions is less straight forward than bias detection of search results [23]. Unless a person performing online search does not have a clear information need, very little attention is paid to the query suggestions. Because of the brief exposure, search engine users perceive query suggestions distinctly, even though certain effects like the diminishing attention paid to elements further down the list still applies [5,8]. Summarizing these findings, we are left with two research questions to focus on as we develop a bias detection pipeline:

© Springer Nature Switzerland AG 2021
L. Boratto et al. (Eds.): BIAS 2021, CCIS 1418, pp. 130–142, 2021.
https://doi.org/10.1007/978-3-030-78818-6_12

– RQ1: To what extent can bias towards metadata on the persons searched (e.g., gender, age, party membership) be uncovered in query suggestions to person-related searches using perception-aware metrics?
– RQ2: How do perception-aware metrics perform compared to simpler metrics in detecting bias in query suggestions to person-related searches?

To answer these research questions, we extend the bias identification pipeline developed by Bonart et al. by introducing perception-aware metrics. Doing so, the pipeline identifies bias in a more realistic manner. This should in turn result in a better indication of present bias. By testing the updated pipeline on the same data, the results produced by both pipelines are directly comparable.

2 Related Work

Findings of various studies show that search engines such as Google are seen as a trustworthy source of information on many topics, including political information [4,22]. According to Houle, search engines significantly impact political opinion formation [10]. The trust in search engines is problematic because their results are prone to be biased. This might be due to bias induced by algorithms [11], or by representing bias inherent in mental models: Although not at all true by definition of these words, a doctor is usually assumed to be male, while a nurse is typically expected to be female [1]. Similar biased patterns exist plentiful, and because search engines show the information inherent in data, bias is as omnipresent in search results as it is in peoples' minds and natural language texts [6,18]. Even Google acknowledges this in a white paper, stating their awareness of disinforming and biased contents presented by their search engine [7]. Biased search results have been widely discussed and researched. Kulshrestha et al. investigated and compared bias in Google search results and search on Twitter [13]. Their bias detection methodology relies on peripheral information, such as the author, publishing and distribution platforms, as well as information gathered from these sources [13].

Aside from search results, *query suggestions* play a key role in what people search for [17]. There are many types of query suggestions such as query expansions, auto completions, query predictions, or query refinements [3,20]. We use the term query suggestion as an umbrella term for all facets of the previously mentioned terms, to describe the list of suggested search queries returned by search engines for an input query or search term. Although it is unclear how exactly they are formed, there is no doubt that query suggestions are derived from what other users search for in a location and language [24]. Also, they can be manipulated [24]. Query suggestions are assumed to be as bias-laden as search results, with a study by Olteanu et al. illustrating how diverse and hard to detect the forms of problematic and biased search results are [19]. The difficulty in detecting bias in query suggestions lies in their sparseness. Without context, they neither offer author or source information nor is input bias available to judge their ranking. Furthermore, bias in query suggestions is often context-dependent and not derivable from the terms themselves [19]. For these reasons, approaches like the one utilized by Kulshrestha et al. do not work for query suggestions.

To overcome the hurdles of identifying bias in sparse, contextless search query suggestions, Bonart et al. developed a bias identification pipeline for person-related search [2]. It represents a natural language processing pipeline with three modules: Data acquisition, data preprocessing, and bias analysis (cf. Fig. 1). The collection they used to develop and test the pipeline consists of search queries and their corresponding lists of query suggestions, gathered since 2017 in German from Google, DuckDuckGo, and Bing. The search terms consist primarily of names of German politicians. With the developed pipeline, Bonart et al. tried to find a way to automatically identify *systematic topical biases* towards certain groups of people with shared meta-attributes (e.g., gender, age, party membership) [2]. Topical bias describes content bias as misrepresented information in the documents themselves [21]. Concerning the meta-attributes, systematic topical bias refers to differences in the distribution of topics in query suggestions of groups of politicians of different meta-attribute characteristics (e.g., male/ female). Due to their aforementioned sparseness, this type of bias is the easiest to detect in query suggestions.

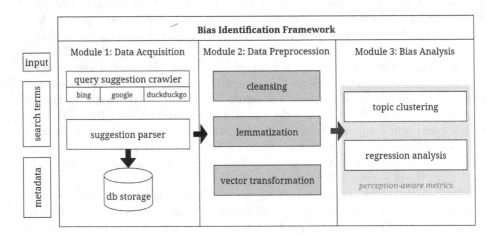

Fig. 1. Bias detection pipeline for person-related query suggestions developed by Bonart et al. [2]. The highlighted steps have been modified.

The metric Bonart et al. used for detecting bias is the number of unique topical cluster terms in the query suggestions for each search term (cf. section 3). Bias is then identified by comparing the differences between certain groups of search terms. The results produced by the bias identification pipeline only revealed minor indicators of bias within the groups of politicians. In addition to the insignificant findings, the metric employed by Bonart et al. does not consider two critical aspects of how query suggestions are perceived: (A) The *frequency of the suggestions* throughout data collection is disregarded. A suggestion that appears once influences the metric as much as a suggestion that appeared many times. (B) The *order of items* in the list of query suggestions is ignored. Although the rank in the list of query suggestions has a strong influence on the visibility of a query suggestion [8], it was not taken into account. Because of these flaws in the metrics, it is doubtful whether the detected bias would have been perceivable by search engine users. Therefore, the bias identification pipeline is reworked and expanded to produce more meaningful results and consider how query suggestions are perceived.

3   Methodology

The following section briefly outlines the bias detection pipeline and highlights changes and additions made to it.

Data Acquisition. The bias analysis is based on a set of N search terms t_i with $i = 1, ..., N$ which share a set of P meta-attributes $x_{i,1}, ..., x_{i,P}$ [2]. The dataset consists of a collection of query suggestions returned for these terms, which consist of names of German politicians or politically relevant people from Germany. Twice per day, for all search terms, a specialized web crawler collects query suggestions in German by HTTP request from three search engines' auto-complete APIs: Google, DuckDuckGo and Bing. Requests only contain the input query as well as language and location information. Therefore, no user profiles or search histories can influence the results.

Preprocessing. Preprocessing is the first module of the pipeline that was changed significantly. The lemmatizer was changed from pattern.de to the german_news standard model made available within the spacy module by Honnibal et al. [9]. An entity recognition step was introduced and is performed using spacy, as well. It is performed after lemmatization on all query suggestions that do not consist of a single word. After cleaning and lemmatization, about 20% of the query suggestions are discarded in the original pipeline because clustering can only be performed on single-word-suggestions. By employing an entity recognition system, many suggestions such as "summer festival" are condensable to a single term, which can be used in the cluster analysis. Since query suggestions are most probably formed considering entities to not deliver multiple very similar suggestions to the user (cf. [3]), the suggestions shortened by entity recognition are not expected to change significantly in meaning. The last step in the preprocessing module consists of the unmodified vectorization of the single term query suggestions using the word2vec module [15]. Although there are newer and more elaborate vectorizers, word2vec performed best on the given collection of German terms.

Bias Analysis. The first step in the bias analysis module, topic clustering, has not been changed methodically. The vectorized query suggestions are assigned to topical clusters utilizing a k-means approach.

Most importantly, new metrics have been introduced. These metrics are perception-aware, meaning that they aim to determine bias analog to how a user would perceive it. Due to the sparseness of metadata around the suggestions and the often context dependant bias, topical bias is the most promising approach to automatically detecting bias. A main characteristic of the perception of query suggestions is the low attention given to them, especially suggestions on lower ranks [8,16]. Therefore, the main factors influencing the exposure of a topic over a time span are the percentage of relevant topical suggestions and their ranks.

As a first step to derive the new metrics, a matrix is created, from which the metrics are calculated. This matrix contains rows for all search terms t_{ir} with $i = 1, ..., N$ being the identifier of the term and $r = 1, ..., 10$ signifying the rank in the list of query suggestions for the term. Search terms and suggestion rank form the multi-index structure for the rows of the matrix. These rows are paired with all M preprocessed single-term query suggestions s_j with $j = 1, ..., M$, that have been assigned to a cluster. This results in a structure where the frequency for every search term-suggestion combination at every rank is stored. Based on this, the number and percentage of suggestions of each of the topical clusters at each rank can be calculated for each search term.

The problem of judging the systematic topical bias in the query suggestions approximates the relevance judgment. Relevance judgments usually describe the probability of a document to fulfill a given information need. Likewise, the percentage of suggestions for a certain cluster for a rank describes the probability of a randomly selected single term belonging to that topic. Thus, using a discounted relevance measure to judge the rank- and perception-aware topical affiliation is not far-fetched. Hence, discounted cumulative gain and its normalized variety are introduced as metrics for detecting bias. Both are usually employed to rank the relevance of a list of documents, for example, as returned by a search query [14]. The metrics put an emphasis on the rank of the judged elements, which is what we want our metric to do. Discounted Cumulative Gain (DCG) is implemented adopted as a bias metric for query suggestions as [12]:

$$DCG(C_x, q) = \sum_{i=1}^{10} \frac{2^{P(C_x(i),q)} - 1}{log_2(i + 1)}, \tag{1}$$

where $DCG(C_x, q)$ describes the DCG of a term q for cluster x and $P(C_x(i), q)$ is the percentage of total appearances of clustered query suggestions at rank i of the list of query suggestions for the term. Instead of relevance, we employ the percentage of suggestions for a topical cluster, which can be interpreted as the topical affiliation for that cluster. Counting appearances of cluster words and using the percentages as key measurements is similar to using graded instead of dichotomous relevance judgments. In essence, instead of a measure of gain, DCG as a metric for topical affiliation describes the average degree of perceived exposure to a topic within the query suggestions of a search term. By revealing differences in the topical affiliation between groups, topical bias towards these groups can be identified and quantified.

The nDCG (normalized Discounted Cumulative Gain) for cluster x of a term is expressed as the DCG divided by the DCG of the percentages $P(C_x(i), q)$ sorted in descending order ($IDCG(C_x, q)$):

$$nDCG(C_x, q) = \frac{DCG(C_x, q)}{IDCG(C_x, q)} \tag{2}$$

By normalizing, the nDCG expresses how every cluster is distributed over the ranks of the query suggestions of a term, neglecting the overall number of cluster words and other clusters. Thereby it expresses, what average rank the suggestions of the topical cluster appear on. A high nDCG score means that a topical cluster appears on average on the first ranks of the suggestions. However, it does not indicate how often suggestions of the topic appear over the span of data acquisition. The nDCG could be a useful metric if the lengths of query suggestions vary, when particular clusters or terms are uncommon or when very little data is available. For example, when trying to judge how prominent a term appeared in searches, that coined only in a very brief time in search suggestions (e.g., suggestion "flu" with names of different states). These terms do not appear often enough over a year to impact the DCG score, but the nDCG allows for differentiated insight anyway by only emphasizing the rank.

Regression Analysis. The metrics describe how the identified topical clusters would manifest in the query suggestions for the search terms. The goal is to identify significant differences between the groups of meta-attributes $x_{i,p}$ (e.g., female, SPD-member) in the perception-aware metrics for each cluster $y_{i,c}$ (e.g., DCG, nDCG). By doing so, topical bias (e.g., towards terms that describe private or family topics) is detectable. To reveal significant differences, multiple linear regression is performed using dichotomous dummy variables for the meta-attributes as independent variables and the perception-aware metrics nDCG and DCG as dependent variables. The model of this regression for topical clusters $c \in 1, ..., k$ can be expressed as

$$y_{i,c} = \beta_0 + \beta_1 x_{i,1} + ... + \beta_p x_{i,p} + \epsilon_i, \tag{3}$$

where ϵ_i is the independent error term and $i = 1, ..., N$ are the observation indices. To avoid multicollinearity, one variable per attribute is used as the base category and omitted.

4   Results of Bias Analysis of German Politicians Dataset

After describing the main changes to the bias detection pipeline in the previous section, this section explores its effectiveness by performing an analysis using the pipeline on the most recent version of the same dataset of German politicians used to test the first version of the pipeline.

Data Acquisition. As mentioned, the dataset consists of German politicians' names as search terms and the corresponding returned query suggestions. Compared to when the bias identification pipeline was first developed, the list was expanded significantly. The number of search terms was raised from 630 to 3047. The additional terms consist of politicians that are currently members of the Bundestag (the federal parliament) but have not been in 2017 when the dataset was created. Additionally, political figures that are not members of a German government body, were added to the dataset. Some names of politicians with a city name attached to it have also been added (e.g. "Volker Beck (Köln)"), along with some terms that either do not describe a person or are for some reason misspelled variants of names (e.g. "spd" or "goeringeckardt"). Both types have been filtered out. As meta-attributes, further information was gathered both manually and with a scraper tool, accessing publicly available resources such as personal websites and databases such as Abgeordnetenwatch[1] or Wikidata[2]. For each person, the socio-demographic factors age, gender, party affiliation and federated state of political origin were collected. For 1227 of the search terms, all information was aggregated, doubling the search terms. Furthermore, the period of data collection now spans 34 instead of 4 months, expanding the collection vastly. The data set and corresponding results of analyses will be published after the publication of this paper. The data set includes 33.4% female politicians. The average age is 54. Most politicians in the dataset originate from the German federal state of North Rhine-Westphalia (16%), while the smallest part originates from the German federal state of Bremen (1.5%). The biggest party in the sample is the CDU ("Christian Democratic Union") with a proportion of about 25%. These proportions correspond roughly to the actual distributions of these attributes among German politicians.

Preprocessing. The updated preprocessing module with the added entity detection step still has to omit some of the crawled query suggestions. Albeit, with a loss of around 18%, there is less potential loss of information due to the removal of longer query suggestions. After cleaning, lemmatization, and entity detection, 5405 unique single word suggestions remained. The vector-transformation algorithm was able to vectorize 3979 of these words.

Bias Analysis. The word embedding vectors for each of the suggestions were used to perform a cluster analysis. A k-means approach was performed with three clusters, as suggested by the employed heuristics. By manually evaluating the clusters, we assigned a label that best describes the topic of each cluster (cf. Table 1). The first cluster includes terms with personal meaning. The second cluster consists mostly of names of cities and places that are of no political significance. The third group contains words with political meaning ranging from topics (e.g. "drug report") over other political persons (e.g. "Guelen") to cities and counties that are of political significance (e.g. "Afghanistan").

---

[1] https://www.abgeordnetenwatch.de/.
[2] https://www.wikidata.org/wiki/Wikidata:MainPage.

Table 1. Examples for terms of the clusters found by performing a k-means clustering approach on the preprocessed single-word query suggestions. Translated from German to English.

Cluster 1: Personal	Cluster 2: Cities and Places	Cluster 3: Politics and Economics
Losing weight	Aachen	Airbus
Events	Cologne	Stocks
Hair	Bielefeld	Guelen
...	...	...

As described in Sect. 3, bias metrics are calculated based on the position and frequency of suggestions corresponding to the clusters assigned in the previous step. Before calculating the metrics, search terms with less than 10 cluster words are dropped. This reduces the number of search terms to 2510, 1321 of which have a federated state, 1146 a Party, 1238 a gender, and 1253 an age assigned. 1227 of the politicians have all meta-attributes assigned.

Table 2 shows the results of the multiple linear regression analysis performed on the DCG and nDCG. The CDU and Baden-Württemberg were chosen as base-categories for the attributes party and federated state. For all metrics, the F-test rejected the joint null hypothesis that all coefficients are zero. Therefore, relevant biased patterns towards each of the metrics can be considered. Although there are biased patterns for each cluster, cluster 2 shows notably less. Very few attributes show biased patterns towards suggestions of that topical cluster. This reflects in the amount of variance explained by the models for the clusters. The regression model using the DCG scores could explain 7%, 1% and 5% of the variance for clusters 1, 2 and 3. The nDCG performed very similarly with 5%, 2% and 6%, respectively.

For cluster 2 (names of cities and countries), only politicians of the CSU (christian social union in bavaria) and the LINKE (democratic socialist party) exhibit significantly higher DCG values than the base category. The members of the LINKE also have significantly higher nDCG values. Cluster 2 suggestions, names of places without political significance, appear on average 1.5 ranks higher for LINKE politicians than for other parties. The perception-aware metrics show a significant topical gender bias towards the cluster of political and economic-related suggestions. The results show significantly ($P < 0.01$) lower average DCG scores (cluster 3: male 0.7, female 0.49, cf. Fig. 2) for suggestions of cluster 3 if the search term is a female person. This also shows in the corresponding nDCG values. With a coefficient of roughly -0.1 (nDCG scores for cluster 3: male 0.46, female 0.36, cf. Fig. 2), query suggestions with political topics appear on average one rank lower if the searched person is female. Age was identified as a biased factor for both cluster 1 and cluster 3. The older the politician, the more politics- and the less personal-related are the query suggestions. Figure 2 shows the mean scores for politicians over and under 40 years of age. The DCG score for cluster

1 is significantly higher for younger politicians, while for cluster 3 the opposite is the case. This also reflects in the regression results. We found some significant bias for both metrics within the political parties and the federated states towards suggestions of the cluster of political terms as well as the cluster of private terms (cf. Table 2).

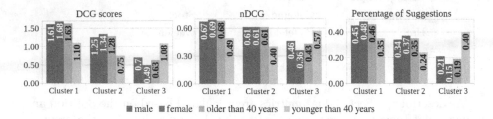

Fig. 2. DCG and nDCG scores as well as total appearance percentages for gender and age meta-attributes. The dataset includes 818 male and 420 female politicians, 1096 older than or exactly 40 years old and 1414 younger than 40 years.

5 Discussion

The developed pipeline was able to detect a significant systematic topical gender bias that presents searches for female German politicians with less suggestions on lower average ranks that can be associated with politics and economics. Similarly, the findings show a topical age bias. Query suggestions for older politicians consist of less and lower ranked suggestions associated with the cluster of personal topics and more and higher ranked suggestions that fit the politics and economics cluster. The overall percentage of explained variance in the metrics seems low, but without comparison and assuming that many unknown factors influence the topics of query suggestions, the results are satisfactory. It seems that the quality of the identified clusters is essential for the effectiveness of the bias identification abilities and the insights the pipeline can produce. By introducing more carefully selected groups of query suggestions as topical clusters, possibly by full or partial manual selection of topic words or utilizing a language model based methodology, the bias identification capabilities could be enhanced further. Another subject for a follow-up study is to test how the pipeline performs on non-person-related searches.

DCG has shown to be a useful metric for describing the perceived topical affiliation but can only be interpreted relative to other DCG scores. It can therefore be used to describe systematic topical bias. The nDCG score can describe the average rank of a cluster or single suggestion. This leads to results similar to the DCG scores if the percentages of terms of the clusters are comparable. For rare or single terms, or if the cluster sizes differ greatly, the metric might be a very useful measure. This could not be tested with the used dataset, however. Compared to the simple percentages of cluster words, the ranking aware metrics

Table 2. Results of the regression analysis for nDCG and DCG scores for each of the clusters. Shown are the coefficients B along with the significance value of the test for coefficients P, for all metric-attribute-combinations. The F-test score for overall significance and the adjusted R^2 measure R^2_c can be found in the row labeled "Model". All values are rounded, significant results ($P < 0.05$) are highlighted.

	nDCG_1		nDCG_2		nCDG_3		DCG_1		DCG_2		DCG_3	
	B	P	B	P	B	P	B	P	B	P	B	P
(Constant)	**0.80**	**0.00**	**0.60**	**0.00**	**0.38**	**0.00**	**2.24**	**0.00**	**1.28**	**0.00**	**0.43**	**0.00**
Female	0.02	0.31	−0.01	0.74	**−0.09**	**0.00**	0.05	0.38	0.08	0.19	**−0.20**	**0.00**
Age (groups of 10 years)	**−0.03**	**0.00**	0.00	0.96	**0.02**	**0.01**	**−0.14**	**0.00**	0.00	0.94	**0.07**	**0.00**
Baden-Württemberg	Reference category											
Bayern	0.05	0.18	0.02	0.60	0.02	0.71	0.25	0.05	−0.12	0.36	0.02	0.85
Berlin	0.02	0.56	−0.04	0.33	**−0.13**	**0.00**	0.04	0.75	−0.09	0.47	−0.03	0.78
Brandenburg	0.08	0.10	0.00	0.99	−0.08	0.18	0.21	0.26	0.03	0.86	−0.17	0.23
Bremen	−0.06	0.36	−0.16	0.05	**0.34**	**0.00**	−0.25	0.34	−0.34	0.19	**0.46**	**0.03**
Hamburg	0.09	0.06	0.01	0.80	−0.11	0.05	0.06	0.75	0.04	0.80	−0.09	0.51
Hessen	−0.03	0.44	0.02	0.63	0.03	0.45	−0.05	0.69	−0.07	0.56	0.16	0.11
Mecklenburg-Vorpommern	−0.05	0.37	0.03	0.62	−0.03	0.61	−0.23	0.25	0.10	0.60	−0.17	0.27
Niedersachsen	0.03	0.28	−0.02	0.57	0.00	0.91	0.04	0.71	−0.19	0.10	−0.02	0.87
Nordrhein-Westfalen	0.05	0.07	−0.01	0.80	0.02	0.65	**0.22**	**0.03**	−0.07	0.50	−0.06	0.43
Rheinland-Pfalz	0.06	0.16	0.01	0.78	0.03	0.63	0.11	0.48	0.06	0.70	−0.03	0.81
Saarland	**0.13**	**0.04**	−0.04	0.58	−0.09	0.24	0.16	0.49	0.00	0.99	−0.25	0.16
Sachsen	0.01	0.77	0.01	0.82	0.02	0.71	−0.03	0.82	0.01	0.94	0.05	0.60
Schleswig-Holstein	−0.01	0.78	−0.01	0.80	−0.01	0.88	−0.08	0.60	0.03	0.83	−0.16	0.18
Thüringen	0.06	0.18	−0.03	0.55	**0.12**	**0.04**	0.04	0.82	−0.13	0.43	0.15	0.26
Sachsen-Anhalt	0.01	0.85	0.00	0.96	0.01	0.94	−0.09	0.66	−0.01	0.97	0.02	0.90
CDU	Reference category											
SPD	0.02	0.36	0.03	0.29	−0.05	0.07	0.07	0.36	0.09	0.22	−0.12	0.05
CSU	−0.03	0.52	0.08	0.11	−0.05	0.37	−0.22	0.19	**0.53**	**0.00**	−0.21	0.11
other parties	0.06	0.31	0.02	0.71	0.03	0.73	0.22	0.30	−0.02	0.94	−0.15	0.36
AFD	**0.11**	**0.00**	−0.01	0.83	**−0.13**	**0.00**	**0.65**	**0.00**	−0.12	0.25	**−0.41**	**0.00**
LINKE	−0.01	0.78	**0.17**	**0.00**	**−0.08**	**0.02**	−0.04	0.69	**0.29**	**0.01**	**−0.23**	**0.01**
FDP	0.01	0.68	−0.03	0.37	−0.07	0.07	0.08	0.47	−0.08	0.45	**−0.18**	**0.04**
GRÜNE	**0.11**	**0.00**	−0.02	0.54	**−0.10**	**0.00**	**0.42**	**0.00**	−0.10	0.28	**−0.23**	**0.00**
Model	R^2_c	P	R^2_c	P	R^2_c	P	R^2_c	P	R^2_c	P	R^2_c	P
	0.05	**0.00**	**0.02**	**0.00**	**0.06**	**0.00**	**0.07**	**0.00**	**0.01**	**0.02**	**0.05**	**0.00**

DCG and nDCG did reveal more bias. Since the rank- and frequency-aware metrics offer more insight without compromising effectiveness, this speaks in favor of the introduced metrics. Directly comparing the new metrics to the old metric is difficult because the primary defining attribute of the perception-aware metrics is, that a different kind of bias is measured. The ability of the pipeline to reveal bias was enhanced by introducing the perception-aware metrics. The results by Bonart et al. explained little more of the variance inherent in the used metric in cluster 3. However, more significant topical bias was discovered towards more of the groups of meta-attributes and in more of the topical clusters. The new pipeline showed significant biases for clusters 1 and 2 and identified systematic topical biases towards the age and gender and some of the parties and federated states. Overall, the findings and the number of groups in which bias was discovered suggest an improvement to the bias detection capabilities. Due to the biased nature of language and mental representations, natural language data inherits bias as well. For this reason, minimizing the perceptible bias might be more reasonable than trying to completely debias data.

The developed metrics are applicable to any other topical bias analysis of ranked lists, for example, online search results. However, the pipeline does not scale well to other domains. Tests have shown the pipeline's application in the analysis of non-person-related search to be less effective. Search queries and query suggestions beginning with politicians' names seem to follow limited patterns. They consist primarily of the name and single or few keywords that show a precise information need. As the produced clusters demonstrate, these terms further fit a limited amount of clusters considerably well. Since the quality and precision of the defined topical clusters are critical for the topical bias analysis, the produced clusters' quality is essential for the bias detection capabilities. Brief tests on a collection of more diverse search queries have shown the pipeline's performance deteriorating. Therefore, to make the pipeline more universally applicable, the clustering needs to be reworked. Since this work focuses on introducing more effective metrics, reworking this drawback of the pipeline has not been addressed. Nevertheless, future work could solve this issue by introducing a more effective topical clustering methodology.

6   Conclusion

The main goal was to introduce perception-aware metrics for bias detection in query suggestions of person-related searches. Integrating rank and frequency of cluster words into the bias detection pipeline enables detecting bias that considers how query suggestions are perceived. This is achieved by adopting the DCG and nDCG metrics for bias detection.

By combining perception-aware metrics with topical clustering of query suggestions, the bias detection pipeline is able to overcome the challenges posed by the sparse character of query suggestions. The results presented in Sect. 4 are more meaningful and better interpretable than the results produced by the pipeline by Bonart et al. Perception-aware bias metrics represent a novel approach to bias detection in query suggestions that could prove useful for other bias detection scenarios as well.

References

1. Bolukbasi, T., Chang, K.W., Zou, J., Saligrama, V., Kalai, A.: Man is to computer programmer as woman is to homemaker? Debiasing word embeddings (2016). http://arxiv.org/abs/1607.06520
2. Bonart, M., Samokhina, A., Heisenberg, G., Schaer, P.: An investigation of biases in web search engine query suggestions. Online Inf. Rev. 44(2), 365–381 (2019). https://doi.org/10.1108/oir-11-2018-0341
3. Cai, F., de Rijke, M.: A survey of query auto completion in information retrieval. Found. Trends Inf. Retr. 10(4), 273–363 (2016). https://doi.org/10.1561/1500000055

4. Daniel J. Edelman Holdings, Inc.: 2020 Edelman Trust Barometer (2020). https://www.edelman.com/trustbarometer

5. Dean, B.: We analyzed 5 million google search results. Here's what we learned about organic CTR (2019). https://backlinko.com/google-ctr-stats

6. Dev, S., Phillips, J.M.: Attenuating bias in word vectors. CoRR (2019). http://arxiv.org/abs/1901.07656

7. Google: How Google Fights disinformation (2019). https://kstatic.googleusercontent.com/files/388aa7d18189665e5f5579aef18e181c2d4283fb7b0d4691689dfd1bf9 2f7ac2ea6816e09c02eb98d5501b8e5705ead65af653cdf94071c47361821e362da55b

8. Hofmann, K., Mitra, B., Radlinski, F., Shokouhi, M.: An eye-tracking study of user interactions with query auto completion. In: Li, J., Wang, X.S., Garofalakis, M.N., Soboroff, I., Suel, T., Wang, M. (eds.) Proceedings of the 23rd ACM International Conference on Conference on Information and Knowledge Management, CIKM 2014, Shanghai, China, 3–7 November 2014, pp. 549–558. ACM (2014). https://doi.org/10.1145/2661829.2661922

9. Honnibal, M., Montani, I., Van Landeghem, S., Boyd, A.: spaCy: industrial-strength natural language processing in Python (2020). https://doi.org/10.5281/zenodo.1212303

10. Houle, C.S.: The search engine manipulation effect (SEME) and its possible impact on the outcomes of elections. Proc. Natl. Acad. Sci. 112(33), E4512–E4521 (2015). https://doi.org/10.1073/pnas.1419828112

11. Introna, L., Nissenbaum, H.: Defining the web: the politics of search engines. Computer. 33, 54–62 (2000). https://doi.org/10.1109/2.816269

12. Järvelin, K., Kekäläinen, J.: Cumulated gain-based evaluation of IR techniques. ACM Trans. Inf. Syst. 20(4), 422–446 (2002). https://doi.org/10.1145/582415.582418

13. Kulshrestha, J., et al.: Search bias quantification: investigating political bias in social media and web search. Inf. Retriev. J. 188–227 (2018). https://doi.org/10.1007/s10791-018-9341-2

14. Lin, J., Nogueira, R., Yates, A.: Pretrained transformers for text ranking: BERT and beyond (2020). https://arxiv.org/abs/2010.06467

15. Mikolov, T., Chen, K., Corrado, G., Dean, J.: Efficient estimation of word representations in vector space (2013). https://arxiv.org/abs/1301.3781

16. Mitra, B., Shokouhi, M., Radlinski, F., Hofmann, K.: On user interactions with query auto-completion. In: Proceedings of the 37th International ACM SIGIR Conference on Research & Development in Information Retrieval, SIGIR 2014, pp. 1055–1058. Association for Computing Machinery, New York (2014). https://doi.org/10.1145/2600428.2609508

17. Niu, X., Kelly, D.: The use of query suggestions during information search. Inf. Process. Manag. 50(1), 218–234 (2014). https://doi.org/10.1016/j.ipm.2013.09.002

18. Noble, S.U.: Algorithms of Oppression: How Search Engines Reinforce Racism. NYU Press (2018). http://www.jstor.org/stable/j.ctt1pwt9w5

19. Olteanu, A., Diaz, F., Kazai, G.: When are search completion suggestions problematic? In: Computer Supported Collaborative Work and Social Computing (CSCW). ACM (2020)

20. Ooi, J., Ma, X., Qin, H., Liew, S.C.: A survey of query expansion, query suggestion and query refinement techniques. In: 4th International Conference on Software Engineering and Computer Systems (2015). https://doi.org/10.1109/ICSECS.2015.7333094

21. Pitoura, E., et al.: On measuring bias in online information. CoRR. vol. abs/1704.05730 (2017). http://arxiv.org/abs/1704.05730

22. Ray, L.: 2020 google search survey: How much do users trust their search results? (2020). https://moz.com/blog/2020-google-search-survey
23. Robertson, R.E., Jiang, S., Lazer, D., Wilson, C.: Auditing autocomplete: suggestion networks and recursive algorithm interrogation. In: Boldi, P., Welles, B.F., Kinder-Kurlanda, K., Wilson, C., Peters, I., Jr., W.M. (eds.) Proceedings of the 11th ACM Conference on Web Science, WebSci 2019, Boston, MA, USA, 30 June–03 July 2019, pp. 235–244. ACM (2019). https://doi.org/10.1145/3292522.3326047
24. Wang, P., et al.: Game of missuggestions: semantic analysis of search-autocomplete manipulations. In: NDSS (2018)

Crucial Challenges in Large-Scale Black Box Analyses

Tobias D. Krafft[1]([✉]) [iD], Martin Reber[1] [iD], Roman Krafft[1] [iD], Anna Coutrier[2] [iD], and Katharina A. Zweig[1] [iD]

[1] Algorithm Accountability Lab, Technische Universität Kaiserslautern, Kaiserslautern, Germany
{krafft,zweig}@cs.uni-kl.de
[2] Science, Technology and Innovation Studies, University of Edinburgh, Edinburgh, Scotland, UK

Abstract. To hold software service and platform providers accountable, it is necessary to create trustworthy, quantified evidence of problematic algorithmic decisions, e.g., by large-scale black box analyses. In this article, we summarize typical and general challenges that arise when such studies are conducted. Those challenges were encountered in multiple black box analyses we conducted, among others in a recent study to quantify, whether Google searches result in search results and ads for unproven stem cell therapies when patients research their disease and possible therapies online. We characterize the challenges by the approach to the black box analysis, and summarize some of the lessons we learned and solutions, that will generalize well to all kinds of large-scale black box analyses. While the studies we base this article on where one-time studies with an explorative character, we conclude the article with some challenges and open questions that need to be solved to hold software service and platform providers accountable with the help of permanent, large-scale black box analyses.

Keywords: Algorithmic accountability · Black box analysis · Socio-technical systems · Challenges · Learnings

1 Introduction

When triggered by keywords, search engines recommend lists of resources and information to users, which help them to navigate the vastness of the world wide web. They enable websites to be found, content creators to be heard, and commercial actors like advertisers to conduct business. Thus, providers of search engines and ad exchanges like Google take up a central position in the socio-technical system [21,32] of web search and search engine marketing. Since this socio-technical system is comprised of multiple actors and technical components, it has proven difficult to assign clear responsibilities for problematic search results or ads. For example, political ads can be erroneous and targeted

L. Boratto et al. (Eds.): BIAS 2021, CCIS 1418, pp. 143–155, 2021.
https://doi.org/10.1007/978-3-030-78818-6_13

to deceive voters [6], search engine results can reinforce racism [25], or ads with deceiving medical advice can be distributed to users with a severe illness [28]. Some of these actions are illegal, others are only ethically questionable. Some of them fall in the clear responsibility of the ad designer, e.g., factual correctness, others more on the side of the technical system, like the targeting of tainted political ads or the targeted distribution of medical ads with dubious content, which are difficult to assign.

Missing regulation in assigning responsibility is one problem, another obstacle is that these cases are often discussed on anecdotal evidence instead of clear cut data. For example, in the course of the Brexit, the journalist Carole Cadwalladr noticed that many people in her hometown voted leave because they saw targeted political ads on facebook [6]. However, ads on facebook that a user was seeing cannot be retrieved after the fact, resulting in no quantifiable evidence.

To enable an analysis of who gets to see what, there are in principle two solutions: getting insight into the algorithmic systems and all processes around it or, if that is not attainable, a so-called *black box analysis*, which observes and analyzes patterns in the input and output of such a system without insight into its inner workings.

Black box analyses can be used to audit the decisions of an algorithmic system and to detect problematic patterns in them. This is a first and necessary, but not sufficient, step to hold the providers of an algorithmic system accountable. Accountability in general can be defined as "a relationship between an actor and a forum, in which the actor has an obligation to explain and to justify his or her conduct, the forum can pose questions and pass judgement, and the actor may face consequences [4, p.442]. Following Bovens' definition, Wieringa defined algorithmic accountability as follows: Instead of explaining and justifying its own conduct, algorithmic accountability now focuses on the behavior of the algorithm or the algorithmic system in question, which has to be justified and explained by the person or company who puts it in use. Accordingly, this framework requires (1) an actor (individual, collective or organizational) who explains the behavior of the algorithm to (2) a forum which then challenges this account. The (3) relationship between the two is shaped by disclosure and discussion of (4) the account and its criteria, and ultimately (5) the consequences imposed by the forum [31]. If the actor is held accountable for the results of proprietary algorithms, the latter usually remain undisclosed or obfuscated by design as they constitute trade secrets whose disclosure would allow *gaming* the system [18]. Thus, without any real insight into the algorithmic system and without any hard facts, any demand regarding algorithmic accountability is a toothless tiger and must fail: If the forum has no means to challenge the account of the actor, the actor can in essence not be held accountable.

So far, there have been only a handful of successful attempts to scrutinise the services these platforms provide with such black box analyses, e.g. [1,7,23]. Most of these were sparked by a concrete evidence or tangible suspicion which determined the subsequent process of analysis. Why are there not more black box analyses on this important topic, if they are the necessary basis for a public discourse?

In this paper, we want to discuss the design process and the challenges that arise when conducting a large-scale black box analysis, mainly based on a recent study we conducted in 2019/20.

The study arose from the work of Anna Couturier at the University of Edinburgh and EuroStemCell in the area of public information, patient decision-making, and stem cell research. Her work's focus on the development of patient and researcher co-development of resources on stem cell treatments pointed to a larger question of how information about medical treatments moves through digital spaces. In particular, she investigated the impact of search engines as primary means for patient-led information gathering on their conditions and diseases and subsequent decision making. Feedback from patient advocates from the Parkinson's Disease and Multiple Sclerosis community noted that patients anecdotally noted that their search queries around their conditions often returned advertisements from private clinics offering unproven treatments [1]. This led to an initial study of advertisements of unproven stem cell treatments within the United Kingdom [13]. These initial investigations, however, were unable to address the largest actor within this network of knowledge dissemination; Google Search itself. This blind spot led Anna Couturier to reach out to us to conduct a black box analysis on how often these ads appear and whether they seem to be targeted to patients rather than a healthy control group. In our "2019 Eurostemcell Data Donation Project" we were able to collect evidence that patients do actually see more of these ads [28], despite a new policy by Google to ban stem cell therapy ads [3]. In Sect. 2 the concept of black analysis and its limitations are presented. In the following section, the above mentioned Eurostemcell Data Donation with its design and results are showcased. Section 4 derives general challenges in conducting a black box analysis, based on the different experiences that were made. In Sect. 5 the basis for the demand for a long term watchdog analyses to ensure algorithmic accountability is lain out and finally Sect. 6 gives a short summary.

2   Black Box Analysis

The concept of black box analysis can be seen as a descendant of reverse engineering. Diakopoulos defines *Reverse Engineering* as "the process of articulating the specifications of a system through a rigorous examination drawing on domain knowledge, observation, and deduction to unearth a model of how that system works" [10]. It allows the analysis of an opaque system (the black box) by observation of in- and outputs and deduction of the inner mechanics that transforms the former into the latter. It can be best achieved if next to the observation of the

---

[1] These initial impressions were collected during the Wellcome Trust Seed project-funded workshop "Patienthood and Participation in the Digital Era: findings and future directions" hosted by the Usher Institute at the University of Edinburgh in August 2018. (Erikainen et al. [14]).

behavior of the machine it is possible to also generate or manipulate the input, to draw specific conclusions about the relationship between input and output [2]. The central questions for this approach are *What is the analysis process?*, *Which properties can be uncovered, which remain disclosed?* or *What methods should be used?* [2].

An analysis of the relationship between input and output of search engines can only be achieved by a black box analysis, as long as it is not done within the companies themselves. Search engines are based on a composition of multiple algorithms which establish a relationship between input and output and are thus amenable to such an analysis.

2.1   Limits of a Black Box Analysis

Of course, not all kind of questions can be answered by such an analysis [30]: A problem is that search engines, like most other algorithmic systems embedded in a complex socio-technical system, are not a stable research subject:

1. The constant evolution of their code in a constantly improving software development process.
2. User experience is in most cases not the same for all users: It might be altered in A/B tests and shaped by personalization [5,16,20].
3. The complexity of the socio-technical system in which they are embedded. Complexity emerges from the algorithmic system's embedding in a heterogeneous assemblage of various types of social and technical entities that all feedback into the system [30]. Furthermore, algorithms in socio-technical systems are ontogenic, performative and contingent in nature [22]. This means, examining a stable representation of this sort of system is almost impossible due to their "contextual, contingent unfolding across situation, time and space [22, p.21].
4. Finally, inspection itself can affect the examination [2].

Despite the above limits of a black box analysis, it is still a useful tool: To assess social consequences of an algorithm's deployment, absolute knowledge about its workings may not always be necessary [9]. A "critical understanding of the mechanisms and operational logic [5, p. 86] is sufficient, as long as it considers those conditions that are required to understand a phenomenon [19].

If that can be achieved, the results of a black box analysis can constitute a meaningful algorithmic accountability relationship in the sense of Wieringa [31] between those, who can access its results (as the forum) and the algorithm provider (as the actor who is held accountable).

However, designing and conducting a reliable black box analysis of search results and ad distributions proves to be challenging as we will report in the next section on the example of our 2019 Eurostemcell Data Donation Project (EDD) and other black box analyses conducted in the last years.

3 A Case Study: Eurostemcell Data Donation

This study was a joint venture between EuroStemCell, the Algorithm Account-ability Lab at the TU Kaiserslautern and University of Edinburgh. The main goal was to examine, whether Google was exposing users with a severe illness searching for stem cell treatments to advertisements of unproven and possibly dangerous medical therapies as discussed in the introduction. These "on the ground" observations led to the joint venture of a black box analysis study and subsequent analysis of search engine results and ads to assess the influence of questionable advertising in the realm of digital health digital marketing on search engines. As the study was induced by such an observation of a probably troublesome phenomenon, it was obvious what exactly had to be measured: the number of search results and ads that patients and non-patients get on (proven or unproven) stem cell therapies. Armed with that, we went into the study design.

3.1 Study Design and Results

Based on an earlier large-scale black box analysis of Google's search results in the context of the German federal election 2017 [23], we used a conceptualised process of a black box analysis by Krafft, Hauer & Zweig [24], shown in Fig. 1. It consists of five phases: The set-up of the accounts which collects the data (1), the data collection phase at the participants' and at the server side (2), the data cleaning phase (3), analysis (4) and finally, the presentation and interpretation of the data (5). For the scope of this article, only the design decisions for phases 1 and 2 are of interest.

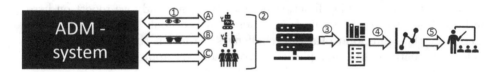

Fig. 1. Conceptualised, technical phases of a black box analysis according to [24].

Design decisions in Phase 1: In the design of the study, the first phase requires the choice of an analysis strategy, namely whether the data is collected based on bot accounts (which is called a *scraping audit*) (1a), on bot accounts simulating humans (1b) or real peoples' user accounts, which is called a *crowd-sourced audit* or *data donation* (1c) following [29]. We chose to use both, the first and third approach.

By choosing the crowdsourced approach, patients can contribute to scientific progress and be invited to take an active stand in enacting their autonomy, express solidarity and benefit from indirect reciprocity [27]. For the analysis, we recruited voluntary participants through patient advocacy groups to donate their data. A second group consisted of users without any of the diseases we were looking at, recruited by newsletters and social media. We further added bot accounts with no search history to ensure a baseline, against which we could compare our findings to understand whether patients would get more ads than user accounts without any known health information.

Design Decisions for Phase 2: The scraping audit was enabled by a browser plugin. It is important to note that we would rather use a way to integrate the data collection into the mobile Google app - however, this would be technically challenging and possibly illegal at the time being. In any case, the plugin automates the search queries and data collection, i.e., once it is installed and runs, the users did not have to do anything. It thus provided a scalable, platform independent and accessible solution that required minimal interaction from the user during the donation. For more than 4 months, the plugins of our participants searched 6 times per day for keywords related to stem cells or specific diseases as long as the browser was running. The plugin scraped the search engine result pages delivered by Google to extract search results and ads.

Our investigation of the crawled data showed that despite an official ban of stem cell therapy related ads by Google at the beginning of the study [17], the captured search results still included ads offering unproven stem cell therapy treatments [28]. On top of that, participants that self-identified as affected, received more advertisement than the control.

4   Challenges in Conducting a Black Box Analysis

In the last years, we have conducted black box analyses with respect to search engine results [23], dynamic pricing, filtering of news items on Facebook [24], an analysis of the autoplay function on YouTube, the study we report on here, and, in ongoing work, the collection of ads from Facebook accounts. We always encounter the same kind of severe challenges, based on the choice of how we collect the data in the first phase: a crowd-sourced approach or a bot-based approach.

4.1   Challenges in a Crowd-Sourced Approach

As our study question was whether patients got search results and ads for (unproven) stem cell therapies, we needed to involve real patients in the study. This also entailed that we needed a control group of real people not suffering from the diseases under study.

Problems with Participant Engagement and Enrollment. In general, participant enrollment is the more cumbersome, the more technical proficiency it requires. This is particularly salient in the case of our study as the conditions faced by our targeted study groups may, in fact, contribute to difficulties in on-boarding. For example, patients with Parkinson's Disease are on average over the age of 65 years old at first diagnosis [26]. This may lead to challenges with enrollment due to a age demographic unfamiliarity with the technology necessary to take part. In our final study iteration, we were pleased to enroll around 100 patients participants. This number is comparatively large for a socio-anthropological medical study. However, for a large scale statistical analysis of the results, this number is comparatively small.

It would be easiest, if participants could grant scientific study teams a restricted access to their account on the given platform [24]. For example, if they were able to go to their Google account, enroll to the study, and search results and ads would be automatically collected and sent to the conductor of the study. However, at the time being, there is no way to access specific information of social media accounts even if users give their full consent, neither for platforms such as the various Google services, Facebook, or Twitter. Facebook actually offered the Facebook Graph API that granted targeted access to users' accounts if they gave their permission - however, following the Cambridge Analytica Scandal, they restricted this access so much that black box analyses targeting specific aspects like ad distribution or specific messages in the timeline are not possible anymore from outside of Facebook.

Diversity of Hardware and Software Environments. Enrolling real persons also entails being confronted with a multitude of devices, operating systems, browsers (that come in different versions), and other software running on the device and interfering with the data collection. In our black box analysis regarding the election in 2017, multiple participants were not able to install the plugin, or it would not send any data, or it would hinder the normal usage of their browsers, e.g., by excessive consumption of computing power. In the running study, we were not able to figure out whether any of this was caused, e.g., by their ad blocking software. Another small problem arose from the different settings of the participant's Google user account, e.g., the setting of the preferred language or the preferred number of search results displayed on one page.

Problems Scraping Websites. The only technology left to collect data that real people see in their search results, was the browser plugin. It is basically a scraper, which is very susceptible to any changes of how the result page in the browser is structured. For example, in our black box analysis study concerning the German election in 2017, Google's layout for their result page changed midway. This resulted in empty data columns in our data collection for some days until we noticed the problem. In our study on dynamic pricing, we learned that web shops are actively fighting against price scraping by changing the structural design of their page regularly, which makes any attempt to investigate personal pricing based on scraping very difficult.

We learned on the one hand that it is absolutely necessary to check the collected data regularly and on the other hand to make any updating procedure of the data collecting software as smooth as possible. Participants are very likely to drop out of the study, if they have to re-install or manually update the data collecting application, as we learned in our black box analysis study in 2017 where one of our plugins had a severe bug: We could not update it remotely and thus a re-installation was necessary. Here we encountered the double-edged challenge of ensuring privacy. In order to maintain the privacy of the data donors, we did not collect contact information, but rather relied on the donor themselves to install and run the donation plugin. We did not even have an email list or other communication channel to make our participants aware of the problem.

Problems Caused by Dynamic Internet Content. Another general problem in the data collection is the dynamic nature of the content advertised in ads or search results: very often, we collected links from ads that at the time of the analysis were already invalid. We learned that it might have been better to crawl these links at collection time and to save the respective pages for future analysis. However, with A/B-testing being abundant, where part of the users following a link get version A of some website and others get version B (or C, D,...) of it [11], it would be necessary to follow the link from within the plugin. That is, the participant's browser would not only open the Google webpage but also any other webpage advertised or displayed on the results' page. This entails problems of safety and data privacy that are difficult to solve plus it might be illegal w.r.t. general terms and conditions of Google's search engine service.

Almost No Manipulation of Input Possible. While the crowd-sourced approach has the huge advantage to collect data that users would see, it is almost impossible to change the "input to the search engine" in any meaningful way, to better understand the real behavior of the system. The "input" to the search engine in a personalised account is not only given by the keywords, time of day the search is conducted, the IP-address of the machine used to conduct the search, and so on, but also by the personal history of searches, of web usage in general, induced properties of the human user imputed by the software (like age, income, gender, etc.). None of this can be easily changed such that a wanted user profile can be consistently achieved. It was this restriction that prompted us to adopt the dual approach of virtual bot-based data gathering. However, the bot-based approach came with its own challenges.

4.2   Challenges in a Bot-Based Approach

Our study was conducted in four countries, where we rented a set of so-called *virtual private servers* to run searches from IP addresses located in the same country.

Problems with Bot Detections. An unfortunate drawback of bot-based approaches is that they are routinely identified by most popular online platforms and then blocked. While these measures are necessary to detect malicious bot attacks, it hinders the mainly benign and public interest-driven scientific investigations. This would include any regular black box analyses by NGOs or the government established to hold software or platform providers accountable.

Problems with Regionalisation. A small problem that we encountered is the localisation of services by IP-addresses and other indicators of the place from where a service is approached: when using virtual private servers, the IP addresses are not as distributed over the country as if persons would use the service. Moreover, the IP address might be assigned with an industrial area rather than a residential area, resulting in different search result.

Problems with Fake Account Generation. In our study, we were lucky that search engine results can be a) obtained without logging into some account and b) analysed rather easily via an HTML-scraping approach. A bot-based approach is nearly impossible if it is necessary to set up fake accounts and/or to use an app by the software provider. We have discussed some of the problems we encountered when setting up fake accounts with Facebook in Krafft, Hauer & Zweig [24].

However, some of the challenges we identified above can be mitigated by conducting a pre-study.

4.3   Arguments for Including a Pre-study

Next to profane bugs in the plugin software, a pre-study of reduced length and number of participants can, e.g., help to estimate the size of the effect that is to be studied, thereby indicating the number of participants needed to run reliable statistical analyses. It helps to discover problems with the technical setup that occur very often, giving room for a technical improvement of the user experience. It might also detect problems with quickly changing website layouts, e.g., when website owners use that tactic to hinder scraping as discussed above.

It will also help to reveal at least some of the weaknesses of the study design and to mitigate unanticipated problems: For example, in the study concerning the election of 2017 [23], we were not aware of the fact that searches on Google could result in Google+ pages to be displayed. Google+ was the attempt of Google to create a social network platform and it allowed to build up contacts and to post and comment on URLs. When a person was searched on Google, who was in the contact list, all their contact data would be shown on the result page, in a special area reserved for that information. Similarly, if a key word was searched for, that was associated with any content on the user's Google+-account, that could also become part of the search results. We did not scrape this reserved area of the result page which could possibly contain personal data of contacts of our participants. However, we did scrape the search engine results and thus needed to make sure to delete all results from the Google+-accounts because otherwise these could have been used to deanonymise our participants. Since we did not have time for a pre-study, we were confronted with this problem in the full study which created some problems in the data collection.

We also discovered only in the analysis of the fully collected data, that most probably, the preferred language setting of our participants in their Google account, produced some of the anomalies that we encountered [23]. However, because we were not aware of this additional "input" to the search engine, we did not collect this information and thus, cannot be sure about its effect.

5   From Experimental Studies to Establishing Accountability with the Help of Large-Scale Black Box Analyses

As discussed in the introduction, accountability for problematic algorithmic results can only be established if there is a *forum* questioning the conduct of the actor, i.e., the provider of the algorithm-based service. Without reliable, large-scale, quantified evidence and only based on anecdotal evidence or hunches, this has proven to be difficult in the last decades. We conclude that at least for those questions that concern, e.g. fundamental rights of citizens or the protection of vulnerable persons like the patients in our study, an experimental study like ours is not sufficient. It is necessary to implement a permanent large-scale black box analysis based on a sufficiently sized and representative sample of users. In contrast to the phenomenon-induced study we presented here, which searched for evidence to back up anecdotal evidence, we call this the *watchdog approach*: it refers to (institutionalised) continuous scrutiny over an algorithm.

Study Design for Watchdog Analyses. To implement a watchdog as part of the forum to hold a software or platform provider accountable [31], the study design needs to be focused on the goal to enable the watchdog's role in the forum. The evidence created by the black box analysis needs to be clear and strong to challenge the actors and to hold them accountable. However, given the state of affairs, especially the lacking access to the necessary data to actually conduct these studies, the above stated technical challenges weaken the collected evidence, or make it impossible to collect it.

Solution to Technical Challenges. It is thus also necessary to overcome the technical challenges that cannot be solved on the side of the watchdog. While the analysis of search engine results including presented ads is technically relatively straight forward, other important analyses can simply not be conducted with state of the art access to platform data. For example, we failed to analyse from a news provider's perspective which of his followers saw what portion of his news [24]. We failed despite the fact that we had **full access** to the Facebook account of the news provider because it did not contain the data we needed. We also failed to set up fake accounts to retrieve the data in another way. This is a problem as German's media structure strives for diversity of news and information. Thus, any subsequent filtering of news outside of the media outlet diminishing that diversity needs to be analyzable and contestable to comply with the rules. Multiple policy consulting committees in Germany and the EU commission have acknowledged the need for the access to relevant data from algorithmic service providers, e.g., the data ethics commission, the Enquete Commission on artificial intelligence, and the EU commission.

6   Summary

In this paper we showed that there are a number of technical challenges that hinder large scale black box analysis of digital platforms. Our group found it an important reminder that the final output of these algorithms was not simply search results, but the potential of an individual impacted by life-altering disease to be exposed to at-best economically exploitative practices and at-worst potentially risky, unproven medical treatments. Some of the challenges discussed in this paper can be mitigated by a careful study design including a pre-study. However, the resources for this and for a large-scale analysis that includes high numbers of patients, should not be underestimated. Next to the technical challenges that can be mitigated there are mayor technical obstacles that can only be resolves together with platform providers. To enable accountability, where it is necessary, a watchdog approach cannot be realized without solving these problems. The study we conducted show that this is a societal problem that cannot be ignored any longer. We see that political bodies like the Deutsche Bundestag [12], the Data Ethics Commission [8] and the European Parliament [15] are currently searching for solutions.

Acknowledgment. The presented project EDD has been partially funded by the EU stem cell public engagement project, EuroStemCell[2] and by a generous grant from the University of Edinburgh School of Social and Political Science. The research was supported by the project GOAL "Governance of and by algorithms (Funding code 01IS19020) which is funded by the German Federal Ministry of Education and Research.

References

1. Andreou, A., Venkatadri, G., Goga, O., Gummadi, K., Loiseau, P., Mislove, A.: Investigating Ad transparency mechanisms in social media: a case study of Facebook's explanations. In: NDSS 2018 - Network and Distributed System Security Symposium, San Diego, CA, United States, pp. 1–15 (2018)
2. Ashby, W.R.: An Introduction to Cybernetics. Chapman & Hall Ltd., London (1957)
3. Biddings, A.: A new policy on advertising for speculative and experimental medical treatments. Google Ads Help (2019). https://support.google.com/google-ads/answer/9475042. Accessed 11 Mar 2021
4. Bovens, M.: Analysing and assessing accountability: a conceptual framework1. Eur. Law J. **13**(4), 447–468 (2007). https://doi.org/10.1111/j.1468-0386.2007.00378.x
5. Bucher, T.: Neither black nor box: ways of knowing algorithms. In: Kubitschko, S., Kaun, A. (eds.) Innovative Methods in Media and Communication Research, pp. 81–98. Palgrave Macmillan, Cham (2016). https://doi.org/10.1007/978-3-319-40700-5_5
6. Cadwalladr, C.: Facebook's role in Brexit - and the threat to democracy (2019). TED Talk. https://www.ted.com/talks/carole_cadwalladr_facebook_s_role_in_brexit_and_the_threat_to_democracy. Accessed Mar 11 2021
7. Datta, A., Tschantz, M.C., Datta, A.: Automated experiments on Ad privacy settings. Proc. Priv. Enhancing Technol. **2015**(1), 92–112 (2015). https://doi.org/10.1515/popets-2015-0007

---

[2] www.eurostemcell.org.

8. DEK: Gutachten der Datenethikkommission der deutschen Bundesregierung. Bundesministerium des Innern, für Bau und Heimat (2019). https://www.bmi. bund.de/SharedDocs/downloads/DE/publikationen/themen/it-digitalpolitik/ gutachten-datenethikkommission.pdf. Accessed 11 Mar 2021

9. Diakopoulos, N.: Algorithmic accountability reporting: on the investigation of black boxes, tow center for digital journalism/knight brief. Columbia Journal. School (2014). https://doi.org/10.7916/D8ZK5TW2

10. Diakopoulos, N.: Algorithmic accountability. Journalistic investigation of computational power structures. Digit. Journal. **3**(3), 398–415 (2015). https://doi.org/ 10.1080/21670811.2014.976411

11. Dixon, E., Enos, E., Brodmerkle, S.: A/B testing of a webpage. United States Patent (2011). https://patentimages.storage.googleapis.com/35/bf/a3/ 2a1ee861e2adaf/US7975000.pdf. Accessed 11 Mar 2021

12. Enquete-Kommission: Künstliche Intelligenz – GesellschaftlicheVerantwortung und wirtschaftliche, soziale und ökologische Potenzialedes Deutschen Bundestags: Abschlussbericht. Berlin, Drucksache 19/23700 (2020). Accessed 11 Mar 2021

13. Erikainen, S., Couturier, A., Chan, S.: Marketing experimental stem cell therapies in the UK: biomedical lifestyle products and the promise of regenerative medicine in the digital era. Sci. Cult. **29**(2), 219–244 (2020). https://doi.org/10.1080/09505431. 2019.1656183

14. Erikainen, S., Pickersgill, M., Cunningham-Burley, S., Chan, S.: Patienthood and participation in the digital era. Digit. Health (2019). https://doi.org/10.1177/ 2055207619845546

15. Europäische Kommission: Weißbuch Zur Künstlichen Intelligenz - ein europäisches Konzept für Exzellenz und Vertrauen (2020). Europäische Kommission https:// ec.europa.eu/info/sites/info/files/commission-white-paper-artificial-intelligence-feb2020_de.pdf. Accessed 11 Mar 2021

16. Gillespie, T.: The relevance of algorithms. In: Media Technologies: Essays on Communication, Materiality, and Society, p. 167 (2014)

17. Google: Healthcare and medicines. Google advertising policies help (2019). https:// support.google.com/adspolicy/answer/176031. Accessed 11 Mar 2021

18. Granka, L.A.: The politics of search: a decade retrospective. Inf. Soc. **26**(5), 364–374 (2010). https://doi.org/10.1080/01972243.2010.511560

19. Grunwald, A.: Technikfolgenabschätzung - Eine Einführung. Edition Sigma, Berlin (2002)

20. Introna, L.D.: Algorithms, governance, and governmentality: on governing academic writing. Sci. Technol. Human Values **41**(1), 17–49 (2016). https://doi.org/ 10.1177/0162243915587360

21. Kienle, A.: Integration von Wissensmanagement und kollaborativem Lernen durch technisch unterstützte Kommunikationsprozesse. Dissertation, Universität Dortmund, Dortmund (2003)

22. Kitchin, R.: Thinking critically about and researching algorithms. Inf. Commun. Soc. **20**(1), 14–29 (2017). https://doi.org/10.1080/1369118X.2016.1154087

23. Krafft, T.D., Gamer, M., Zweig, K.A.: What did you see? A study to measure personalization in Google's search engine. EPJ Data Sci. **8**(1), 38 (2019)

24. Krafft, T.D., Hauer, M.P., Zweig, K.A.: Why do we need to be bots? What prevents society from detecting biases in recommendation systems. In: Boratto, L., Faralli, S., Marras, M., Stilo, G. (eds.) BIAS 2020. CCIS, vol. 1245, pp. 27–34. Springer, Cham (2020). https://doi.org/10.1007/978-3-030-52485-2_3

25. Noble, S.U.: Algorithms of Oppression - How Search Engines Reinforce Racism. New York United Press, New York (2018)

26. Pagano, G., Ferrara, N., Brooks, D.J., Pavese, N.: Age at onset and Parkinson disease phenotype. Neurology **86**(15), 1400–1407 (2016). https://doi.org/10.1212/WNL.0000000000002461

27. Prainsack, B.: Data donation: how to resist the iLeviathan. In: Krutzinna, J., Floridi, L. (eds.) The Ethics of Medical Data Donation. PSS, vol. 137, pp. 9–22. Springer, Cham (2019). https://doi.org/10.1007/978-3-030-04363-6_2

28. Reber, M., Krafft, T.D., Krafft, R., Zweig, K.A., Couturier, A.: Data donations for mapping risk in google search of health queries: a case study of unproven stem cell treatments in SEM. In: IEEE Symposium Series on Computational Intelligence (SSCI), pp. 2985–2992 (2020)

29. Sandvig, C., Hamilton, K., Karahalios, K., Langbort, C.: Auditing algorithms: research methods for detecting discrimination on internet platforms. Data Discrim. Conv. Crit. Concerns Prod. **22**, 4349–4357 (2014)

30. Seaver, N.: Knowing algorithms. In: Media in Transition, Cambridge, MA, vol. 8 (2014)

31. Wieringa, M.: What to account for when accounting for algorithms: a systematic literature review on algorithmic accountability. In: Proceedings of the 2020 Conference on Fairness, Accountability, and Transparency, pp. 1–18 (2020)

32. Zweig, K.A., Krafft, T.D., Klingel, A., Park, E.: Sozioinformatik Ein neuer Blick auf Informatik und Gesellschaft. Carl Hanser Verlag (2021, in publication)

New Performance Metrics for Offline Content-Based TV Recommender System

Luisa Simões, Vaibhav Shah[(✉)], João Silva, Nelson Rodrigues, Nuno Leite, and Nuno Lopes

DTx - Digital Transformation CoLAB, University of Minho, Campus of Azurém Ed. 1, 4800-058 Guimarães, Portugal
{luisa.simoes,vaibhav.shah,joao.silva,nelson.rodrigues,nuno.leite, nuno.lopes}@dtx-colab.pt

Abstract. The past decade has seen a fast rise in popularity of recommendation systems provided by many entertainment and social media services. However, despite the recognised advances in different recommendation approaches and technologies, there remain many challenges, particularly in TV content recommendation systems. More precisely, machine learning based TV content recommendation systems suffer from a class imbalance problem; hence, it is difficult to evaluate the system using traditional metrics. Moreover, specific challenges arise during the development phase, when the system operates in 'offline' mode. This means the recommendations are not actually presented to users - making it even more difficult to measure the quality of those recommendations. This paper presents a proof-of-concept demonstrator of a television recommendation system, based on Content-based Filtering, as a contribution towards building a full-scale intelligent recommendation system. New evaluation metrics are proposed for 'offline' testing mode, while also tackling the class imbalance problem. The experimental results, based on real usage data, are promising and help in defining the future path as presented along with the conclusion.

Keywords: Recommendation system · Content-based filtering · Evaluation metrics

1 Introduction

In the age of digital media, the increase in entertainment content consumption has been almost exponential. With huge growth in digital media and entertainment industry, it is pertinent for content providers to present customised content lists according to the consumers' 'taste' in order to gain an edge over their competitors. More specifically, in the context of a cable TV service with a set-top box, the viewers of such service select contents from a long list of items - such as movies and TV series - in their device's entertainment menu. Since there are multiple possible contents that a subscriber might be interested in,

L. Boratto et al. (Eds.): BIAS 2021, CCIS 1418, pp. 156–169, 2021.
https://doi.org/10.1007/978-3-030-78818-6_14

a content Recommendation System (RS) that highlights/presents a customised list of most interesting 'unseen' contents is a handy approach to facilitate the selection. This paper presents a proof-of-concept (PoC) of such a system. This is an ongoing work, building on the agile development model, i.e. starting from a working prototype of a simple RS, and gradually up-scaling it towards a more sophisticated system. There are two major approaches for building a recommendation system - namely the Content-Based Filtering (CBF) and Collaborative Filtering (CF), and a third approach is to merge these two approaches in different ways, i.e. a hybrid approach. This work explores a content-based filtering approach, currently being developed in an 'offline' manner, which means the recommendations are never presented to the target users. This causes a major challenge, quite common in this type of systems, which is the evaluation process of a Recommendation System in an offline environment. Performance metrics in 'offline' testing usually measure accuracy of the RS based on the ground-truth, as well as the novelty or serendipity [8]. In the literature, Accuracy is one of the most used techniques in an 'offline' environment, which shows the ability of the RS to correctly predict a class as discussed by [16]. For example, [4] carry out an extensive study on RS that used accuracy as an evaluation metric. Out of those 62 studies, the performance was measured by means of precision in 31 studies, mean absolute error (MAE) in 27 studies, recall in 23 studies, F1-Score in 14 studies, root mean square error (RMSE) in 6 studies. There are also other metrics that were used more sporadically, for example the metrics of mean squared error (MSE), normalised discounted cumulative gain (nDCG), and area under the curve (AUC) were used in 15 studies. In [5], the RS developed uses several common metrics such as precision, recall, mean average precision, average percentile-rank, and nDCG. However, Ferraro et al. understood the need for diversity in the results of the recommendation system, thus contributing to another analysis of the metrics, namely Diversity and the Repetition.

Bell and Langer, in [2] also studied the possibility of using offline recommendation tests, and used precision, mean reciprocal rank (MRR) and nDCG as accuracy metrics. [17] studied the different concepts of evaluating RS approaches, and addressed the Precision, Recall, RMSE and MAE as the accuracy metrics used to verify the utility of a RS. [15] developed a RS for courses recommendation having as accuracy metrics precision, recall and the skill-coverage, which calculates the number of courses recommended with the required skills for the end user. It is stated in the literature that none of the recent studies introduces novel or useful metrics to analyse the evaluation of a RS in an 'offline' environment, and many authors have reservations regarding the evaluation of such systems. [4] concluded that none of the cases presented innovative metrics for the evaluation of RS. The same author studied the recent developments to improve the current performance and accuracy metrics, especially in the situations of high data sparsity, and stated that there is still work to do in order to improve evaluation metrics in an 'offline' environment. [2] concluded in their study that *'offline evaluations probably are not suitable to evaluate RS, particularly in the domain of experimental RSs'*, this challenge is still supported by recent works [3]. In fact, a recent manifesto discusses the topic of the need for a science of forecasting system performance rather than only focusing on intrinsic evaluation [6]. In an attempt to overcome these and other issues, important events and competitions in the area (e.g., Netflix Prize, RecSsys challange) have been contributing over the years with a wide range of strategies to optimise recommendation systems [1] without forgetting the challenge of '*offline evaluation*', determining whether all metrics evaluated offline are necessary and provide additional valuable information for an RS in a real environment [14]. But for more than a decade it is possible to witness multiple strategies that are being explored by industry and academia to predict user feedback and historical models of user behaviour [9]. This trend in research aims to predict items from implicit feedback [10], rather than rely on a set of explicitly generated ratings that are possible in online systems. To overcome this challenge some authors are using models of user interaction (i.e., click models) to construct estimators that learn statistically efficiently in an offline evaluation environment [12]. Although an offline environment is not the ideal setup to evaluate a recommender system, it is always necessary to perform some kind of evaluation before implementing an algorithm in a production environment. Other relevant work that adressed offline evaluation metrics was performed in [11,13].

Which leaves the authors to conclude that new metrics should be explored to analyse and compare different algorithms. Three new metrics are proposed, namely Genre Hit-Ratio, User Hit-Ratio and True Positives Quality, to help the system developers with an insight on how well a user's preferences were predicted, firstly in terms of genres recommended/predicted (since genre was the principal 'feature' in this phase of the system development), secondly how many of the users actually watched at least one of the recommended contents, and finally the quality of visualisation to verify how well the selected recommendations served the users' interests.

2   Content-Based TV Recommendation System

In the presented work, several recommender algorithms were developed, based on the Content-Based approach with small differences in the recommendation's listing and three different pre-processing alternatives. This section provides a description of each module and the steps of the recommendation pipeline.

2.1   Architecture

The current phase of the development cycle involves a simple content-based recommendation engine that outputs filtered lists of recommendations based on each user's content genre based preferences. The idea is to place this engine eventually as a functional component inside the broader framework of a cable TV service provider, i.e. the system operates on a real-life setup with real data. Nevertheless, the presented engine is a fully functional system that can operate in a standalone mode as well, with all the required modules. The complete pipeline of the presented system consists of the following main components or phases: input, pre-processing, feature engineering, the recommendation engine and finally the output and reporting of the recommendations (see Fig. 1).

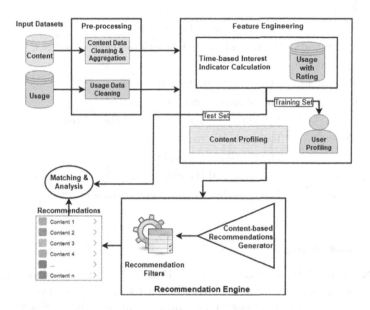

Fig. 1. Architecture of the proposed content-based recommendation system.

The following sub-sections describe the input datasets and each of the steps in the recommendation pipeline.

2.2   Input Datasets

The input data is supplied in two datasets - Usage and Content, and can be summarised as follows: 3 months of visualisation history (usage) data; from 100k total devices; having 12M content visualisations of total 332k unique contents. The content dataset is an exhaustive list of all the contents offered by the service provider, out of which the recommendations are prepared. The usage dataset is a list of all the visualisations, by all the users, during a specific period, considering which the recommendations are generated. Both these datasets contain several columns to describe the visualisations history and the contents. Table 1 describes the most relevant features for the presented use-case, for each dataset.

Table 1. Most relevant features of Usage and Content Datasets

Usage dataset	
Id	Device id
Start	Visualisation start datetime
End	Visualisation end datetime
Content_id	Content id, to match with the content dataset
Content dataset	
Content_id	Unique id to identify the content
Content_dur	The content duration in seconds
Genre	The genre, or list of genres of the content
Title	The content's title
Sub_title	The content's original title
Season	The season of the content (in case of a tv series)
Episode	The episode of the content (in case of a tv series)

2.3 Pre-processing

Data Cleaning - The entries for visualisations under 5 min were also discarded, since they reveal little to no information about the user's interests and with this the whole data becomes lighter. Then, invalid entries, i.e. entries with crucial parameters missing or with undefined values were removed.

Aggregation and Popularity - The pre-processing encompasses three different pre-processing blocks, which differ only on how the popularity of contents is calculated and whether or not it contains an aggregation process.

Pre-Processing 1 has no aggregation, which means the recommendations are individual and can contain specific episodes instead of the whole series, furthermore the popularity of an item is computed based on the number counting of visualisation. For *Pre-Processing 2*, the popularity calculation is the same but the aggregation process is included. And finally, *Pre-Processing 3* also contains the aggregation of contents but the "popularity" feature is calculated based on the number of users that watched each content.

Implicit Ratings - The input datasets do not contain a rating for each visualisation (or each content), based on the users' explicit feedback, and so a rating inference for the contents is performed. The rating R is inferred based on the visualisation time in comparison to the content's actual duration time. In this case, the visualisation time matches the time between the selection and play (t_{start}) of a content, and the action of closing (t_{end}) the visualisation panel of that content, hich causes a percentage bigger than 100% in some cases. The rating R is calculated as is denoted in Eq. (1):

$$R = Norm \left(\frac{t_{end} - t_{start}}{d} \right) * 10 \tag{1}$$

$$where,$$

$$R \in \mathbb{Z},\ 1 \leq R \leq 10\ and\ Norm(x) = \begin{cases} x, & \text{if } x \leq 1 \\ 1, & \text{if } x > 1 \end{cases},$$

$$t_{start} = visualisation\ start\ time,$$
$$t_{end} = visualisation\ end\ time,$$
$$d = content\ duration.$$

The normalisation function in Eq. (1) assumes that every value bigger than 1 (a percentage bigger than 100%), must be assigned to the ideal maximum value of 1, and then scale these values to have ratings as integers in the [1,10] interval.

Data Splitting - The data was split into train and test datasets, in which the former uses approximately 11 weeks of data, and the latter uses the last 1 week. The following block only applies to the training data, as seen in Fig. 1, and the testing data is used in the final step to evaluate the recommendation system.

2.4   Feature Engineering

Content and User Profiling - In the Content Profile, the goal is to describe the contents by their genre in a balanced manner. Using this information and the user's visualisation history, it is possible to compute the User Profile. Firstly, a *user x content* matrix with the implicit ratings is created, and then the genre relevance must be calculated individually for each user.

Matching Profiles - To make the recommendations, the algorithm needs to match the information in the user and content's profiles. With this information it is finally possible to compute the recommendation ratings for each user, by computing the sum product of the content and user profile.

2.5   Recommendation Engine

Filter Recommendations - This work encompasses three CBF algorithms, that differ in the selection of items after the recommendation rating calculation. In **CBF1**, the lists of recommendations are simply the ten contents with the highest recommendation rating for that user, excluding those that were already watched. Since the only factor of interest is the content's genre, the list of items at most times will be dreary, with no diversification at all. To overcome this, two other content-based lists were created that force more diverse recommendations. **CBF2** takes the top five preferred genres for each user, and selects the two most popular contents of each of them.

This filtering of contents certainly creates more diverse recommendations, however it does not always match exactly the user preferences. To obtain this, the system requires another listing that mimics the percentages in the user profile. **CBF3** does exactly that, by using the percentages to select the number of recommendation for each genre.

3   Evaluating the Recommendation System

Typically, evaluating a recommendation system means calculating how many of the recommendations are 'accepted' by the users, i.e. finding the recommendation to selection conversion ratio. The objective of a recommendation system is to have a high conversion rate, by correctly guessing the users' preferences, or by presenting recommendations which the users are more likely to accept, thus creating a more positive user experience in terms of contents being recommended. However, such a measure of recommendations is possible when the system is 'online', meaning the recommendations are actually presented and the user selection feedback is recorded. On the other hand, in an 'offline' scenario, it is difficult to measure whether a user would like a recommendation or not, since the recommendations are not really presented to users. Thus the task is to predict the visualisations in the test period, and the challenge is to measure the quality of 'predictions'. A key difference between recommendations and predictions is that the former has the power to actually influence a user's ultimate choice, while the latter is only a passive measure. Nevertheless, it is important to calculate whether the predictions were in the right direction or not. Moreover, it is also important if the recommended (predicted) content that was selected by a user was actually watched for a significant period of time, i.e. measuring the user satisfaction as far as the quality of recommendation is concerned. In this section, first some of the traditional evaluation metrics are presented, and briefly explained why they are not effective in the context of a TV recommendation system. Then, the new evaluation metrics are proposed, to measure a system's performance in a way that gives a better insight into the quality of recommendations, especially in an 'offline' context.

3.1   Traditional Metrics

The machine learning systems, including recommendation systems, are typically evaluated using the four metrics: precision, recall, false positive rate and accuracy. For a TV recommendation system, these metrics are calculated using the values filling the confusion matrix considering the number of contents that were or weren't recommended and which contents were watched, and which were not. Thus, in the evaluation phase, each content visualisation in the testing dataset will be classified to one of the categories in the confusion matrix as per Table 2.

Table 2. Confusion matrix

	Watched	Not watched
Recommended	True Positive (TP)	False Positive (FP)
Not recommended	False Negative (FN)	True Negative (TN)

Based on the values obtained from the confusion matrix, the Table 3 shows the calculations as well as meanings of the traditional metrics in the present context. These measures are of little significance, due to several reasons:

Table 3. Traditional metrics

Metric	Calculation	Interpretation
Precision	$\frac{TP}{(TP+FN)}$	Positive Predictive Value. The rate of recommendations/predictions that were indeed watched
Recall	$\frac{TP}{(TP+FN)}$	True Positive Rate. The number of contents that were recommended/predicted and were watched out of all the contents watched
False positive rate	$\frac{FP}{(FP+TN)}$	The number of contents that were recommended/predicted but not watched, out of all the contents that were not watched
Accuracy	$\frac{(TP+TN)}{(TP+TN+FP+FN)}$	The rate of correct predictions, including both watched and not watched

- Only 10, out of large number of, classes are recommended for selection;
- Number of items recommended (predicted) are always hugely inferior to the number of items not recommended (class imbalance);
- Multiple interesting items are left out of the final list of recommendations;
- A True Positive implies a selection of even 1 of the 10 recommendations.

For example, in the case of precision, out of the 10 recommendations presented (or predicted visualisations), a success would mean at least one of the recommended contents being watched. A viewer is not expected to select and go through all 10 of them. On the other hand, there is a huge class imbalance. There are only 10 recommendations presented to the user, which means the rest of the thousands of contents are 'not recommended'. Naturally, in a normal case a user would anyways not watch all of them. So the true negatives would always be very high. These two facts mean, the precision would always be very low, whereas the accuracy will always be very high. Additionally, since in the present scenario there are no recommendations being actually presented, the user may select practically any content from the menu. In such case, the recall or hit-ratio (true positive rate) would always be very low, since the user may watch many more contents other than those predicted. Similarly, the false positive rate, meaning the recommended/predicted contents that were not watched out of all the contents that were not watched, shall be very low as well since there is always a high number of contents that are not watched than the ones that were in a small list of recommendations/predictions and were not watched.

Considering these issues with the traditional metrics for a TV recommendation system, as well as given the challenge of testing the system in offline mode, new metrics were proposed.

3.2   Proposed New Metrics

In an offline context, it is not possible to measure the recommender system's performance since there are no users to give feedback about the recommendations that were given. It is however, quite straight forward to measure how accurately a system can predict what the user will most likely watch (without any external influence) based on his visualisation history. These two evaluations can be easily mistaken, so it's important to keep in mind that the main goal of a recommender system is not to predict what a user will watch next, but instead to find the most relevant contents in all the database, and possibly recommended an item that the user would never even know existed if it wasn't for the recommendation given. A first approach was to consider the most common traditional metrics to evaluate the system but then it also created new metrics that can be a bit more suitable for an offline context.

User Hit-Ratio (UHR). Intends to measure the conversion rate in terms of users, instead of measuring how many of the recommended contents were actually watched. The precision metric obtains a perfect score only when all the recommended contents were watched by all users, which is an extremely unlikely event and does not give much insight about the recommendation system's performance. However, UHR aims at measuring this performance by counting the amount of satisfied users, i.e. the number of users that 'accepted' at least one of the recommendations given, and comparing it to the total number of users. This tells the system if the recommendations given are being relevant to the users or not. To formulate the calculation, let U be the total number of users. Then the User-Hit Ratio is denoted as in Eq. (2).

$$UHR = \frac{\sum_{i=1}^{U} u_i}{U}, \quad where \ u_i = \begin{cases} 0, & if \ TP_i = 0 \\ 1, & if \ TP_i > 1 \end{cases} \tag{2}$$

In Eq. 2, u_i is the ith user with any visualisation, and TP_i is the True Positive rate of the ith user.

Genre Hit-Ratio (GHR). Since content-based algorithm is focused on the user's taste and in the content or feature set items, it seems obvious to measure the performance of this prediction. In this context, the content *Genre* is one of the chosen features, therefore, *GHR* was developed to measure the accuracy of the predictions of users' genre-wise preferences. With this new metric it is possible to observe how many of the watched contents belong to the predicted genres. This metric is crucial to evaluate whether or not the recommendations are similar to the users' taste. If a user watches only comedy and drama contents, the recommendations will be other contents that contain these two genres. Even if the user does not select any of the ten recommendations, it is important to evaluate if the genre was accurately 'predicted'. To illustrate, consider that the user watched five new contents after he/she received the recommendations. Four out of these five were from comedy or drama genres, which gives a GHR of 80%. In this example, although the user never watched any of the recommendations, the contents on this list were compatible with the user's genre taste.

To formulate the calculation, let C_i be the total number of contents watched by the ith user. Further, consider a genre calculation function $G()$, such that $G(C)$ gives the list of all the genres of content C; additionally consider a user-wise genre calculation function $GU()$, such that $GU(u)$ returns the preferred genres of user u. Then, the Genre-Hit Ratio is denoted in Eq. (3),

$$GHR = \frac{\sum_{i=1}^{U}\left(\sum_{j=1}^{10} w_{ij}\right)}{\sum_{i=1}^{U} C_i}, \quad where \quad w_{ij} = \begin{cases} 1, & \text{if } G(c_{ij}) \cap GU(u_i) \neq \emptyset \\ 0, & \text{if } G(c_{ij}) \cap GU(u_i) = \emptyset \end{cases} \quad (3)$$

In Eq. (3), w_{ij} is an indicator whether the jth content watched by the ith user had that user's recommended/predicted genres or not.

True Positive Quality (TPQ). The traditional metrics discussed before, measure the system's performance merely based on quantity parameters. However, even when a user watches all the recommended contents (100% precision), it does not mean that they were relevant to him/her. To assess relevance, it is necessary to look at the quality of the watched recommendations, which is commonly evaluated based on user feedback. For offline contexts, the authors propose an implicit feedback approach - *True Positive Quality* - which is the mean value of the True Positive (Table 2) content's implicit ratings. With this, it is possible to evaluate how much the user enjoyed the recommendations that were presented as in Eq. (4). These values range from 1 to 10, and if the system obtains a 9 TPQ it means that the 'accepted recommendations' were extremely relevant to the users. On the other hand, if this value is 5 or below, it means that the users found the recommendations to be mediocre.

$$TPQ = \frac{\sum_{i=1}^{U}\left(\sum_{j=1}^{N_i} R_{ij}\right)}{\sum_{i=1}^{U} N_i} \quad (4)$$

$$where,$$
$$R_{ij} = rating\ of\ j^{th}\ true\ positive\ content\ for\ the\ i^{th}\ user(fromeq.(1)),$$
$$N_i = number\ of\ true\ positive\ contents\ for\ the\ i^{th}\ user.$$

4   Results Analysis and Concluding Remarks

The present recommendation system had a two-dimensional evolution, in the pre-processing and algorithm planes, as described in the previous sections. Given this, nine individual tests were performed, that correspond to all the possible combinations of the content-based algorithms (CBF1, CBF2 and CBF3) and the pre-processing blocks (PP1, PP2 and PP3). The results considering both traditional and proposed metrics obtained, are analysed in Table 4.

Table 4. Traditional and proposed metrics

	Traditional Metrics				Proposed Metrics		
PP1	Precision	Recall	FPR	Accuracy	UHR	GHR	TPQ
CBF1	0.13%	0.26%	0.05%	99.92%	0.97%	69.12%	8.09
CBF2	0.39%	0.72%	0.05%	99.93%	3.09%	83.30 %	7.30
CBF3	0.44%	0.84%	0.05%	99.92%	3.41%	82.32%	7.31
PP2	Precision	Recall	FPR	Accuracy	UHR	GHR	TPQ
CBF1	0.16%	0.69%	0.11%	99.87%	1.62%	74.73%	8.57
CBF2	0.75%	2.78%	0.10%	99.88%	6.42%	85.19%	8.18
CBF3	0.81%	2.34%	0.11%	99.9%	5.50%	85.17%	8.13
PP3	Precision	Recall	FPR	Accuracy	UHR	GHR	TPQ
CBF1	0.16%	0.69%	0.11%	99.87%	1.62%	74.73%	8.57
CBF2	0.73%	2.72%	0.10%	99.88%	6.31%	85.19%	7.97
CBF3	0.80%	2.31%	0.11%	99.90%	5.42%	85.17%	7.90

Analysing the *Traditional Metrics*, it is possible to realise that the values for each metrics are either extremely low, or extremely high. All tests have precision and false positive rate values under 1%. Recall values show a bit more variance (2.52%) in comparison, and have slightly higher values, though still under 3%. However, the Recall values increase when the data contains sparse values, which is the case of the presented work. Accuracy is on the other side of the spectrum, with all tests scoring higher than 99.8%, with a variance of 0.06%. In general, none of these metrics give good insights about the recommendation system, as none of them reflect the dimensions of the advances between pre-processing blocks and the different algorithms.

As described in the *Proposed New Metrics*, it is possible to observe a bigger variance in the test's results, i.e. 5.45%, 16.07% and 1.27% respectively, but most importantly these metrics give more relevant information about the system:

1. User Hit-Ratio measures the users that watched the recommended contents
2. Genre Hit-Ratio compares the watched content to those that were recommended (considering that *genre* is a factor of interest in this work)
3. True Positive Quality expresses the quality of the accepted items, by calculating the mean of the implicit ratings.

4.1   Conclusion

When launched, the recommendation systems operate by interacting with users, i.e. presenting the globally popular recommendations to users, and learning from the users' choices. However, before going 'online', there is a phase in the development cycle when the 'recommender algorithm' must be tested to provide a proof of concept, or test its efficiency. The challenge in the presented work was to measure the quality of recommendations before the recommendation system is integrated with the client's larger infrastructure to actually start presenting the recommendations to viewers. In other words, in the 'offline' mode these recommendations become predictions, and instead of influencing the users' choices, the task is to analyse the quality of these predictions. New metrics were proposed to help measure how well a user's genre-based preferences were predicted, or how effective were the recommendations, or predictions, by comparing with actual content visualisations by the users. Besides, these metrics can also help measure a recommendation system in 'online' mode. For example, even if a particular recommendation is 'not accepted' by the user, by analysing the 'genre' of the actual content selected by the user, it is possible to evaluate if that parameter was correctly predicted or not. This further helps in improving the final filtering of the recommendation lists.

4.2   Future Work

This is an ongoing work, and there are already several lessons learned from the presented experiments. Some of the shortcomings are planned, on multiple levels, to be corrected in the next development cycle that is ongoing at the time of this publication. For example, improved input datasets will be used with more information regarding the visualisations and contents, to correctly predict a user's visualisation rating as well as prepare a better (more relevant) content list for recommendation. Also, the current methodology of preparing training and test sets introduced a time-bias. To address this, the new phase includes implementation of a 'prequential methodology' [7] that splits the data into shorter periods of time, in a sliding window like manner. The feature engineering section is also being enhanced to lessen the bias in the implicit ratings and prepare new features to include currently discarded content information, such as namely cast and crew. Additionally, a collaborative filtering approach based algorithm is being implemented, to generate recommendations based on the users' similarity in terms of watched contents. Testing the proposed evaluation metrics on this new algorithm, and comparing the current and new results will give a clear insight on the effectiveness of the algorithms. Finally, new evaluation metrics are planned to measure other aspects of the algorithms to be implemented, and the authors also suggest the inclusion of Novelty and Diversity to evaluate the system performance. Novelty refers to the extent to which users receive new and alluring recommendations that are perceived as interesting discoveries, and Diversity refers to the presence of different types of contents in terms of genres, actors, directors, and TV channel in the recommendation list.

Acknowledgment. This work has been supported by NORTE-06-3559-FSE-000018, integrated in the invitation NORTE-59-2018-41, aimed at Hiring of Highly Qualified Human Resources, co-financed by the Regional Operational Programme of the North 2020, thematic area of Competitiveness and Employment, through the European Social Fund (ESF).

References

1. Abel, F., Deldjoo, Y., Elahi, M., Kohlsdorf, D.: RecSys challenge 2017: offline and online evaluation. In: RecSys 2017 - Proceedings of the 11th ACM Conference on Recommender Systems (2017). https://doi.org/10.1145/3109859.3109954
2. Beel, J., Langer, S.: A comparison of offline evaluations, online evaluations, and user studies in the context of research-paper recommender systems. In: Kapidakis, S., Mazurek, C., Werla, M. (eds.) TPDL 2015. LNCS, vol. 9316, pp. 153–168. Springer, Cham (2015). https://doi.org/10.1007/978-3-319-24592-8_12
3. Cañamares, R., Castells, P., Moffat, A.: Offline evaluation options for recommender systems. Inf. Retriev. J. **23**(4), 387–410 (2020). https://doi.org/10.1007/s10791-020-09371-3
4. Çano, E., Morisio, M.: Hybrid recommender systems: a systematic literature review. Intell. Data Anal. **21**(6), 1487–1524 (2017)
5. Ferraro, A., Bogdanov, D., Choi, K., Serra, X.: Using offline metrics and user behavior analysis to combine multiple systems for music recommendation (2019)
6. Ferro, N., et al.: From evaluating to forecasting performance: how to turn information retrieval, natural language processing and recommender systems into predictive sciences: manifesto from dagstuhl perspectives workshop 17442, Dagstuhl Manifestos, vol. 7, no. 1, pp. 96–139 (2018)
7. Gama, J., Sebastião, R., Rodrigues, P.P.: On evaluating stream learning algorithms. Mach. Learn. **90**(3), 317–346 (2012). https://doi.org/10.1007/s10994-012-5320-9
8. Ge, M., Delgado-Battenfeld, C., Jannach, D.: Beyond accuracy: evaluating recommender systems by coverage and serendipity. In: 4th ACM Conference on Recommender Systems, pp. 257–260 (2010)
9. Hu, Y., Volinsky, C., Koren, Y.: Collaborative filtering for implicit feedback datasets. In: IEEE International Conference on Data Mining, ICDM (2008)

10. Jeunen, O.: Revisiting offline evaluation for implicit-feedback recommender systems. In: Proceedings of the 13th ACM Conference on Recommender Systems, pp. 596–600. ACM, NY, USA (2019)
11. Krauth, K., et al.: Do offline metrics predict online performance in recommender systems? (2020)
12. Li, S., Abbasi-Yadkori, Y., Kveton, B., Muthukrishnan, S., Vinay, V., Wen, Z.: Offline evaluation of ranking policies with click models. In: 24th International Conference on Knowledge Discovery & Data Mining, NY, USA, pp. 1685–1694 (2018)
13. Myttenaere, A.D., Grand, B.L., Golden, B., Rossi, F.: Reducing offline evaluation bias in recommendation systems (2014)
14. Peska, L., Vojtas, P.: Off-line vs. on-line evaluation of recommender systems in small e-commerce. In: Proceedings of the 31st ACM Conference on Hypertext and Social Media, pp. 291–300. ACM, NY, USA (2020)
15. Rao, S., et al.: Learning to be Relevant. In: Proceedings of the 28th ACM International Conference on Information and Knowledge Management, pp. 2625–2633. ACM, New York (2019)
16. Shani, G., Gunawardana, A.: Evaluating recommendation systems. In: Ricci, F., Rokach, L., Shapira, B., Kantor, P.B. (eds.) Recommender Systems Handbook, pp. 257–297. Springer, Boston, MA (2011). https://doi.org/10.1007/978-0-387-85820-3_8
17. Silveira, T., Zhang, M., Lin, X., Liu, Y., Ma, S.: How good your recommender system is? A survey on evaluations in recommendation. Int. J. Mach. Learn. Cybern. 10(5), 813–831 (2017). https://doi.org/10.1007/s13042-017-0762-9

Author Index

Printed in the United States
by Baker & Taylor Publisher Services

Printed in the United States
by Baker & Taylor Publisher Services